MICROECONOMICS

MICROECONOMICS

CONCEPTS AND APPLICATION

FIRST EDITION

Mack Bean

Franklin Pierce University

cognella

SAN DIEGO

Bassim Hamadeh, CEO and Publisher
Susana Christie, Senior Developmental Editor
Alia Bales, Production Manager
Emely Villavicencio, Senior Graphic Designer
Alexa Lucido, Licensing Manager
Natalie Piccotti, Director of Marketing
Kassie Graves, Senior Vice President, Editorial
Jamie Giganti, Director of Academic Publishing

Printed in the United States of America.

cognella® | ACADEMIC PUBLISHING
320 South Cedros Ave., Ste. 400, Solana Beach, CA 92075

Brief Contents

PART I **Introduction . . . 1**

CHAPTER 1 Economics . . . 3
Basics

CHAPTER 2 Five Key Principles of Economics . . . 15

CHAPTER 3 The Economy, Markets, Production, Income, and Exchange . . . 25

PART II **Demand, Supply, and Equilibrium . . . 35**

CHAPTER 4 Demand and Supply . . . 37

CHAPTER 5 Equilibrium and Market Failure . . . 55

CHAPTER 6 The Causes of Demand and Supply and How it Is Measured . . . 65

CHAPTER 7 Market Surpluses . . . 78

PART III **Production Cost and Markets . . . 89**

CHAPTER 8 A Business' Production Cost . . . 90

CHAPTER 9 Types of Markets . . . 102
Perfectly Competitive Markets

CHAPTER 10 Types of Markets . . . 115
Monopolies

CHAPTER 11 Types of Markets . . . 124
Oligopolies

CHAPTER 12 Types of Markets . . . 135
Monopolistic Competitive Markets

PART IV **Regulation . . . 141**

CHAPTER 13 Business Regulation . . . 142

CHAPTER 14 Environmental Pollution and Societal Cost . . . 152

PART V **Asymmetric Information and Financial Markets** **161**

CHAPTER 15 Knowledgeable and Unknowledgeable Market Players 163

CHAPTER 16 The Role of Financial Markets in the Economy 170

PART VI **Labor and International Trade** **185**

CHAPTER 17 The Labor Market Environment 187

CHAPTER 18 International Trade 201

Detailed Contents

PART I **Introduction** ... **1**

CHAPTER 1 **Economics** ... **3**
Basics
Concept Highlight ... 3
Real Life Example: What Does This Mean to You? ... 3
Introduction ... 4
Objectives ... 4
1.1 What Is Economics? ... 5
1.2 Factors of Production ... 6
1.3 Economy ... 9
1.4 Economic Thought ... 10
1.5 Two Types of Economic Analysis ... 12
Summary ... 12
End-of-Chapter Application ... 13
References ... 14

CHAPTER 2 **Five Key Principles of Economics** ... **15**
Concept Highlight ... 15
Real Life Example: What Does This Mean to You? ... 15
Introduction ... 15
Objectives ... 16
2.1 The Principle of Opportunity Cost ... 17
2.2 The Marginal Principle ... 18
2.3 The Principle of Voluntary Exchange ... 19
2.4 The Principle of Diminishing Returns ... 19
2.5 The Reality Principle ... 22
Summary ... 23
End-of-Chapter Application ... 23
Bibliography ... 24

CHAPTER 3 **The Economy, Markets, Production, Income, and Exchange** ... **25**
Concept Highlight ... 25
Real Life Example: What Does This Mean to You? ... 25
Introduction ... 26
Objectives ... 26

3.1 Economies and Markets 27
3.2 Production and Income 27
3.3 Circular Flow Diagram 29
3.4 Exchange 30
Summary 32
End-of-Chapter Application 32
Bibliography 33

PART II **Demand, Supply, and Equilibrium 35**

CHAPTER 4 **Demand and Supply 37**
Concept Highlight 37
Real Life Example: What Does This Mean to You? 37
Introduction 38
Objectives 38
4.1 What is Demand? 39
4.2 Calculating the Slope of a Demand Curve 45
4.3 What Is Supply? 46
4.4 Calculating the Slope of a Supply Curve 50
4.5 Equilibrium 50
Summary 52
End-of-Chapter Application 53
Bibliography 54

CHAPTER 5 **Equilibrium and Market Failure 55**
Concept Highlight 55
Real Life Example: What Does This Mean to You? 55
Introduction 56
Objectives 56
5.1 Review: Demand, Supply, and Equilibrium 57
5.2 What is the Optimal Mix of Output? 58
5.3 Sources of Market Failure 60
Summary 63
End-of-Chapter Application 64
Bibliography 64

CHAPTER 6 **The Causes of Demand and Supply and How it Is Measured 65**
Concept Highlight 65
Real Life Example: What Does This Mean to You? 65
Introduction 66
Objectives 66
6.1 Determinants of Demand and Elasticity 67
6.2 Price Elasticity of Demand 68

6.3 Cross-Price Elasticity of Demand: Substitute Goods vs. Complementary Goods. 70
6.4 The Effect of Time on Price Elasticity of Demand 72
6.5 The Effect of Budgets on Price Elasticity of Demand: Income 72
6.6 Price Elasticity of Supply 74
6.7 The Effect of Time on Price Elasticity of Supply 75
Summary 76
End of Chapter Application 76
Bibliography 77

CHAPTER 7 **Market Surpluses 78**
Concept Highlight 78
Real Life Example: What Does This Mean to You? 78
Introduction 79
Objectives 79
7.1 Review: Determinants of Demand 80
7.2 Utilitarianism 82
Summary 85
End-of-Chapter Application 86
Bibliography 87

PART III **Production Cost and Markets 89**

CHAPTER 8 **A Business' Production Cost 90**
Concept Highlight 90
Real Life Example: What Does This Mean to You? 90
Introduction 91
Objectives 91
8.1 What is Economic Cost? 93
8.2 A Business's Production Cost in the Short Run 93
8.3 A Business's Production Cost in the Long Run 96
8.4 The Short Run vs. the Long Run in Production: A Review 98
Summary 99
End of Chapter Application 100
References 101

CHAPTER 9 **Types of Markets 102**
Perfectly Competitive Markets
Concept Highlight 102
Real Life Example: What Does This Mean to You? 102
Introduction 103
Objectives 103
9.1 What Is a Perfectly Competitive Market? 105
9.2 What is Economic Profit? 105

9.3 The Shutdown Decision ... 108
9.4 The Short Run and Long Run for Businesses in a Perfectly Competitive Market 110
Summary ... 112
End-of-Chapter Application ... 113
Bibliography ... 114

CHAPTER 10 **Types of Markets ... 115**
Monopolies
Concept Highlight ... 115
Real Life Example: What Does This Mean to You? ... 115
Introduction ... 115
Objectives ... 115
10.1 What Is a Monopoly? ... 117
10.2 Strategies Used by a Monopolist to Earn Economic Profit ... 117
10.3 Societal Costs Caused by Monopolies ... 119
10.4 What Is a Natural Monopoly? ... 119
10.5 The Difference Between the Short Run and the Long Run for a Monopoly ... 121
Summary ... 121
End-of-Chapter Application ... 122
References ... 123

CHAPTER 11 **Types of Markets ... 124**
Oligopolies
Concept Highlight ... 124
Real Life Example: What Does This Mean to You? ... 124
Introduction ... 125
Objectives ... 125
11.1 What Is an Oligopoly? ... 127
11.2 Acting Strategically ... 127
11.3 What Is a Duopoly? ... 127
11.4 The Game Tree ... 128
11.5 Strategies Used to Avoid the Duopolist's Dilemma ... 129
11.6 Retaliating Against Businesses That Don't Price Fix ... 130
11.7 Oligopoly Behavioral Qualities ... 131
11.8 The Difference Between the Short Run and the Long Run for Businesses in an Oligopoly ... 132
Summary ... 132
End-of-Chapter Application ... 133
Bibliography ... 134

CHAPTER 12 **Types of Markets ... 135**
Monopolistic Competitive Markets
Concept Highlight ... 135

Real Life Example: What Does This Mean to You? 135
Introduction 136
Objectives 136
12.1 What Is a Monopolistic Competitive Market? 137
12.2 Differentiating Products and Services 137
12.3 The Difference Between the Short Run and the Long Run for Businesses in a Monopolistic Competitive Market 138
Summary 138
End-of-Chapter Application 139
References 140

PART IV **Regulation** **141**

CHAPTER 13 **Business Regulation** **142**
Concept Highlight 142
Real Life Example: What Does This Mean to You? 142
Introduction 143
Objectives 143
13.1 Review: The Free Market System 145
13.2 Regulation: Anti-trust vs. Trust 146
13.3 Regulation's Effect on Businesses vs. a Natural Monopoly 147
Summary 149
End-of-Chapter Application 150
References 151

CHAPTER 14 **Environmental Pollution and Societal Cost** **152**
Concept Highlight 152
Real Life Example: What Does This Mean to You? 152
Introduction 153
Objectives 153
14.1 What Is Pollution? 154
14.2 Market Incentives' Effect on Business Pollution 154
14.3 Costs Associated With Pollution 155
14.4 A Business's Response vs. a Natural Monopoly's Response to Pollution Regulation 155
14.5 A Business's Response vs. a Natural Monopoly's Response to Pollution Regulation 156
Summary 158
End-of-Chapter Application 158
Bibliography 159

PART V **Asymmetric Information and Financial Markets** 161

CHAPTER 15 **Knowledgeable and Unknowledgeable Market Players** 163
Concept Highlight 163
Real Life Example: What Does This Mean to You? 163
Introduction 164
Objectives 164
15.1 What Is the Asymmetric Information Problem? 165
15.2 The Adverse-Selection Problem 166
Summary 168
End-of-Chapter Application 168
References 169

CHAPTER 16 **The Role of Financial Markets in the Economy** 170
Concept Highlight 170
Real Life Example: What Does This Mean to You? 170
Introduction 171
Objectives 171
16.1 What Is a Financial Market? 173
16.2 How Changes in Interest Rates Affect the Demand for Money 175
16.3 Types of Interest Rates 176
16.4 Time Value of Money 176
16.5 Demand for Loanable Funds 177
16.6 Types of Financial Securities Offered on the Financial Market 179
Summary 182
End-of-Chapter Application 182
Bibliography 184

PART VI **Labor and International Trade** 185

CHAPTER 17 **The Labor Market Environment** 187
Concept Highlight 187
Real Life Example: What Does This Mean to You? 187
Introduction 188
Objectives 188
17.1 What is the Labor Market? 189
17.2 The Demand for Labor 191
17.3 The Supply of Labor 194
17.4 Labor Market Equilibrium 196
Summary 197
End-of-Chapter Application 198
Bibliography 200

CHAPTER 18 **International Trade**........ **201**

Concept Highlight 201
Real Life Example: What Does This Mean to You? 201
Introduction........ 202
Objectives 202
18.1 A Review of Efficiency and the Production Possibilities Graph (Frontier)........ 203
18.2 Specialization and Trade: A Review of Absolute and Comparative Advantages........ 206
18.3 What Is Free Trade, and How Does it Affect Employment?........ 207
18.4 Protectionism 208
Summary 209
End-of-Chapter Application........ 210
Bibliogrpahy........ 211

Part I
Introduction

Source: NASA Earth Observatory, https://commons.wikimedia.org/wiki/File:City_Lights_of_the_United_States_2012.jpg, National Aeronautics and Space Administration (NASA), 2012.

CHAPTER 1

Economics

Basics

Concept Highlight

Chapter 1 provides an introduction to economics.

Real Life Example: What Does This Mean to You?

Economics is used daily to understand decisions regarding how best to use limited resources. An example of this includes a country that possesses limited resources to produce various goods and services.

The government must decide on the different types of goods and services to produce based on those limited resources.

Introduction

Having a basic understanding of economics provides us with a basic foundation for examining microeconomics. This foundation begins with learning the definition of economics as well as learning the key economic questions we must address regarding the use of limited resources. From here, the chapter introduces one of the tools nations use to determine the best possible combination of goods and services to be produced with its limited resources. Then, the chapter introduces the concept of an economy in which economics is employed as well as the concept of a market. The chapter ends with an examination of the two types of economic analyses used to understand the economy.

OBJECTIVES

While reading this chapter, readers should be able to

LO 1.1. define "economics"

LO 1.1. identify the three key economic questions that must be addressed

LO 1.2. identify the five resources that make up the factors of production

LO 1.2. illustrate and explain the production possibilities graph (frontier)

LO 1.3. define "economy"

LO 1.3. define "market"

LO 1.3. explain the free market system

LO 1.3. define "invisible hand theory"

LO 1.3. explain the mixed economy

LO 1.4. identify the two economic thoughts

LO 1.4. identify the two assumptions that economists make about people in the market

LO 1.4. define "variable"

LO 1.4. define "ceteris paribus"

LO 1.5. explain the two economic analyses

OUTCOMES

After completing this chapter, readers will be able to do the following:

- Identify the three key economic questions that must be addressed.

- Illustrate a production possibilities graph (frontier), explain what the production possibilities curve indicates, and explain whether the production possibilities curve can move.
- Explain the invisible hand theory.
- Identify the two assumptions economists make about people in the market.
- Explain the two economic thoughts.
- Explain the two economic analyses.

Key Terms

The following key terms are discussed in this chapter:

- economics
- scarcity
- factors of production
- efficiency
- production possibilities graph (frontier)
- production possibilities curve
- economy
- market
- free market system
- invisible hand theory
- mixed economy
- positive economics
- normative economics
- variable
- ceteris paribus
- macroeconomics
- microeconomics

1.1 What Is Economics?

Economics is defined as the study of the choices made by people regarding the use of scarce resources. Within this definition, **scarcity** refers to limited resources being used to fulfill unlimited wants and desires. Therefore, in conditions of scarcity, we are forced to make decisions about how to use limited resources. Understanding this, economics examines the process by which people make these choices. Individuals, businesses, and governments must work together in this process. As a group, they decide how to allocate resources by addressing three questions:

1. What do we produce?
2. How do we produce it?
3. Who will consume it?

FIGURE 1.1 Making Decisions Based on Scarce Resources

1.2 Factors of Production

economics: the study of the choices made by people regarding the use of scarce resources

scarcity: a situation in which there are limited resources to fulfill unlimited wants and desires

Among these important questions, the most important for a nation is, "What do we produce?" The answer to this question is influenced by the factors of production. The **factors of production** are the resources used in the production of goods and services. Such resources consist of natural resources (made by nature), human effort (labor), human capital (knowledge and skill), physical capital (facilities and equipment), and entrepreneurship (someone taking the risk to start a business). These five resources are required to produce goods and services, and therefore, they make up the factors of production. However, no single person, business, or government has an unlimited number of these resources at their disposal. So each must decide how best to use the resources for the purpose of production.

From the national perspective, it is more important to expand the question of what we produce to, "What combination of goods and services should we be produce to be most efficient with our limited resources?" **Efficiency** refers to having the ability to maximize resources in production. In other words, producing multiple products and services allows us to get the most out of our resources. As such, one tool that can help determine possible combinations of goods and services to produce is the production possibilities graph (frontier). The **production possibilities graph (frontier**; PPG) is a graph that shows the possible combinations of goods and services produced based on the resources available. The production possibilities provide a picture of the difference combinations of goods and services for production, which, in turn, allows us to make decisions on production levels. An example of this includes a nation determining to produce both agricultural and manufacturing goods with its resources. With its resources, the nation determines it could produce the number (in tons) of agricultural and manufacturing goods shown in Table 1.1 based on the resources it possesses.

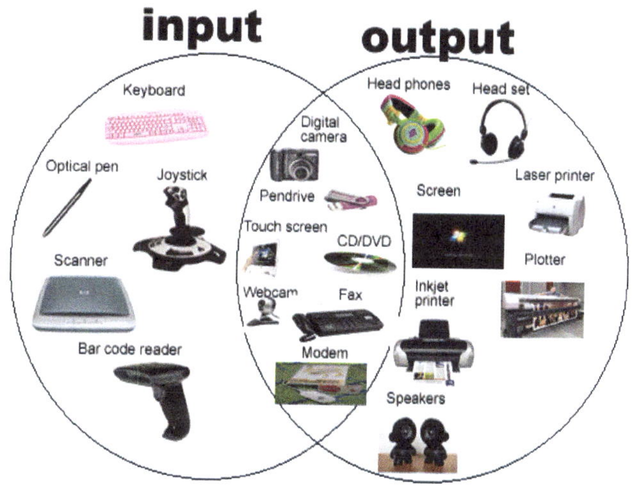

FIGURE 1.2 An Example of Factors of Production: Resources (Inputs) and Products (Output)

TABLE 1.1 An Example of Production Choices Based on Scarcity

Agricultural goods	Manufacturing goods
100	700
200	600
300	500
400	400
500	300
600	200
700	100

As mentioned, in this example, the nation determined its production capabilities in agricultural and manufacturing goods based on the resources it possessed. However, due to its limited resources, the production of one good comes at the expense of producing the other good. In doing so, the PPG (frontier) allows us to see the sacrifice in production associated with limited resources. An illustration of this graph is shown in Figure 1.3.

Each point on this graph represents a production combination level. When the points are connected, it creates a production possibilities curve. A **production possibilities curve** (PPC) is a curve that shows the possible combinations of goods and services produced based on the resources available. This curve represents what is and is not attainable. Everything inside the curve is attainable because the nation has the resources, while nothing outside of the curve is attainable because there are not enough resources.

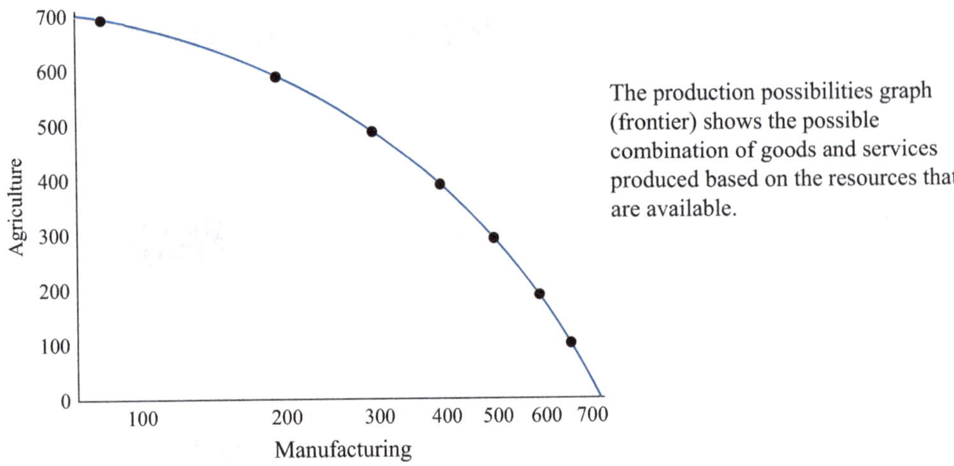

FIGURE 1.3 An Example of a Production Possibilities Graph (Frontier)

Therefore, the production possibilities curve establishes the boundary between what can be produced and what can't be produced.

The production possibilities curve isn't stationary. This curve can shift to the right or to the left. The curve will shift to the left if resources are not replaced as they are used. This shift represents a decline in production. However, the curve will shift to the right if resources are replaced as they are used. This shift represents an increase in production.

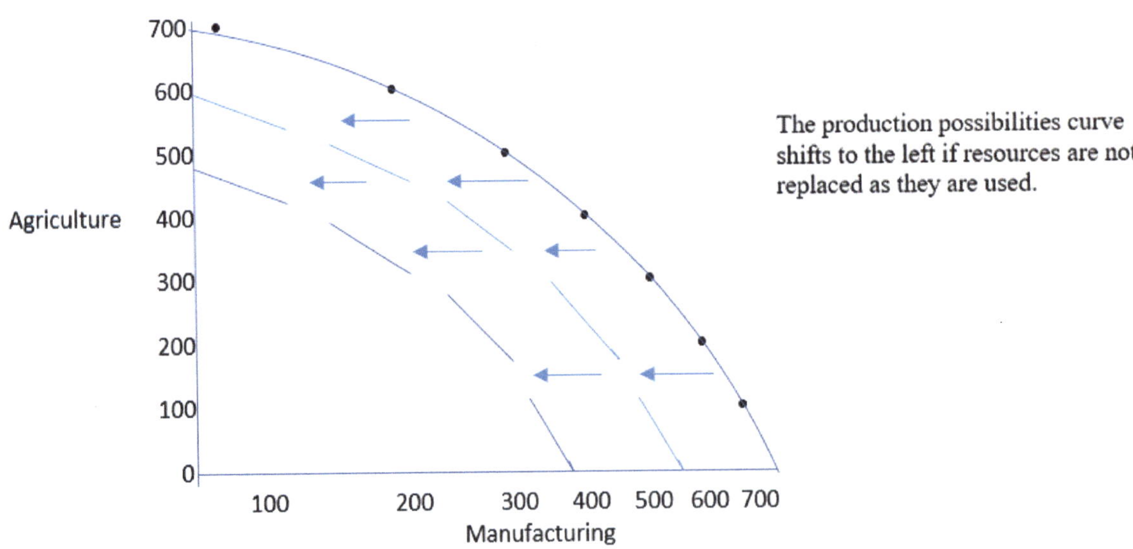

FIGURE 1.4 A Left Shift of the Production Possibilities Curve

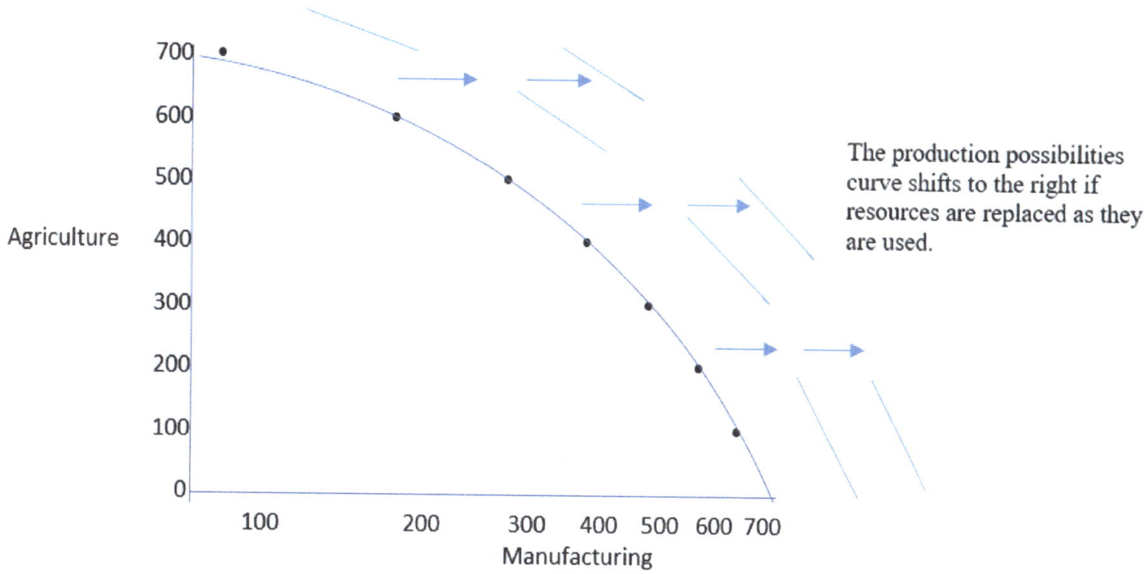

FIGURE 1.5 A Right Shift of the Production Possibilities Curve

1.3 Economy

The study of economics occurs within the economy. An **economy** is a system through which resources are distributed. In other words, an economy refers to a system through which the resources that make up the factors of production move from point A to point B. Economies consists of markets. A **market** is a place where buyers and sellers engage in exchanges (buy and sell). The U.S. economy is built upon the free market system. The **free market system** is one in which sellers have the freedom to sell their products at any price and buyers have the freedom to buy. Adam Smith is given credit for the creation of this system and, therefore, is known as the father of the free market system. Smith was recognized for his writings of the invisible hand theory, from which the free market system idea was founded. The **invisible hand theory** is the belief that if the government were to let the market be, without intervention, eventually, both buyers and sellers would agree upon a price at which they are satisfied. In other words, the invisible hand theory indicates that the market would be better if the government allowed buyers and sellers to negotiate on prices of goods and services without intervention. However, the government intervenes in the market to protect the public. Because of

factors of production: the resources used in the production of goods and services

efficiency: having the ability to maximize resources in production

production possibilities graph (frontier): a graph that shows the possible combinations of goods and services produced based on the available resources

production possibilities curve: a curve that shows the possible combinations of goods and services produced based on the available resources

FIGURE 1.6 Adam Smith

this, the United States actually operates as a mixed economy. A **mixed economy** is one in which there are both market freedoms and government controls.

1.4 Economic Thought

Economists study the economy. When doing so, they think about the economy in one of two ways. One view of the economy is positive economics. **Positive economics** refers to the view of the economy based on examining the factors that affect economic activities and predicting the consequences of actions related to those factors. In other words, positive economists examine the factors that affect the economy and predict what will occur if there are attempts to change those factors. In doing so, positive economists seek to address two questions based on scientific facts and data. Those questions are as follows:

economy: a system through which resources are distributed

market: a place where buyers and sellers engage in exchanges (buy and sell)

free market economy: a system in which sellers have the freedom to sell their products at any price and buyers have the freedom to buy

invisible hand theory: the belief that if the government were to let the market be, without intervention, eventually, both buyers and sellers would agree upon a price at which they are satisfied

mixed economy: an economy in which there are both market freedoms and government controls

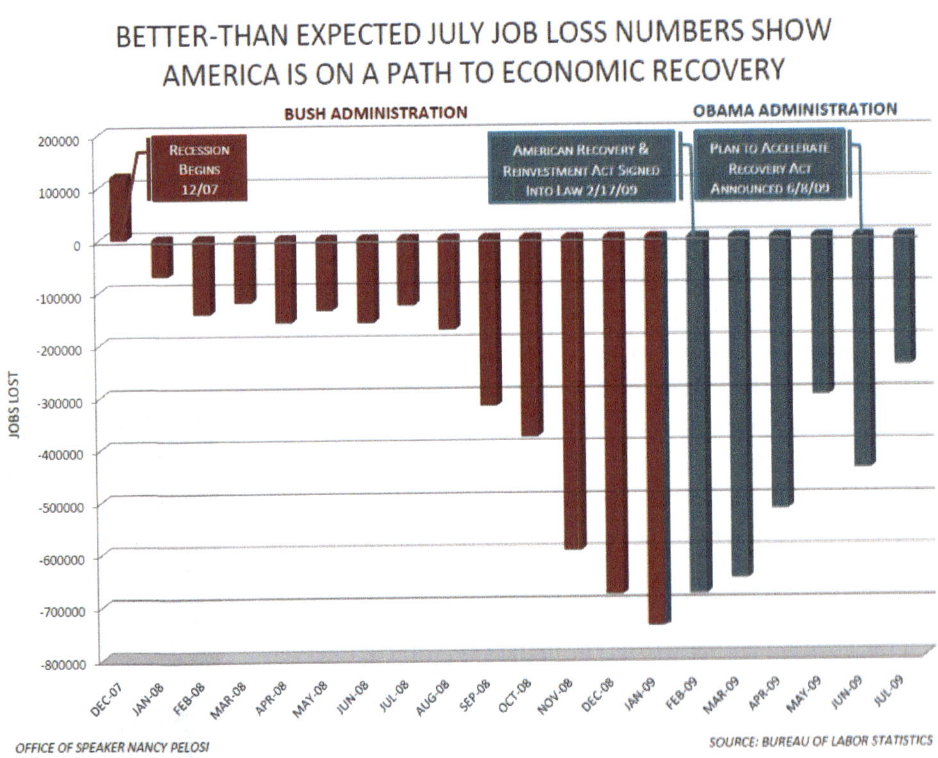

FIGURE 1.7 A Diagram Using Facts to Demonstrate Positive Economic Thought

1. What is?
2. What will be?

The second view of economics is normative economics. **Normative economics** refers to the view of the economy based on examining the factors that affect economic activities and predicting the consequences of actions related to factors. As stated, normative economics has the same definition as positive economics. Thus, normative economists also examine the factors that affect the economy and predict what will occur if there are attempts to change those factors. However, normative economists seek to address one question based on judgement and morals. That one question asked by normative economists is as follows:

1. What ought to be?

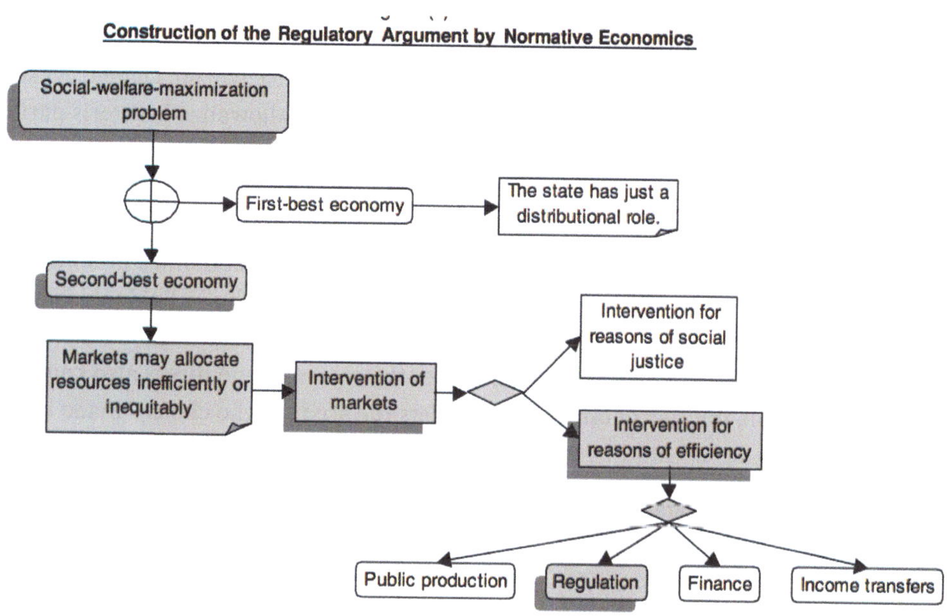

FIGURE 1.8 A Diagram of Normative Economic Thoughts

As economists examine the economy, they make two assumptions about people. The first assumption is that people will act selfishly in the market. This assumption is based on the view that people will seek their own best interest when engaging the market activities. By comparison, the second assumption is that people prefer to make informed decisions. This assumption is based on the view that people prefer to make decisions in the market based on having all relevant information.

Economists use variables when analyzing people within the economy. A **variable** (V) refers to something of value. An example of a variable would be a college student who has a part-time job and receives an allowance from their parents. In this example, the student's income variable consists of the hourly wage from the part-time job, the number of hours worked, and the allowance received from parents:

(college student's income) V = hourly wage + hours worked + allowance

When economists examine two or more variables, they assume that at least one variable will not change. This is known as ceteris paribus. **Ceteris paribus** refers to something that remains fixed or does not change. In the example of the college student who has a part-time job and receives an allowance, economists assume that an increase in the student's income would be derived from either an increase in the number of hours the student works an increase in the student's hourly wage. However, economists assume the student's allowance will not change. As such, the student's allowance is ceteris paribus.

positive economics: the view of the economy based on examining the factors that affect economic activities and predicting the consequences of the actions taken towards those factors; it addresses what is and what will be

normative economics: the view of the economy based on examining the factors that affect economic activities and predicting the consequences of the actions taken towards those factors; it addresses what ought to be

variable: something of value

ceteris paribus: remaining fixed or not changing

1.5 Two Types of Economic Analysis

Economists use two economic analyses to study the economy: macroeconomics and microeconomics analyses. **Macroeconomics** is defined as the study of the choices made by individuals, businesses, and governments as a whole when facing scarcity. Within this analysis, economists examine decisions related to using limited resources among everyone as a whole. Due to this, macroeconomics is also known as the "the big picture." By comparison, **microeconomics** is defined as the study of the choices made by individuals, businesses, and governments separately when facing scarcity. This analysis allows economists to examine decisions of using limited resources among one person, one business, or one level of government. Because of this, microeconomics is also known as "the small picture."

macroeconomics: the study of the choices made by individuals, businesses, and governments as a whole; it is known as "the big picture"

microeconomics: the study of the choices made by individuals, businesses, and governments separately; it is known as the "the small picture"

SUMMARY

- Scarcity forces people to make choices.
- "Economics" is the study of the choices made by people regarding the use of scarce resources.
- Individuals, businesses, and governments must determine what to produce based on the limited resources possessed.
- The factors of production consist of the resources used in production.

- The production possibilities graph (frontier) is one tool used to illustrate the best combination of goods and services to produce based on the available resources.
- An "economy" is a system through which resources are distributed.
- The U.S. economy is built upon the free market system.
- The free market system derives from the invisible hand theory.
- The U.S. economy operates under a mixed economy.
- Two economic viewpoints are positive economics and normative economics.
- Economists use variables to analyze people within the economy.
- Economists assume people are selfish and that they prefer to make informed decisions.
- Economists use both macroeconomics and microeconomics to study the economy.

END-OF-CHAPTER APPLICATION

Comprehension Questions

Directions: Refer to the chapter to correctly respond to the following questions and prompts.

1. List and explain the different types of resources that make up the factors of production. (LO 1.1)
2. Define the production possibilities graph (frontier). Explain what the product possibilities curve indicates. Explain whether the production possibilities curve can move. (LO 1.2)
3. Explain the relationship between free market system and the invisible hand theory. (LO 1.3)
4. Ken is retired and receives monthly social security payments as well as payments from his pension. In addition, he has a part-time job. Identify his income variables. (LO 1.4)
5. Explain the two economic analyses used by economists to study the economy. (LO 1.5)

Case Scenario: The Business of Farming

Directions: Use what you learned in the chapter to respond to the following scenario.

Farmers are in the business of raising animals and growing crops. By comparison, businesses are in the business of providing goods and services. In both cases, farmers and business owners must think about where to conduct business and how to distribute their products. In this context, answer the following questions:

1. Compare and contrast the decisions that go into choosing a location for both farmers and businesses.
2. What resource(s) are important for farmers? What resource(s) are important for businesses?

3. Compare and contrast the distribution process for farmers and businesses.
4. What labor requirements does a farmer have? What labor requirements does a business have?

REFERENCES

Investopedia. (2021). *Positive economics.* https://www.investopedia.com/terms/p/positiveeconomics.asp#:~:text=Key%20 Takeaways%201%20Positive%20economics%20is%20an%20objective,should%20be%20in%20the%20future.%20More%20 items...%20

O'Sullivan, A., Shreffin, S., & Perez, S. (2017). *Microeconomics: Principles, applications, and tools* (9th ed.). Pearson Publishing.

Schiller, B. R. (2016). *The micro economy today* (14th ed.). McGraw-Hill Education.

Thinking Economics. (2002). *Location, location, location.* http://www.thinkingeconomics.net/ch15/s02/c15s2e3.htm

CREDITS

Five Key Principles of Economics

Concept Highlight

Chapter 2 examines the five key principles of economics.

Real Life Example: What Does This Mean to You?

The discipline of economics is governed by five key principles. These principles serve as a guide to explaining the forces that affect economic activity. An example of this would be a college student making decisions about when to study. Such decisions entail putting option (studying) over others (playing video games, hanging out with friends, working additional hours, etc.). In economics, such decisions require trading one thing for another.

Introduction

The five key principles of economics include the principle of opportunity cost, the marginal principle, the principle of voluntary exchange, the principle of diminishing returns, and the reality principle. Each principle is an economic theory that economists use as a guide. As such, these principles are important to understanding the rationale behind the choices made regarding the use of limited resources.

OBJECTIVES

While reading this chapter, readers should be able to

- **LO 2.1.** define the principle of opportunity cost and explain its relationship with the production possibilities graph (frontier)
- **LO 2.2.** define the marginal principle
- **LO 2.2.** explain the difference between marginal benefits and marginal costs
- **LO 2.3.** define the principle of voluntary exchange
- **LO 2.4.** define the principle of diminishing returns
- **LO 2.4.** distinguish between the total product curve and the marginal product of labor
- **LO 2.4.** understand the difference between the short run and the long run
- **LO 2.5.** define the reality principle
- **LO 2.5.** explain real value and nominal value

OUTCOMES

After completing this chapter, readers will be able to do the following:

- Illustrate the production possibilities graph (frontier), and explain why it is negatively sloped, based on the principle of opportunity cost.
- Explain the economic rationale for the marginal principle.
- Explain the economic rationale for the principle of voluntary exchange.
- Explain the economic rationale for the principle of diminishing returns.
- Illustrate and explain the total product curve and the marginal product of labor.
- Explain the economic rationale for the reality principle.

Key Terms

The following key terms are discussed in this chapter:

- opportunity cost
- principle of opportunity cost
- production possibilities graph (frontier)
- marginal principle
- marginal benefits
- marginal cost
- principle of voluntary exchange
- principle of diminishing returns
- output
- inputs

- total product curve
- marginal product of labor
- short run
- long run
- reality principle
- real value
- nominal value

2.1 The Principle of Opportunity Cost

There are five key principles of economics. A "principle" refers to a truth. Therefore, these principles serve as a truth for explaining decisions made regarding the use of limited resources. In doing so, the five principles are (a) the principle of opportunity cost, (b) the marginal principle, (c) the principle of voluntary exchange, (d) the principle of diminishing returns, and (e) the reality principle.

The first principle to be introduced is the principle of opportunity cost. **Opportunity cost** refers to a situation in which one makes sacrifices. Therefore, the **principle of opportunity cost** is the belief that for one to obtain something, something else must be given up in return. As such, this principle explains that everything has a cost; therefore, one must make sacrifice to acquire something else. Such transactions are caused by scarcity. In other words, one must sacrifice resources to acquire other resources due to not having an abundance of all resources. This principle is demonstrated when examining the production possibilities graph (frontier). The **production possibilities graph (frontier**; PPG) is as a graph that shows the possible combinations of goods and services produced based on the resources that are available. Figure 2.1 shows a PPG.

In this figure, the principle of opportunity cost tells us that production possibilities graph is negatively sloped because of scarcity. This means that due to there being limited resources, the production of one

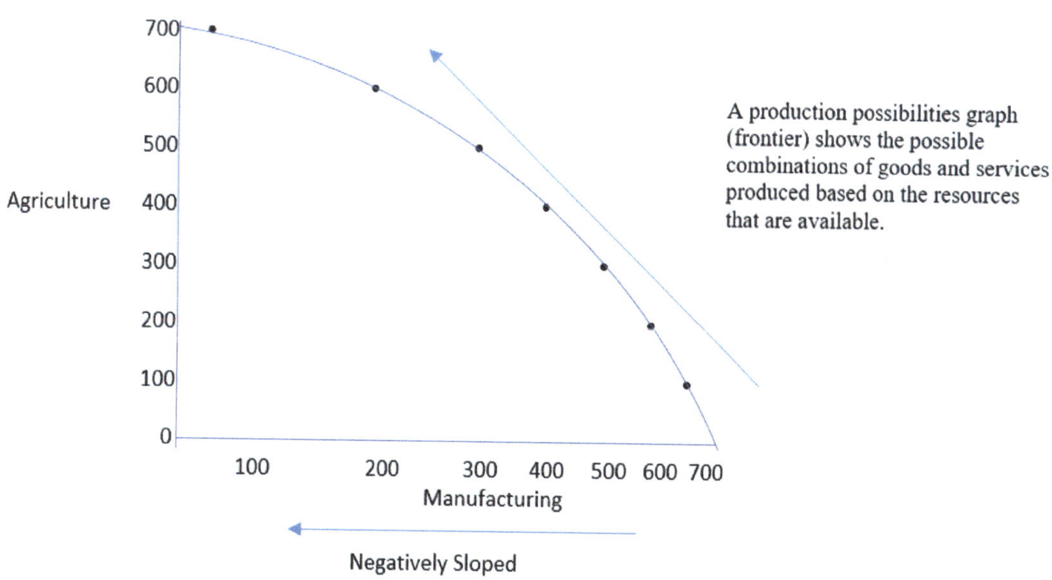

FIGURE 2.1 A Production Possibilities Graph (Frontier)

good will come at the sacrifice of the other good, and therefore, it would be impossible to maximize production of both goods with existing resources. As a result, the principle of opportunity cost demonstrates that there will always be trade-offs.

opportunity cost: a situation in which one makes sacrifices

principle of opportunity cost: the belief that for one to obtain something, something else must be given up in return

production possibilities graph (frontier): a graph that shows the possible combinations of goods and services produced based on the resources that are available

2.2 The Marginal Principle

A second key principle of economics is the marginal principle. This principle has two definitions. The first definition of the **marginal principle** is the belief that a small change in one variable will cause a change in another variable (small $\Delta V \rightarrow$ large ΔV). In doing so, this principle is used daily to help us improve our decision-making by understanding how a change of one thing affects something else. An example of this principle would be a college student who has a part-time job. While at the end of his work shift, the student's supervisor asks the student to remain at work for a few more hours. In this example, the student mentally calculates the additional income earned from working more hours. As such, the student is making their decision about working additional hours by relating the income they will earn to the hours they will work. In doing so, this principle introduces to concepts of marginal benefits and marginal costs. **Marginal benefits** (MB) refer to the additional benefits received from a small increase in an activity. Using the example of the college student who has a part-time job, the marginal benefits are the additional income earned from working additional hours. By comparison, **marginal costs** (MC) are the additional costs incurred from a small increase in an activity. Using the example of the college student who has a part-time job, for each additional hour worked, one less hour will be available for studying.

TABLE 2.1 Using the Marginal Principle to Examine the Costs and Benefits of an Action

Cost-Benefit Analysis Items	Perspectives		
	Department of Corrections	Society	Local Community
Improved prison management	Benefit		
Fewer prison riots and assaults	Benefit		
Improved post-release for the general prison population	Benefit	Benefit	
Strained relationships of supermax prisoners with the outside world		Cost	
Increased mental health problems among supermax prisoners	Cost	Cost	
Increased number of jobs	Cost	Cost	Benefit
Increased property taxes of supermax prison	Cost	Cost	Benefit
Increased taxes to afford expansions and security measures	Cost	Cost	Benefit

The second definition of the marginal principle is the belief that one should increase an activity if one's marginal benefits are greater than its marginal costs, decrease an activity if the marginal costs are greater than the marginal benefits, and choose the level of activity where the marginal benefits equal the marginal costs. Once again, this definition allows us to improve our decision-making by relating our marginal benefits to our marginal costs. Like the first definition, the second definition of the marginal principle assumes that a small change in either marginal benefits or marginal costs will cause a change in an activity (small $\Delta V \rightarrow$ large ΔV). Therefore, this definition states that one should continue an activity as long as the marginal benefits are greater than the marginal costs, one should discontinue an activity when the marginal cost becomes greater than the marginal benefits, and one should choose the level of activity at which the marginal benefits equal the marginal costs.

marginal principle: the belief that a small change in one variable will cause a change in another variable; the belief that one should increase an activity if one's marginal benefits are greater than its marginal costs, decrease an activity if the marginal costs are greater than the marginal benefits, and choose the level of activity where the marginal benefits equal the marginal costs

marginal benefits: the additional benefits received from a small increase in an activity

marginal costs: the additional costs incurred from a small increase in an activity

2.3 The Principle of Voluntary Exchange

A third key principle of economics is the principle of voluntary exchange. The **principle of voluntary exchange** is the belief that society benefits when people act in their own self-interest. In doing so, this theory explains how the free market system operates. Within this explanation, people behave in their own self-interest in the marketplace when they seek to find goods and services at the lowest possible price. This action ensures that goods and services are offered at lower prices if merchants seek to make a sale. In turn, society benefits, as goods and services are offered at lower prices to everyone.

principle of voluntary exchange: the belief that society benefits when people act in their own self-interest

FIGURE 2.2 People in the Market Acting in Their Own Self-Interest

2.4 The Principle of Diminishing Returns

A fourth key principle of economics is the principle of diminishing returns. The **principle of diminishing returns** is the belief that output will increase at a decreasing rate when one input increases while all other inputs remain at a constant rate. Within this definition, "an increase at a decreasing rate" refers to smaller increase in production for each level of output that occurs. An **output** refers to the final goods and services produced and is available for sale, while **inputs** refer to the resources (raw materials, facilities, equipment, etc.) used in the production of the final goods and services. Therefore, the principle of diminishing returns explain that overall production (output) becomes smaller at each level output when only one input (resource) is increased but all other inputs remain constant. As such, this theory is used by businesses to determine the number of employees to be employed.

An example of this principle would be a pizza shop owner who has one employee. This employee can bake 12 pizzas in a day. The pizza shop owner decides to hire a second employee with the hopes of increasing pizza production from 12 to 24 pizzas per day. However, total production between the two employees only increases to 18. In response, the pizza shop owner hires a third employee with the hopes of increasing pizza production to 24. Yet pizza production between the three employees only increases to 21. Table 2.2 shows the pizza production output as the number of workers increase. In addition, this illustration shows the change in output for each additional work.

TABLE 2.2 THE RELATIONSHIP BETWEEN LABOR AND OUTPUT

Number of employees	Pizza production (output)	Change in pizza production (output)
1	12	-
2	18	6
3	21	3

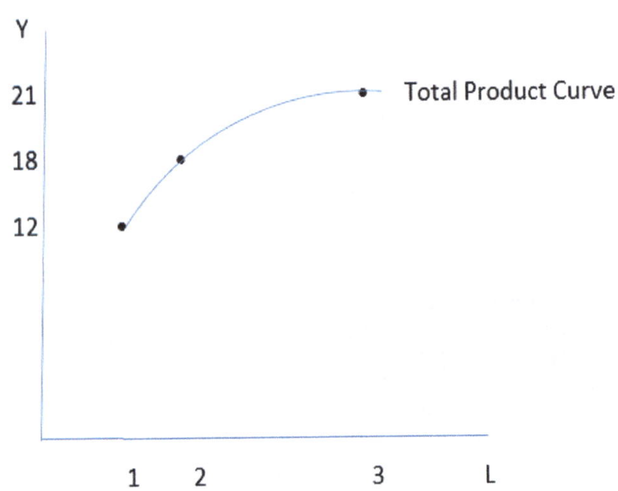

FIGURE 2.3 A Total Product Curve

Figure 2.3 shows *an increase at a decreasing rate* in the last column, as pizza production changes from 12 to 18 to 21 for each additional employee. We can see this change on a total product curve. A total product curve is a curve that shows the relationship between labor (L) and output (Y).

The total product curve also includes the marginal product of labor. The **marginal product of labor** refers to a curve that shows the change in output for each additional worker employed. In doing so, the marginal product of labor shows diminishing returns. In other words, the marginal product of labor shows *an increase at a decreasing rate.* Figure 2.4 shows an example of the marginal product of labor. Using the example provided, this figure shows pizza output per additional worker, changing from 12 to 6 to 3.

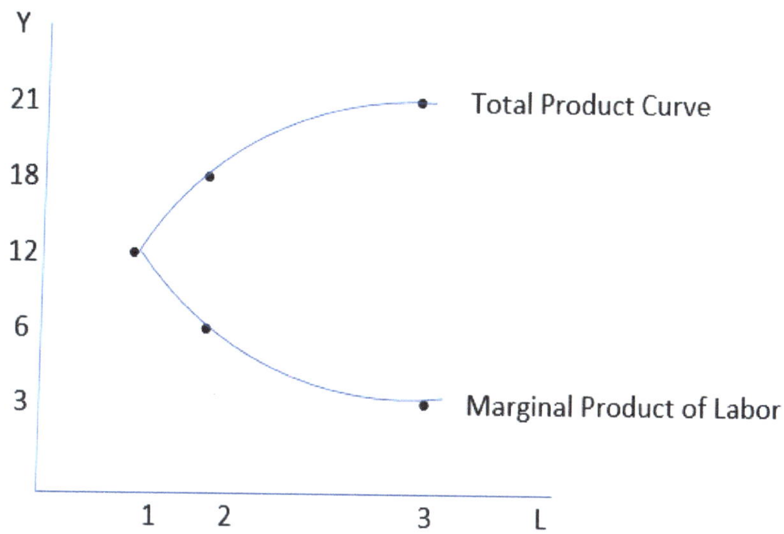

FIGURE 2.4 The Marginal Product of Labor

So why do production increases become smaller with each level of output? This occurs because each resource becomes less efficient and, therefore, less productive. In the example provided, the pizza shop owner only hired workers, while leaving all other resources (stove, ingredients, utensils, etc.) at their current levels. This caused each worker to have less space to work, and therefore, each worker became less efficient as well as less productive. However, each worker would be just as efficient as the others if the pizza shop owner changed all other resources as they hired additional resources.

Diminishing returns occur in the short run. The **short run** has two definitions. The first definition is a period of time in which one or more factors of production remains fixed. It is also defined as a period of time in which a business can't build new facilities or modify existing ones. During the short run, businesses do not have the ability to change at least one of their resources (raw materials, facilities, equipment, etc.) and, therefore, production increases become smaller with each level of output as additional workers are hired.

principle of diminishing returns: the belief that output will increase at a decreasing rate when one input increases, while all other inputs remain at a constant rate

output: final goods and services produced and available for sale

inputs: the resources (raw materials, facilities, equipment, etc.) used in the production of the final goods and services

total product curve: a curve that shows the relationship between labor (l) and output (y)

marginal product of labor: a curve that shows the change in output for each additional worker employed

short run: a period of time in which one or more factors or production remains fixed; a period of time in which a business can't build new facilities or modify existing ones

long run: a period of time in which all the factors of production can be changed; a period of time in which businesses can build new facilities or modify existing ones

Diminishing returns do not occur in the long run. The long run also has two definitions. First, the **long run** is defined as a period of time in which all the factors of production can be changed. It is also defined as a period of time in which businesses can build new facilities or modify existing ones. During this period, diminishing returns do not occur because businesses are able to change their resources as they hire additional workers. As a result, the necessary improvements for additional workers allow each one to be productive.

2.5 The Reality Principle

A fifth key principle of economics is the reality principle. The **reality principle** is the belief that it is more important to know the real value of money than the nominal value of money. The **real value** of money refers to the value of money based on what can be purchased. The **nominal value** of money is the value stated on the currency. Therefore, the reality principle assumes that people prefer to know what can be purchased with money rather than the amount that's stated on the currency. As such, this principle is used to determine the amount of money to carry.

reality principle: the belief that it is more important to know the real value of money than the nominal value of money

real value: the value of money based on what can be purchased

nominal value: the value of money stated on the currency

FIGURE 2.5 Consumer Purchases Based on the Reality Principle

SUMMARY

- The principle of opportunity cost tells us that the production possibilities curve is negatively sloped because of scarcity. (LO 2.1)
- The marginal principle improves our decision-making by allowing us to examine the marginal benefits and marginal costs of an activity. (LO 2.2)
- The principle of voluntary exchange explains how the free market system operates. (LO 2.3)
- The principle of diminishing returns is used by businesses to determine the number of people to employ. (LO 2.4)
- The total product curve shows the relationship between labor and output. (LO 2.4)
- The marginal product of labor shows diminishing returns. (LO 2.4)
- Diminishing returns occur in the short run; they don't occur in the long run. (LO 2.4)
- The reality principle is the notion that the real value of money is most important to people. (LO 2.5)

END-OF-CHAPTER APPLICATION

Comprehension Questions

Directions: Refer to the chapter to correctly respond to the following questions and prompts.

1. The government of the Democratic Republic of the Congo seeks to use its diamonds to maximize production in both microchips and beauty products. Is this realistic? Why, or why not? (LO 2.1)
2. You have been asked to be part of a study group on your campus. How would the marginal principle affect your decision? What factors would you consider in this decision? (LO 2.2)
3. Businesses at a local shopping outlet are offering a major discount day on apparel and shoes. In response, Julie decides to go shopping. Is she applying the principle of voluntary exchange? Why, or why not? (LO 2.3)
4. Suppose you are the manager of a local retail store. As the manager, you are responsible for hiring. This means it is your responsibility to hire the right number of employees. Why would you be concerned with diminishing returns in your hiring decisions? (LO 2.4)
5. Paul is the owner of a shoe manufacturing business. He has one employee who produces 50 shoes per week. Paul wants to increase shoe production to 100 shoes per week. So he hires a second worker. The two employees combine to produce 75 shoes per week. In response, Paul hires a third worker. The three employees combine to product 85 shoes per week. Draw the business's total product curve. Draw its marginal product of labor. (LO 2.4)

6. A local fast-food restaurant is offering $10 per hour to new employees. However, they have been unsuccessful in attracting job applicants. Use the concepts of real value and nominal value to explain why they might be having hiring difficulties. (LO 2.5)

Case Scenario: The Benefits and Costs of Producing Oil in the United States

Directions: Use what you learned in the chapter to respond to the following scenario.

W. W. Norton (2004) reports that the U.S. government offered the U.S. oil industry an incentive to produce oil in the early 1970s in response to OPEC's decision to raise prices. This source reports that to motivate U.S. producers, the U.S. government allowed producers to use international pricing. However, during this period, inflation was increasing, which led to decreases in buying power as well as the real price of oil received by the producers. As a result, there was less incentive for U.S. producers to drill. To encourage U.S. oil production, W. W. Norton (2004) reports that by 1972, as oil prices continued to rise, the U.S. government made the decision to deregulate the market. This spurred domestic production through the early 1980s; however, by the mid-1980s, increased oil production caused oil prices to plummet (Norton, 2004). Answer the following questions:

1. What were the opportunity costs associated with U.S. oil production in the early 1970s?
2. Identify the marginal benefits and marginal costs of U.S. domestic production from the early 1970s to the early 1980s.
3. How does inflation affect purchasing power and oil prices?
4. Identify a government policy you would implement to maintain stable oil prices in the United States for domestic producers in the mid-1980s. Identify some marginal benefits and marginal costs associated with the policy.

BIBLIOGRAPHY

O'Sullivan, A., Shreffin, S., & Perez, S. (2017). *Microeconomics: Principles, applications, and tools* (9th ed.). Pearson Publishing.

Schiller, B. R. (2016). The micro economy today (14th ed.). McGraw-Hill Education.

W. W. Norton. (2004). Producing American oil. https://wwnorton.com/college/econ/ecu7/section16/case-studies.htm

CREDITS

CHAPTER 3

The Economy, Markets, Production, Income, and Exchange

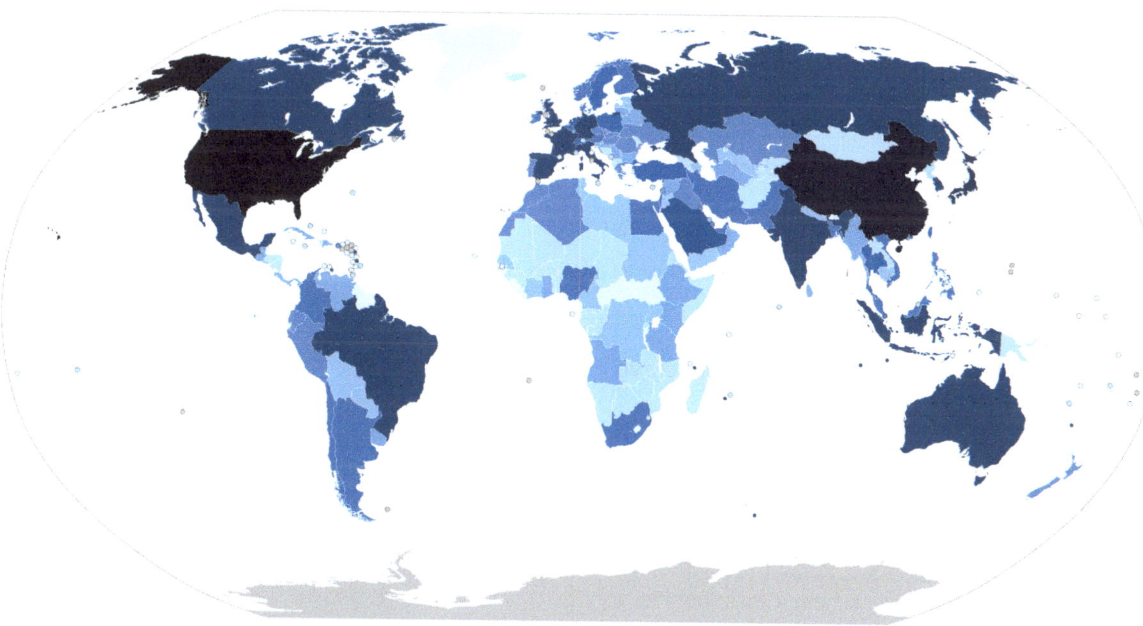

Concept Highlight

Chapter 3 examines production as well as specialization and trade.

Real Life Example: What Does This Mean to You?

Production occurs daily in the economy and leads to economic growth. This production is measured through the gross domestic product, which also provides a measure of national wealth. An example of this includes an entrepreneur who buys land and equipment, builds a facility, and hires labor to manufacture a product. Within this production process, labor earns a wage, which is also their wealth. From this wage, both labor and businesses purchase goods and services. These purchases allow the cycle to grow and repeat itself.

Introduction

A centrally planned economy is an important concept, as it is one of the three types of economies. As such, a centrally planned economy explains how resources are distributed from the public's perspective. In doing so, economists use the GDP to measure the use of these resources in production. Moreover, they explain the movement of these resources with the circular flow diagram.

The consumption possibilities curve is important to economics because it provides a picture of the different consumption options in the economy. In providing consumption in the economy, some producers specialize in the production process. This, in turn, allows them to gain both an absolute and comparative advantage.

OBJECTIVES

While reading this chapter, readers should be able to

LO 3.1. identify a centrally planned economy

LO 3.2. define "gross domestic product"

LO 3.2. define "per capital GDP"

LO 3.2. define "growth rate

LO 3.3. identify a circular flow diagram

LO 3.4. identify a consumption possibilities curve

LO 3.4. define "absolute advantage"

LO 3.4. define "comparative advantage"

OUTCOMES

After completing this chapter, readers will be able to do the following:

- Use the gross domestic product to relate production to national wealth.
- Illustrate the circular flow diagram.
- Explain how specialization and trade makes one better off.
- Illustrate the consumption possibilities curve.

Key Terms

The following key terms are discussed in this chapter:

- centrally planned economy
- gross domestic product
- per capita GDP
- economic growth

- circular flow diagram
- consumption possibilities curve
- absolute advantage
- comparative advantage

3.1 Economies and Markets

As discussed in Chapter 1, "economy" refers to a system through which resources are distributed. The economy is made up of markets. A "market" is a place where buyers and sellers engage in exchanges. The U.S. economy was built upon the free market system. The free market system is a system in which the sellers have the freedom to sell products at any price and buyers have the freedom to buy. However, the U.S. economy operates as a mixed economy. A mixed economy is a system in which there are both market freedoms and government controls.

Beyond the free market and mixed economy, there is also a centrally planned economy. A **centrally planned economy** is defined as a system in which all productive resources are owned and distributed by the government. Under a centrally planned economy, the government decides what products are produced and who gets to consume them.

centrally planned economy: a system in which all productive resources are owned and distributed by the government

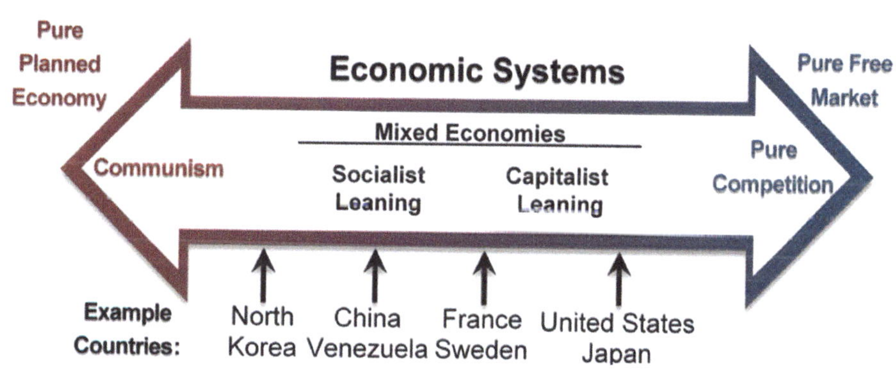

FIGURE 3.1 Economic Systems

3.2 Production and Income

The economy distributes resources. These resources make up the factors of production and are used to produce. Economists seek to determine how much is produced in a nation with these resources. This measurement is called the gross domestic product. The **gross domestic product** (GDP) is defined as a measure of all goods and services produced in a nation within 1 year. In other words, the GDP is a measure of production. This measurement is very important because it also measures national income (NI). Naturally, the question becomes, "How does a measure of production determines national income?"

For businesses to produce, they must hire labor. But laborers do not work for free; they earn a wage. This wage represents income. When all wages in the country are combined, this, in turn, determines national income. An analogy of a river will be used to explain this relationship. In this analogy, assume that the river has a series of streams breaking off it. In addition, assume that resources are flowing downstream. In doing so, economists watch the resources flow downstream to determine what products are produced. The producers of these products will attach a price, which is also their value. These prices consist of money that is paid to labor (L) and money kept by the business (B) to cover its other costs as well as profits. This, in turn, represents wages for both labor and the business; these wages also represent income. Therefore, when economists combine all wages earned in the economy based on the prices charged for the products, the total is the national income. Figure 3.2 shows an example of GDP measurement.

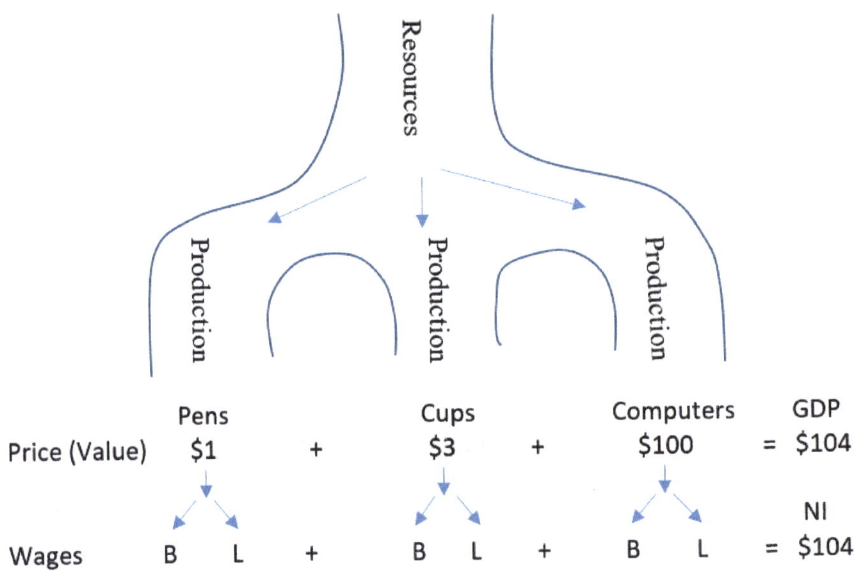

FIGURE 3.2 GDP and National Income Measurement

The U.S. GDP for 2020 was $20.93 trillion. Using the preceding explanation, this number means the U.S. produced $20.93 trillion in goods and services. This value is based on the prices charged. As such, these prices are used to cover wages to labor as well as the business's other cost and profits. In doing so, these prices represent wages (and income) to both. Therefore, $20.93 trillion production also equals $20.93 trillion in national wages (national income).

The GDP measures national production and national wealth. From this, economists seek to determine production by the average person. In doing so, they are concerned with the per capital GDP. The **per capital GDP** is defined as the average level of production per person. This measure is determined by dividing the GDP by the nation's total population, which, in turn, determines the average income per person. Using this calculation, for 2020, the estimated U.S. per capita GDP was $63,416.

In addition to the measures mentioned, economists also track nations' GDP from year to year to determine whether they are producing more or less over time. In doing so, they are seeking to measure economic growth. **Economic growth** is defined as sustained growth in the GDP over a period of time. As such, economic growth provides indication of growth in national income. Table 3.1 shows changes in the U.S. GDP between 2019 and 2021.

TABLE 3.1 U.S. Annual GDP

Year	GDP (in trillions)
2021	$23.32
2020	$20.93
2019	$21.43

Source: Aaron O'Neill, "Gross Domestic Product (GDP) Per Capita in the United States in Current Prices from 1987 to 2027," https://www.statista.com/.

Economists often compare nations' GDP to determine which countries are richer and which are poorer relative to one another. When they make these analyses, they examine both goods and services to determine output produced. In doing so, they use these numbers to rank nations' GDP. Table 3.2 shows the 2020 ranking of the top five nations based on their GDPs.

TABLE 3.2 2021 GDP Rankings of the Top Five Nations

Nations	GDP (in trillions)
United States	$23.32
China	$17.73
Japan	$4.94
Germany	$4.25
India	$3.17

Source: Global PEO Services, "Top 15 Countries by GDP in 2021," https://globalpeoservices.com/.

3.3 Circular Flow Diagram

One of the roles of economists is explaining how the economy operates. This explanation occurs by discussing the circular flow diagram. A **circular flow diagram** describes the flow of income and products between markets. This diagram involves two markets, which include the market of the owners of the factors of production and the market of final products. Between these two markets, two groups exist: individuals and businesses. Using both the markets and groups, economists explain the operation of the economy through the circular flow diagram by stating that the owners of the factors

gross domestic product: a measure of all goods and services produced in a nation within 1 year

per capita GDP: the average level of production per person

economic growth: sustained growth in the GDP over a period of time of production hire the individuals who produce the final goods and sell those goods to both individuals and businesses. From this, the owners of the factors of production earn profit, which, in turn, is used to hire more labor and start the process over again, earning profit. Figure 3.3 demonstrates this process.

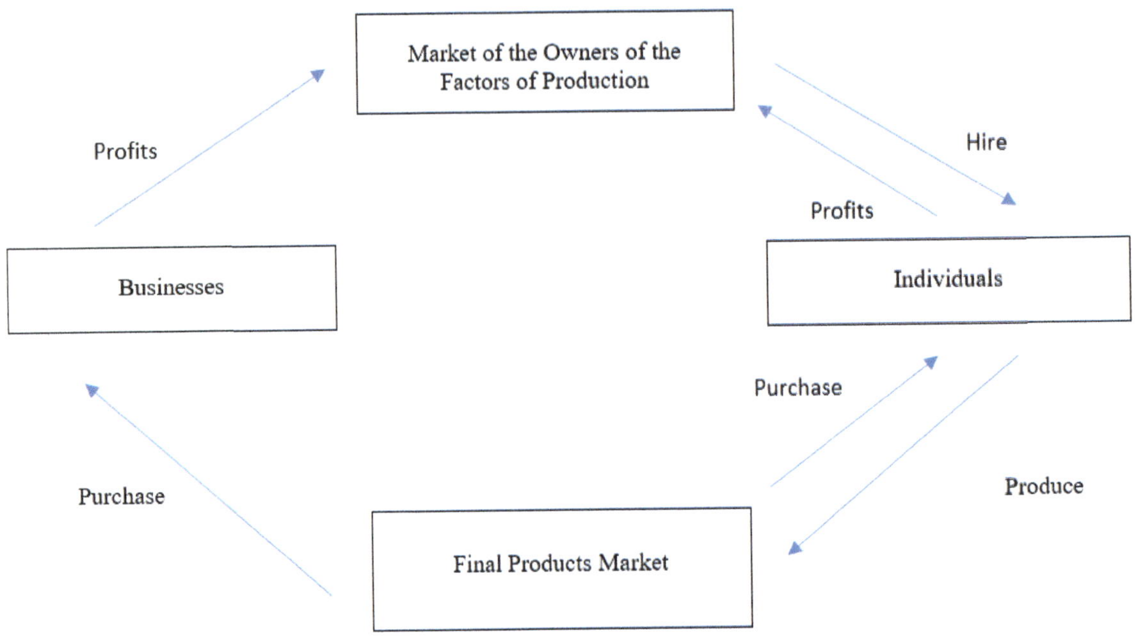

FIGURE 3.3 A Circular Flow Diagram

circular flow diagram: a diagram that describes the flow of income and products between markets

In using the circular flow diagram to explain the operation of the economy, economists are using the GDP. In other words, the circular flow diagram explains that the economy operates through hiring, production, purchases, and income. This process, in turn, explains what occurs in the GDP production process and the income distribution process.

3.4 Exchange

The economy consists of limited resources that are used to produce a variety of products. These products are sold in the market. However, some producers within the economy choose to specialize in the production process and then trade with others. This decision is based on the principle of opportunity cost. The principle of opportunity cost explains that specialization makes people better off because it allows them to be efficient in the production process by producing one or a few goods and trading with others producing other types of products. Therefore, this principle explains that there will always be trade-offs.

An example of this includes two producers, Samantha and Bobby, who possess the same resources. With her resources, Samantha can produce six watermelons and two tomatoes. By comparison, Bobby can produce 1 watermelon or 1 tomato with his resources. What is the opportunity cost of production for

Samantha and Bobby? In this example, Samantha's opportunity cost is three watermelons for one tomato, while Bobby's opportunity cost is one watermelon for one tomato. In analysis, the principle of opportunity cost tells us Samantha should specialize in producing watermelons, and Bobby should specialize in producing tomatoes. In doing so, Samantha can specialize in producing watermelons and trade with Bobby who, in turn, specializes in producing tomatoes. This allows both to be better off. Table 3.3 shows the production capabilities of Samantha and Bobby.

TABLE 3.3 Production Capabilities of Samantha and Bobby

Producer	Watermelon	Tomato
Samantha	6	2
Bobby	1	1

From this example, we can use the consumption possibilities curve to see the consumption possibilities created from specialization and trade. A **consumption possibilities curve** is a curve that shows the possibilities combination of consumptions that result from specialization and trade. Figure 3.7 shows a consumption possibilities curve for Samantha and Bobby. In this figure, Samantha's consumption options move from six watermelons for one tomato to one watermelon from six tomatoes. In doing so, this curve shows us the benefits of specialization and trade.

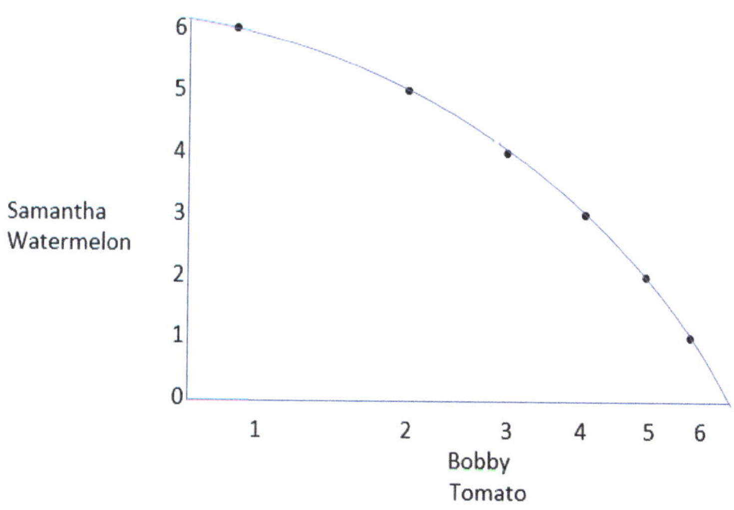

The consumption possibilities curve is a curve that shows the possibilities combination of consumptions that result from specialization and trade.

FIGURE 3.4 A Consumption Possibilities Curve

In addition, in this example, Samantha has an absolute advantage. An **absolute advantage** is an advantage that occurs because one is more productive than another. However, both Samantha and Bobby can achieve a comparative

consumption possibilities curve: a curve that shows the possibilities combination of consumptions resulting from specialization and trade

absolute advantage: an advantage that occurs because one is more productive than another

comparative advantage: an advantage that occurs because one can produce at a lower opportunity cost than another advantage through specialization and trade. A **comparative advantage** is an advantage that occurs because one can produce at a lower opportunity cost than another.

SUMMARY

- A centrally planned economy is one in which all productive resources are distributed by the government. (LO 3.1)
- Economists use the GDP to measure production. The measure also determines national wealth. (LO 3.2)
- Economists use the circular flow diagram to explain how the economy operates. (LO 3.3)
- Specialization and trade in the production process makes one better off by allowing one to produce one or a few goods and trade with others who are producing other types of products. (LO 3.4)
- The consumption possibilities curve shows the consumption possibilities that result from specialization and trade. (LO 3.4)
- An absolute advantage occurs when one is more productive than another. (LO 3.4)
- A comparative advantage occurs when one can produce at a lower opportunity cost than another. (LO 3.4)

END-OF-CHAPTER APPLICATION

Comprehension Questions

Directions: Refer to the chapter to correctly respond to the following questions and prompts.

1. Who makes most of the basic decisions regarding the distribution of resources in a centrally planned economy? Is this considered efficient? Why, or why not? (LO 3.1)
2. Use the GDP to explain the relationship between production and national income. (LO 3.2)
3. Explain how specialization and trade makes one better off. (LO 3.3)
4. Suppose an economy maxes out its production capabilities with its current resources by producing 100,000 shoes and 80,000 shirts. Draw a consumption possibilities graph illustrating this production, using point A for shoes and point D for shirts. Suppose the economy reduces shoe production to 80,000 to produce 20,000 shirts. Illustrate this production on the graph using point B. Suppose the economy reduces shoe production to 40,000 to produce 60,000 shirts. Illustrate this production on this graph using point C. Draw a consumption possibilities curve to connect each point on the graph. (LO 3.4)
5. Jeffrey and Kim are producers who possess the same amount of resources. Jeffrey can produce 100 apples and 50 ears of corn, while Kim can produce 20 apples and 20 ears of corn. To produce this

level of products, Jeffrey must use all his resources, while Kim uses 80% of her resources. Which producer has an absolute advantage? Which producer has a comparative advantage? Explain your answers. (LO 3.4)

Case Scenario: Comparing and Contrasting GDPs

Directions: Use what you learned in the chapter to respond to the following scenario.

Suppose China's GDP overtakes the United States' GDP. However, suppose China's national income lags the United States' national income in the process. Answer the following questions:

1. Compare and contrast the economies of China and the United States.
2. What must have occurred with China's GDP to overtake the United States' GDP?
3. Explain how China could have overtaken the United States in GDP but remain behind the United States in national income.

BIBLIOGRAPHY

BEA. (2021, February 25). *Gross domestic product, fourth quarter and year 2020 (second estimate).* https://www.bea.gov/news/2021/gross-domestic-product-fourth-quarter-and-year-2020-second-estimate

Global Peo Services. (n.d.). *Top 15 countries by GDP in 2020.* https://globalpeoservices.com/top-15-countries-by-gdp-in-2020/

O'Sullivan, A., Shreffin, S., & Perez, S. (2017). *Microeconomics: Principles, applications, and tools* (9th ed.). Pearson Publishing.

Schiller, B. R. (2016). *The micro economy today* (14th ed.). McGraw-Hill Education.

Statista. (2021). *Gross domestic product (GDP) per capita in the United States in current prices from 1986 to 2026.* https://www.statista.com/statistics/263601/gross-domestic-product-gdp-per-capita-in-the-united-states/

Trading Economics. (2021). *United States GDP.* https://tradingeconomics.com/united-states/gdp

CREDITS

Part II
Demand, Supply, and Equilibrium

Source: Shawn P. Eklund/U.S. Navy, https://commons.wikimedia.org/wiki/File:US_Navy_020813-N-3642E-503_Navy_customers_look_for_ripe_apples_at_the_commissary_located_at_Naval_Station_Norfolk.jpg, 2002.

CHAPTER 4

Demand and Supply

Concept Highlight

Chapter 4 examines the concept of demand and supply.

Real Life Example: What Does This Mean to You?

Demand and supply are used daily to understand buying and selling habits in the market in relation to price and other variables. Take, for example, Sam, who owns a pizza restaurant. Sam has been changing the price of his small pepperoni pizza to understand how consumer spending changes in his restaurant. In doing so, Sam noticed that consumer spending on his small pepperoni pizza changed as price changed.

By comparison, Sam has been asked to cater an event in his town. For this event, he was asked to provide large one-topping pizzas. In the negotiations for catering this event, Sam provided the sale of different quantities of large one-topping pizzas at different purchased price points.

Introduction

Demand is an important concept due to its examination in buying habits. As such, the concept of demand allows the reader to understand changing buying habits due to changes in pricing and other variables. Supply is also an important concept due to its examination of selling habits. This concept allows the reader to understand producing selling habits due to changes in pricing and other variables.

OBJECTIVES

While reading this chapter, readers should be able to

LO 4.1. define "demand"

LO 4.1. draw a demand curve

LO 4.1. distinguish between substitute goods and complementary goods

LO 4.2. calculate the slope of a demand curve

LO 4.3. define "supply"

LO 4.3. draw a supply curve

LO 4.3. calculate the slope of a supply curve

LO 4.4. define "equilibrium"

LO 4.4. define "excess supply"

LO 4.4. define "excess demand"

OUTCOMES

After completing this chapter, readers will be able to do the following:

- Illustrate a demand curve.
- Explain how a change price affects the demand curve.
- Explain how a change in variables other than price affects the demand curve.
- Explain how a substitute good affects the demand curve.
- Explain how a complementary good affect the demand curve.
- Calculate the slope of a demand curve.
- Illustrate a supply curve.

- Explain how a change in price affects the supply curve.
- Explain how a change in variables other than price affects the supply curve.
- Calculate the slope of a supply curve.
- Illustrate excess supply on a graph.
- Illustrate excess demand on a graph.

Key Terms

The following key terms are discussed in this chapter:

- demand
- demand schedule
- demand curve
- law of demand
- change in quantity demanded
- change in demand
- substitute good
- complimentary good
- individual demand
- market demand
- supply
- supply schedule
- supply curve
- law of supply
- change in quantity supplied
- change in supply
- individual supply
- market supply
- equilibrium
- efficiency
- excess supply
- excess demand

4.1 What is Demand?

Demand (D) is defined as the number of a particular product consumers are willing and able to buy at various prices, ceteris paribus. The definition of demand implies that it focuses on buying. In doing so, the examination of demand begins with a demand schedule. A **demand schedule** refers to a table that shows the relationship between price and the number of a particular product consumers are willing and able to buy, ceteris paribus. An example of a demand schedule includes a pizza shop owner who is examining the number of small-size pepperoni pizzas being sold at various prices. In this example, Table 4.1 shows the relationship between the price and the number of small-size pepperoni pizzas being sold.

TABLE 4.1 A Demand Schedule

Price for small pepperoni pizza	Number of pizzas purchased
$2	10
$4	8
$6	6
$8	4
$10	2

demand: the number of a particular product consumers are willing and able to buy at various prices, ceteris paribus

demand schedule: a table that shows the relationship between price and the number of a particular product consumers are willing and able to buy, ceteris paribus

The relationship between price and the number of a particular product that consumers are willing to buy can be seen on a demand curve. A **demand curve** is defined as a curve that shows the relationship between price and the number of a particular product that consumers are willing to buy, ceteris paribus. Using the preceding example, Figure 4.1 shows a demand curve. In this example, the demand curve is both negatively sloped and upward sloped because of the law of demand. The **law of demand** is the belief that as price rises, the number of a particular product who consumers buy that product declines, and vice versa. In other words, the law of demand assumes consumers purchase fewer products when they are more expensive. Because of this, demand *moves up* along the demand curve (the demand curve remains stationary). By comparison, if price falls, there will be *downward movement* along the demand curve as purchases become less expensive. Figures 4.2 and 4.3 show these movements. Within this, Figure 4.2 shows upward move, which is a decline in quantity demanded, while Figure 4.3 shows a downward movement, which indicates an increase in quantity demanded. As such, this movement is known as a change in quantity demanded. A **change in quantity demanded** (QD) is defined as a situation in which a change in price causes a change in the number of a particular product purchased by consumers.

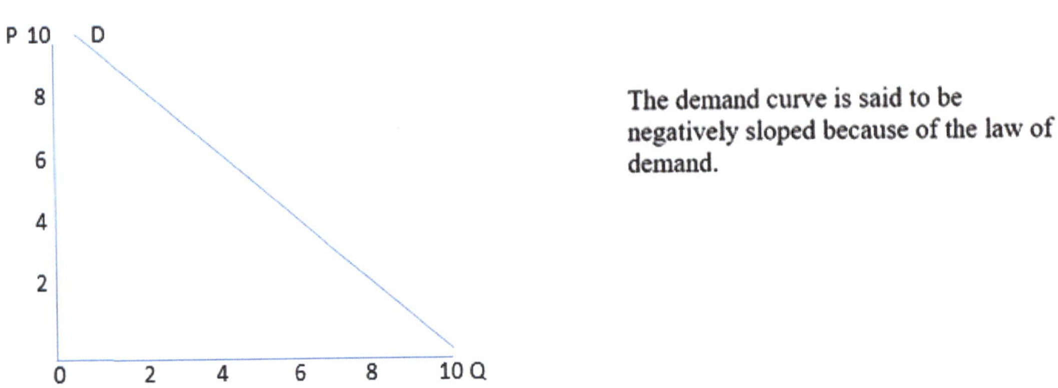

FIGURE 4.1 A Demand Curve

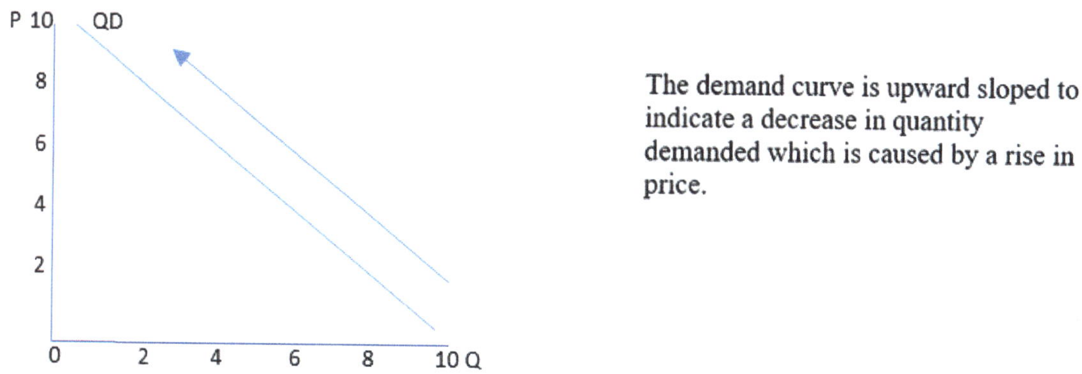

FIGURE 4.2 Upward Movement (Change in Quantity Demanded)

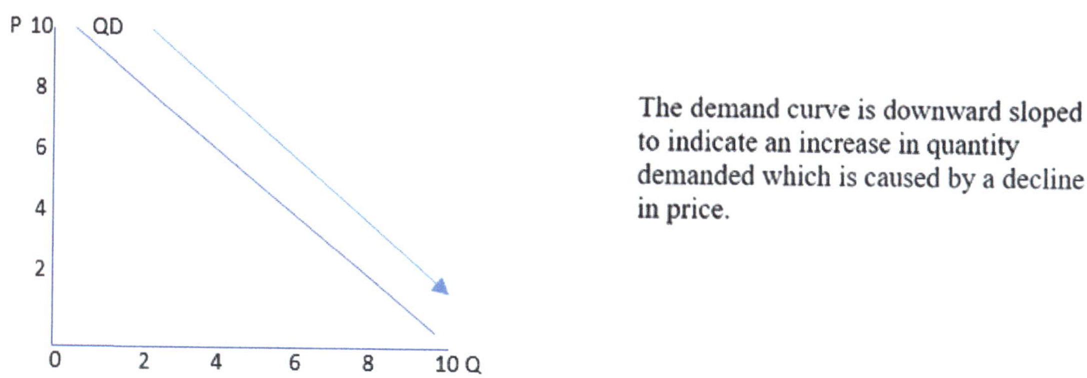

FIGURE 4.3 Downward Movement (Change in Quantity Demanded)

The law of demand assumes that price is the only variable that causes a change in ceteris paribus, holding all other factors constant; however, this is not true. Such other variables include income, taxes, technological changes, tastes, preferences, and much more, which cause the demand curve to shift right or left. Figures 4.4 and 4.5 show these shifts. Within this, Figure 4.4 shows a right shift, which indicates a rise in demand, while Figure 4.5 shows a left shift, which indicates a decline in demand. As such, this shift is known as a change in demand. A **change in demand** is defined as a situation in which a change in a variable other than price causes a change in the number of a particular product purchased by consumers.

demand curve: a curve that shows the relationship between price and the number of a particular product that consumers are willing to buy, ceteris paribus

law of demand: the belief that as price rises, the number of a particular product consumers buy declines, and vice versa

change in quantity demanded: a situation in which a change in prices causes a change in the number of a particular product purchased by consumers

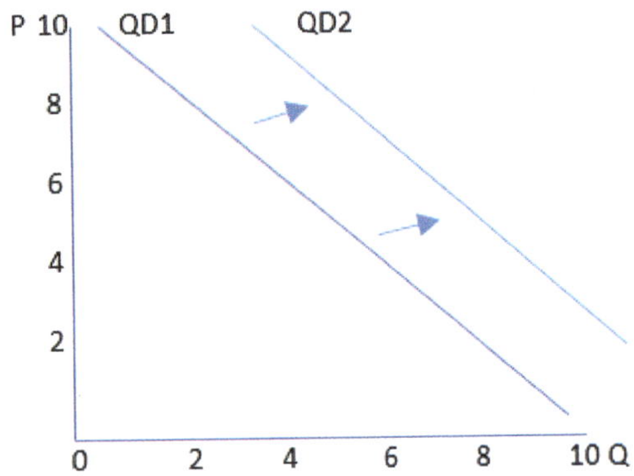

A right shift of the demand curve indicates an increase in demand. This shift is caused by a change in variables other than price.

FIGURE 4.4 A Right Shift (Change in Demand)

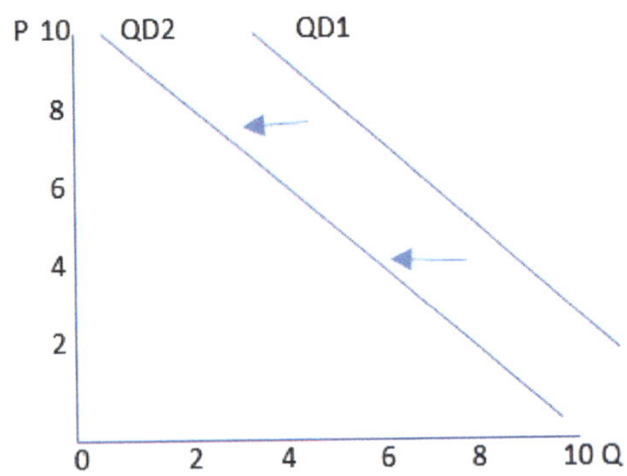

A left shift of the demand curve indicates a decrease in demand. This shift is caused a by a change in variables other than price.

FIGURE 4.5 A Left Shift (Change in Demand)

change in demand: a situation in which a change in a variable other than price causes a change in the number of a particular product purchased by consumers

Substitute and complementary goods are used to help understand the difference between a change in quantity demanded and a change in demand. A **substitute good** refers to a good that replaces another good. In other words, a substitute good is a good that is like a primary good but acts as a second choice. An example of such goods are tea and coffee. In this example, these products have similar qualities, which allows one to be replaced by another. Therefore, using these goods as an example, the price of one good changing will cause the demand for the other to change; Figures 4.6 and 4.7 demonstrate this effect. In Figure 4.6, the price of tea increases, which causes the demand for coffee to rise. In doing so, tea experiences an upward movement along its demand due to a change in its price (change in quantity demanded). In response to this price change in tea, consumers increase their purchase in coffee, which causes a right shift of its demand curve (change in demand). By comparison, in Figure 4.7, the price of tea decreases, which causes the demand for coffee to decline. In doing so, the price change in tea causes downward movement along its demand curve (change in quantity demanded), and in response, consumers buy less coffee, which causes its demand curve to shift to the left (change in demand).

Tea

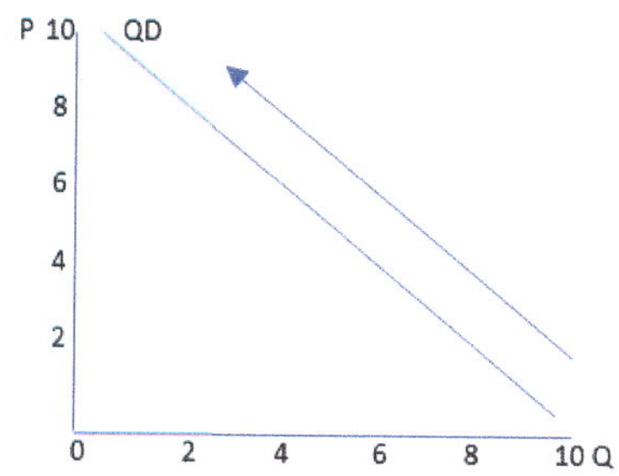

The rise in the price of tea causes a decline in quantity demanded. This, in turn, causes upward movement along the demand curve.

Coffee

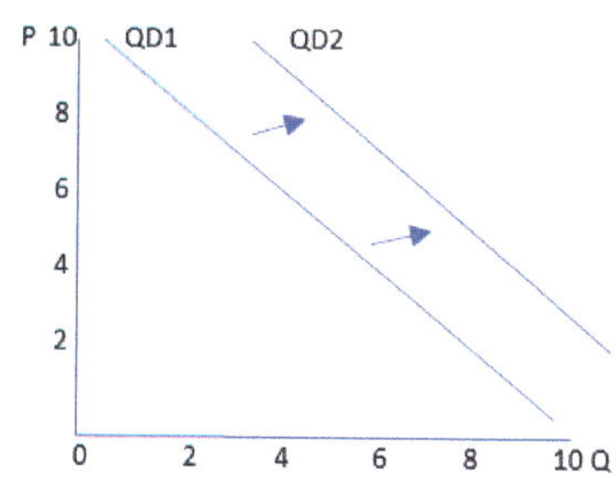

The rise in the price of tea causes an increase in the demand for coffee as the products act as a substitute. This, in turn, causes the demand curve for coffee to shift to the right.

FIGURE 4.6 Substitute Goods: Upward Movement of Tea

Tea

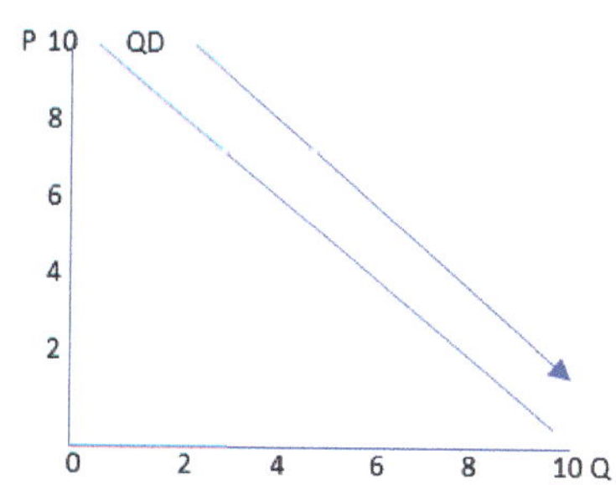

The decline in the price of tea causes an increase in quantity demanded. This, in turn, causes downward movement along the demand curve.

Coffee

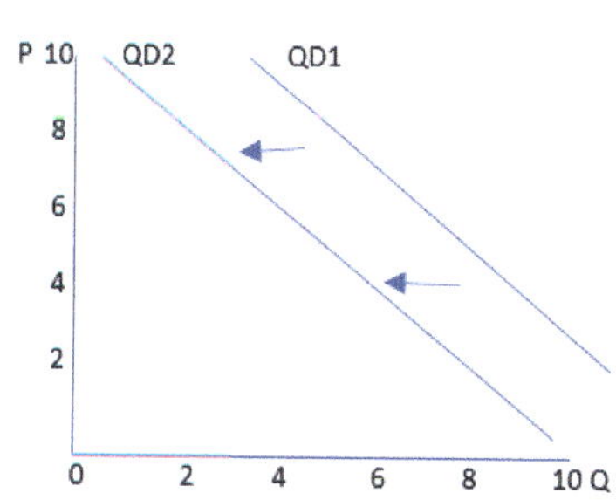

The decline in the price of tea causes a decrease in the demand for coffee as the products act as a substitute. This, in turn, causes the demand curve for coffee to shift to the left.

FIGURE 4.7 Substitute Goods: Downward Movement of Tea

substitute good: a good that replaces another good; in other words, a good that is like a primary good but acts as a second choice

A **complementary good** refers to a good that goes along with another good. In other words, a complementary good is a good that is purchased along with the primary good. Therefore, a change in the price of one good will cause the change in demand for the complementary good to mirror the change in demand for the primary good. Examples of complementary goods are hot dog wieners and buns. Figures 4.8 and 4.9 provide a demonstration. In Figure 4.8, if the price of hot dog wieners rises, consumers will purchase fewer wieners and buns. Therefore, the price change causes upward movement along the demand curve of hot dog wieners (change in quantity demanded) and a left shift of the demand curve of buns (change in demand). By comparison, Figure 4.9 demonstrates what occurs when there is a decrease in the price of hot dog wieners. In this figure, the price decrease causes an increase in the demand for both hot dog wieners and buns. As such, this price change causes downward movement along the demand curve of hot dog wieners (change in quantity demanded) and a right shift of the demand curve for buns (change in demand).

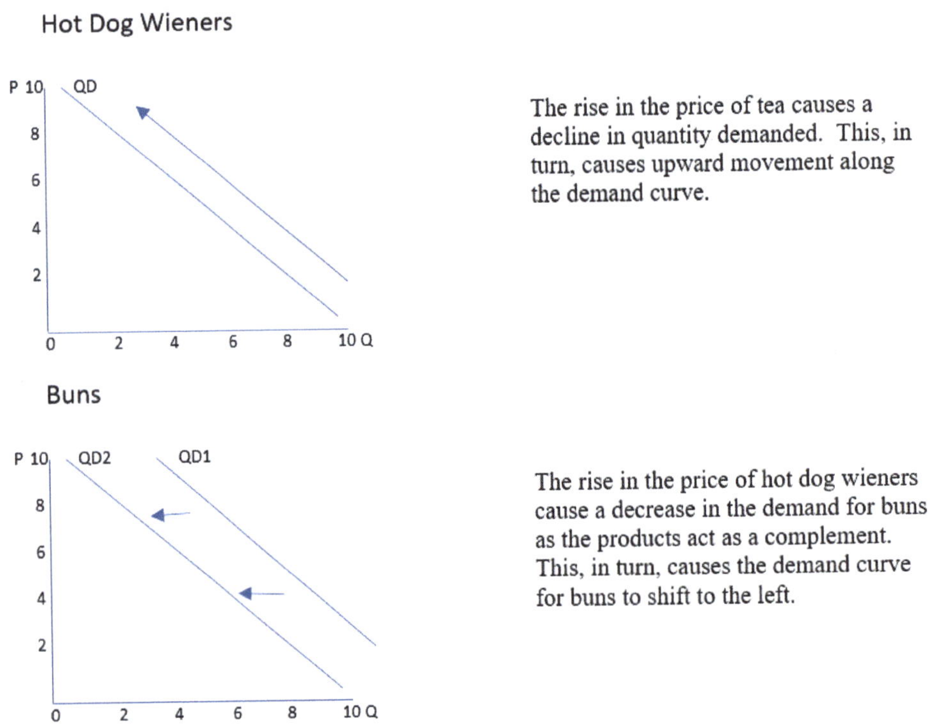

FIGURE 4.8 Complementary Goods

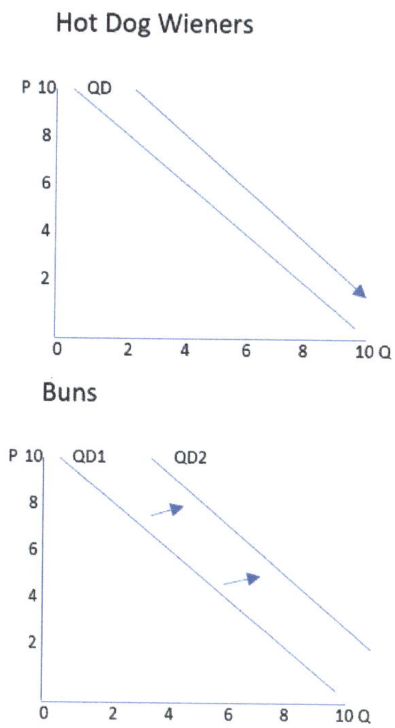

The decline in the price of hot dog wieners cause an increase in quantity demanded. This, in turn, causes downward movement along the demand curve.

The decline in the price of hot dog wieners cause an increase in the quantity demanded for buns as the products act as a complement. This, in turn, causes the demand curve for coffee to shift to the right.

FIGURE 4.9 Complimentary Goods

Within a market, both individual and market demand exists. **Individual demand** is defined as the number of a particular product one consumer is willing to buy at various prices, ceteris paribus. **Market demand** is defined as the number of a particular product that all the consumers in the market are willing to buy at various prices, ceteris paribus.

complementary good: a good that goes along with another good

individual demand: the number of a particular product that one consumer is willing to buy at various price, ceteris paribus

market demand: the number of a particular product that all the consumers in the market are willing to buy at various prices, ceteris paribus

4.2 Calculating the Slope of a Demand Curve

A demand curve is said to be negatively sloped because price and quantity moves in opposite directions. These movements imply that quantity decreases as price rises, and vice versa. As a result, the demand curve also slopes upward or downward as the change in quantity responds to the change in price. Understanding this, economists seek to determine the steepness of the slope of the curve. By doing so, they can measure the rate at which the curve moves up or down. This measurement can be calculated by dividing the run by the rise. The run refers to the change in quantity (ΔQ) while the rise refers to the change in price (ΔP). Therefore, the formula for calculating the slope of a demand curve is as follows:

$$\text{slope} = \Delta P / \Delta QD$$

Figure 4.10 provides an example of determining the steepness of the slope of a demand curve. Within this figure, the example determines both the rise and run. As such, in this example, the rise is determined by the change in price (vertical line), while the run is determined by the change in quantity (horizontal line). Using this in the example, price increased from \$6 to \$10, and quantity demanded decreased from 8 units to 4 units. To determine the steepness of the slope of the demand curve, the equation would look as follows:

$$\text{slope} = AB / BC = (\$10 - \$6) / (4 - 8) = -1$$

The resulting number in the example is negative, due to the law of demand, which indicates that price and quantity will always move in opposite directions. Because of this, the general rule should be if price falls, the change in quantity should be positive, while if the price rises, the change in quantity should be negative. In either case, the resulting number for the slope will always be negative. Furthermore, the resulting number indicates more steepness as it gets larger and flatness as it gets smaller.

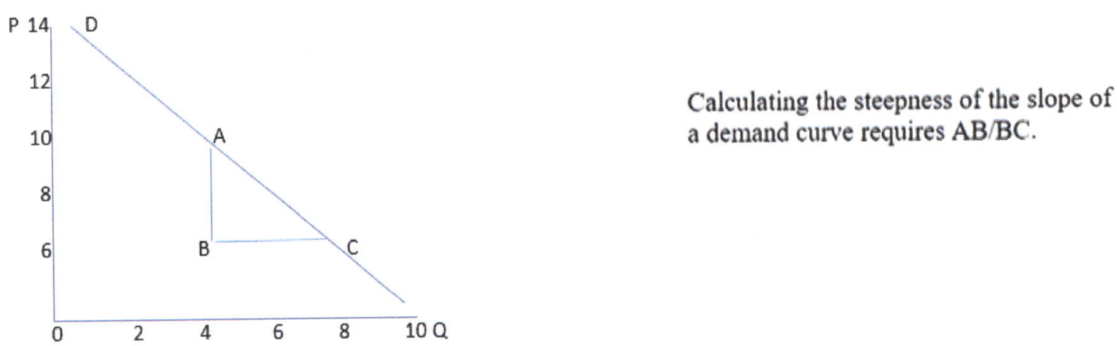

FIGURE 4.10 Calculating the Steepness of a Demand Curve

4.3 What Is Supply?

Supply (S) is defined as the number of a particular product producers are willing to sell at a given price, ceteris paribus. The definition of supply focuses on producers, who are also the manufacturers, selling to resellers and consumers. As such, there is a difference between demand and supply. This difference exists at various prices and at a given price. "At various prices" refers to consumers being willing to buy at any price while "at a given price" refers to a price point at which producers will not sell. This price point occurs when the price falls below the producer's cost. Therefore, producers will be unwilling to sell below a certain cost because they will lose money.

supply: the number of a particular product that producers are willing to sell at a given price, ceteris paribus

supply schedule: a table that shows the relationship between price and the number of a particular product producers are willing to sell

The examination of supply begins with a supply schedule. A **supply schedule** refers to a table that shows the relationship between price and the number of a particular product producers are willing to sell. An example of a supply schedule includes a pizza shop owner who providing quantities of small-size pizzas at different price points for catering. In this example, Table 4.2 shows the relationship between the price and the number of small pizzas being offered.

TABLE 4.2 A Supply Schedule

Price per small pizza	Number of offerings
$2	1
$4	3
$6	5
$8	7
$10	10

The relationship between price and the number of a particular product producers are willing to sell can be seen on a supply curve. A **supply curve** is defined as a curve that shows the relationship between price and the number of a particular product producers are willing to sell. Using the preceding example, Figure 4.11 shows a supply curve. In this example, the supply curve begins at or above the pizza shop owner's production cost. Based on the information provided, the owner's cost is at least $2 because the owner will not provide pizzas below this price. Therefore, the pizza shop owner's supply curve will begin at or above $2. In addition, the supply curve is both positively sloped and upward sloped because of law of supply.

supply curve: a curve that shows the relationship between price and the number of a particular product producers are willing to sell

law of supply: the belief that as price rises, the number of a particular product producers supply increases

change in quantity supplied: a situation in which a change in prices causes a change in the number of a particular product that producers are willing to sell

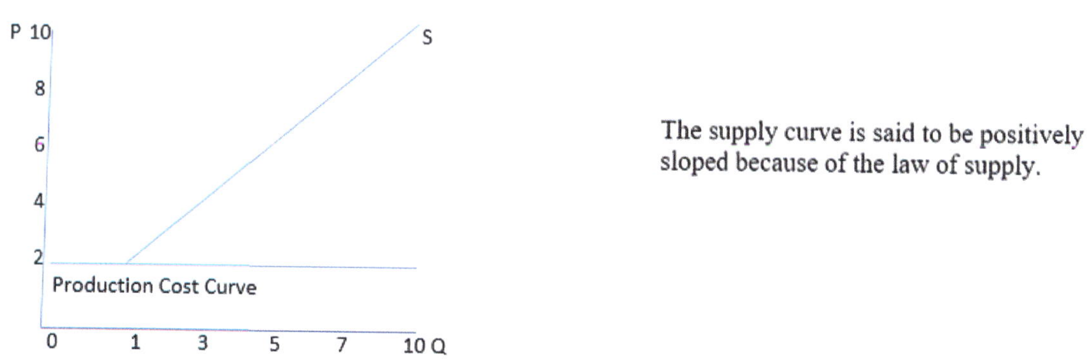

FIGURE 4.11 A Supply Curve

The **law of supply** is the belief that as price rises, the number of a particular product that producers supply increases. In other words, the law of supply assumes that as price rises, producers will supply a greater number of products because they can earn more money. Because of this, supply *moves up* along the supply curve as price increases (the demand curve remains stationary). By comparison, if price falls, there will be *downward movement* along the supply curve, as producers will earn less money. Figures 4.12 and 4.13 show these movements. Within this, Figure 4.12 shows upward movement, which is an increase in quantity supplied, while Figure 4.13 shows a downward movement, which indicates a decrease in quantity supplied. As such, this movement is known as a change in quantity supplied. A **change in quantity supplied (QS)** is defined as a situation in which a change in prices causes a change in the number of a particular product that producers are willing to sell.

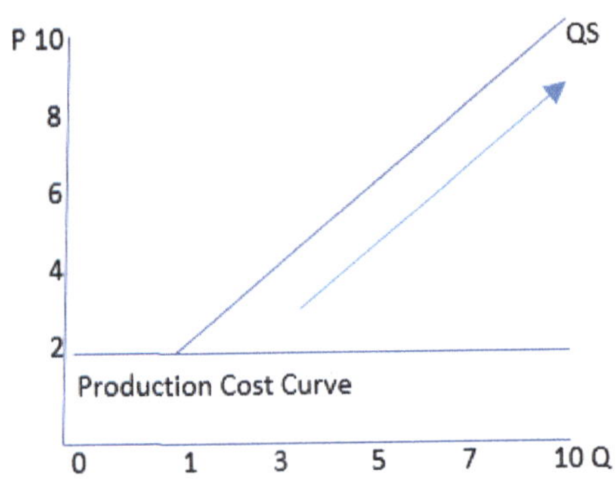

The supply curve is upward sloped to indicate an increase in quantity supplied which is caused by a rise in price.

FIGURE 4.12 Upward Movement (Change in Quantity Supplied)

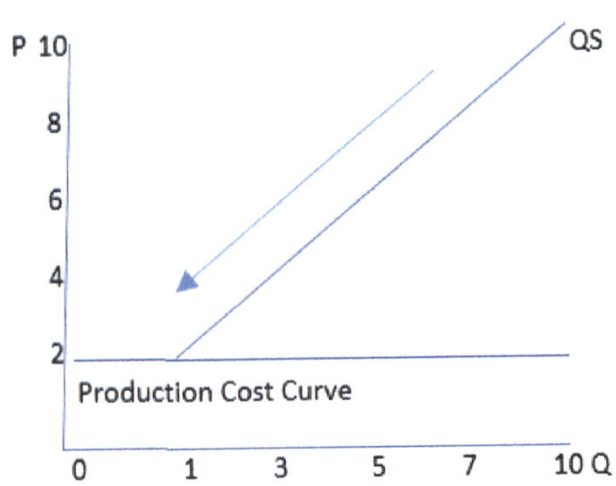

The supply curve is downward sloped to indicate a decrease in quantity supplied which is caused by a decline in price.

FIGURE 4.13 Downward Movement (Change in Quantity Supplied)

The law of supply assumes price is the only variable that causes a change in the number of a particular product producers are willing to sell, holding all other factors constant. However, price is not the only variable that affects the change in the number of a particular product producers are willing to sell. In fact, many of the same variables that affect demand also affect supply. These variables include factor costs, taxes, technological changes, tastes, preferences, and many others, and they will cause the supply curve to shift right or left. Figures 4.15 and 4.16 show these shifts. Within this, Figure 4.14 shows a right shift, which indicates an increase in supply, while Figure 4.15 shows a left shift, which indicates a decline in supply. As such, this shift is known as a change in supply. A **change in supply** is defined as a situation in which a change in a variable other than price causes a change in the number of a particular product producers are willing to sell.

change in supply: a situation in which a change in a variable other than price causes a change in the number of a particular product producers are willing to sell

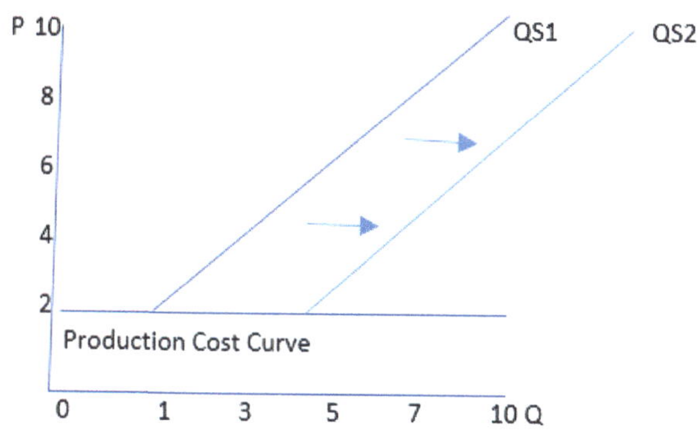

A right shift of the supply curve indicates an increase in supply. This shift is caused by a change in variables other than price.

FIGURE 4.14 A Right Shift (Change in Supply)

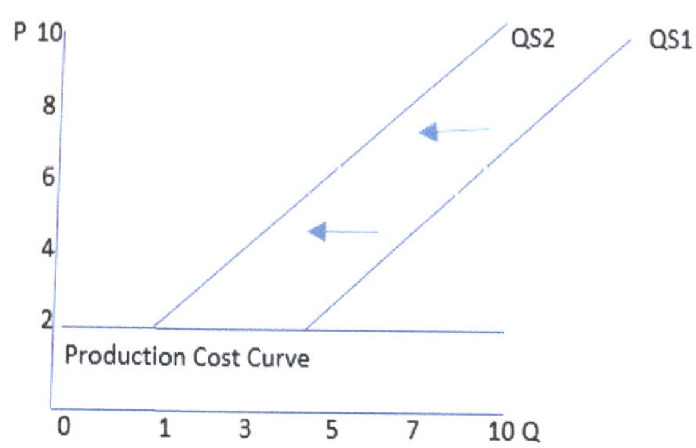

A left shift of the supply curve indicates a decrease in supply. This shift is caused by a change in variables other than price.

FIGURE 4.15 A Left Shift (Change in Supply)

Like demand, within a market, both individual and market supply exists. **Individual supply** is the number of a particular product one producer is willing to sell at a given price, ceteris paribus. **Market supply** is the number of a particular product all producers are willing to sell at a given price, ceteris paribus.

individual supply: the number of a particular product one producer is willing to sell at a given price, ceteris paribus

market supply: the number of a particular product all producers are willing to sell at a given price, ceteris paribus

4.4 Calculating the Slope of a Supply Curve

A supply curve is said to be positively sloped because price and quantity moves in the same direction. This movement implies that quantity increases as price rises, and vice versa. As a result, the supply curve also moves upward or downward as the change in quantity responds to the change in price. In understanding this, economists seek to determine the steepness of the slope of the curve. Like demand, economists can measure the rate at which the curve moves up or down. In doing so, they can determine the rate of the slope by dividing the run by the rise. Therefore, the formula for calculating the slope of a supply curve is as follows:

$$\text{slope} = \Delta P \,/\, \Delta QS$$

Figure 4.16 provides an example of determining the steepness of the slope of a supply curve. Within this figure, the example determines both the rise and run. As such, in this example, the rise is determined by the change in price (vertical line), while the run is determined by the change in quantity (horizontal line). Using this in the example, price increased from \$4 to \$8, and in response, supply increases from 3 units to 7 units. Soto determine the steepness of the slope of the supply curve, the equation looks as follows:

$$\text{slope} = AC \,/\, CB = (\$8 - \$4) \,/\, (7 - 3) = 1$$

In this example, the resulting number is positive due to the law of supply, which indicates price and quantity will always move in the same direction. Therefore, the resulting number for the slope will always be positive. Furthermore, like measuring the slope of the demand curve, the resulting number indicates steepness as it gets larger and flatness as it gets smaller.

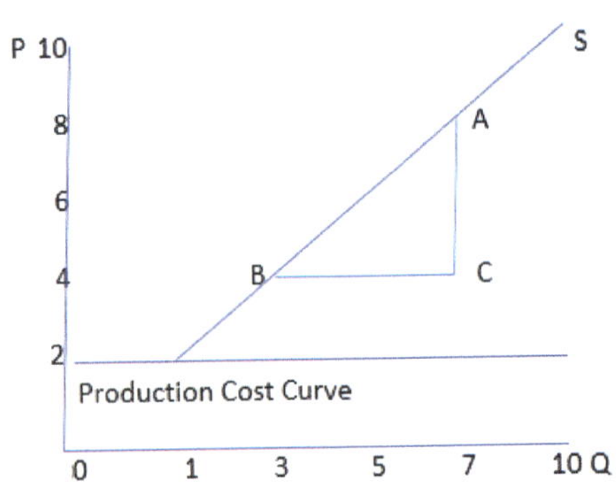

Calculating the steepness of the slope of a supple curve requires AC/CB.

FIGURE 4.16 An Example of Calculating the Steepness of a Supply Curve

4.5 Equilibrium

The point at which the demand curve meets the supply curve is known as equilibrium. **Equilibrium (E)** is defined as the point at which the number of a particular product consumers are willing to buy equals the number of a particular product producers are willing to sell. Figure 4.17 shows equilibrium. When the market experiences equilibrium, it is said to have reached efficiency. **Efficiency** refers to having the ability to maximize resources in production. Therefore, when the market reaches equilibrium, producers maximize the resources used in production by selling them to customers. In doing so, at equilibrium, producers sell to the greatest number of consumers and, thereby, earn the greatest profits. However, how is it known when producers will earn the greatest profits at equilibrium?

When the market reaches equilibrium, producers sell their products at a price point at which the greatest number of consumers are willing to buy. If price rises above this price, it creates excess supply. **Excess supply** is defined as a situation in which there is a greater quantity of a product supplied than what consumers are willing to buy. In other words, excess supply creates a surplus. This means that if price rises above equilibrium, quantity demanded will decline, as some consumers choose not to buy due to the higher price, which causes a surplus. This causes upward movement along the demand curve. To reduce this surplus in inventory, producers are forced to lower prices. As a result, producers will not be earning the greatest profits. Figure 4.18 shows excess supply.

However, if prices fall below equilibrium, it will create excess demand. **Excess demand** is defined as a situation in which there will be a greater number of consumers willing to buy than the number of products available for sale. In other words, excess demand creates a shortage. This means that if price falls below equilibrium, quantity supplied declines, as some producers choose not to sell, as they will not be able to cover their costs. This causes downward movement along the supply curve. As a result, producers will be missing profits, as they will not be able to keep up with demand. To lessen demand, producers will be forced to raise prices. Figure 4.19 shows excess demand.

equilibrium: the point at which the number of a particular product that consumers are willing to buy equals the number of a particular product that producers are willing to sell

efficiency: the ability to maximize resources

excess supply: a situation in which there is greater quantity supplied than what consumers are willing to buy

excess demand: a situation in which there will be a greater number of consumers willing to buy than the number of products available for sale

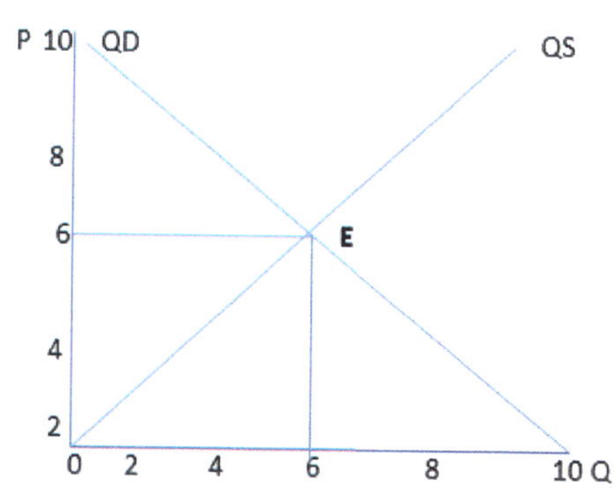

Equilibrium refers to the point where QD equals QS.

FIGURE 4.17 Equilibrium

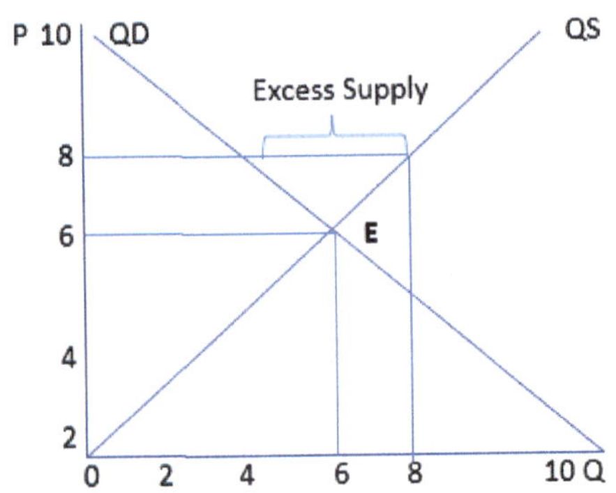

Excess supply occurs when price rises above equilibrium.

FIGURE 4.18 Excess Supply

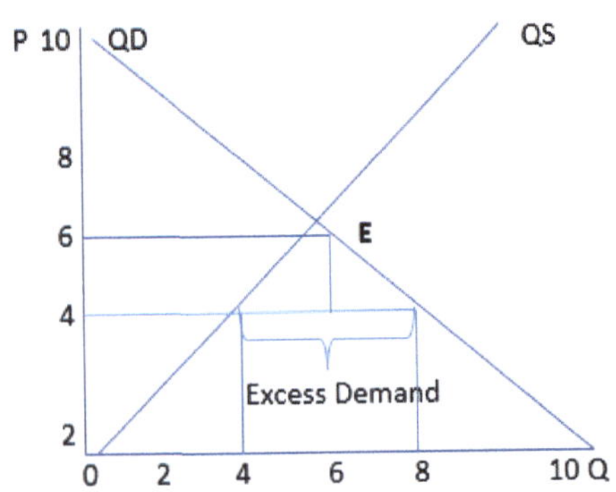

Excess demand occurs when price falls below equilibrium.

FIGURE 4.19 Excess Demand

SUMMARY

- Demand and supply are used daily to understand buying and selling habits in the market in relation to price and other variables. (LO 4.1)
- Demand focuses on people being willing and able to make purchases at various prices, ceteris paribus. This includes both individual demand and market demand. (LO 4.1)
- Demand can be seen on a demand curve. (LO 4.1)
- Substitute and complementary goods can be used to examine demand. (LO 4.1)
- "Supply" is defined as the number of a particular product producers are willing to sell at a given price, ceteris paribus. This includes both individual and market supply.
- Supply can be seen on a supply curve. (LO 4.3)

- Demand and supply curves illustrate the quantity purchased and quantity sold in response to changes in price. In response, the demand curve negatively slopes, while the supply curve positively slopes. (LO 4.1, LO 4.3)
- Economists can use the run and rise to determine the slope of both the demand and supply curves. (LO 4.2, LO 4.4)
- Variables other than price affect both demand and supply. These variables cause the demand and supply curves to shift. (LO 4.1, LO 4.2)
- The point at which the quantity supplied equals the quantity demanded is known as equilibrium. A rise in price causes excess supply, while a decline in price causes excess demand. (LO 4.5)

END-OF-CHAPTER APPLICATION

Comprehension Questions

Directions: Refer to the chapter to correctly respond to the following questions and prompts.

1. Tammy is a college student who has a limited income and a need for software upgrade on her computer. How will price increases on computer software upgrades affect her decision? How will this decision shape her demand curve? (LO 4.1)
2. Assume pencils and pen act as substitutes. If the price of pencils declines, the demand for pens will ____. (LO 4.1)

    a. move up the demand curve

    b. move down the demand curve

    c. shift the demand curve to the right

    d. shift the demand curve to the left

3. The price of a 7.5 ounce can of ravioli decreased from $2 to $1. In response, Sam's demand for ravioli increased from 5 cans to 10 cans per month. Calculate the slope of Sam's demand curve. (LO 4.2)
4. What would happen to energy prices if the government enacted stricter environmental legislation? (LO 4.3)
5. Tasty Pizzas increased the price of its large pizza from $15 to $18. As a result, weekly sales declined from 100 large pizzas to 80 large pizzas. Calculate the slope of the Tasty Pizzas supply curve. (LO 4.4)
6. Suppose the equilibrium price for admission into your local university's football game is $16. What would happen if price increased to $20? What would happen if price decreased to $12? (LO 4.4)

Case Scenario: A Case Analysis on Demand and Supply of Gold in India

Directions: Use what you learned in the chapter to respond to the scenario below.

According to Periyasamy (2016), the Indian market is the second largest consumer of gold. The author states that the demand for gold in this market derives from cultural and religious traditions that involves wearing jewelry. In addition, the author states that the demand for gold in the country is caused by consumers seeking to preserve their wealth, due to its increase in value over time. Because of these factors, Periyasamy (2016) states that price isn't the only driver of demand for gold in India. As a result, as supply becomes strained, the author states that over time, gold's demand curve in this market moves due to price and shifts due to factors other than price.

1. How does cultural and religious traditions affect the demand curve for gold? How does it affect the supply curve for gold?
2. What type of pressure does the desire for preserve wealth have on the supply of gold and its price in India?
3. Suppose the demand for gold in the Indian market is infinite. What would be the shape of the demand curve? Does the shape of the curve reflect the true nature of demand?
4. Based on the reading, what effect would a price increase have on demand in this market?

BIBLIOGRAPHY

O'Sullivan, A., Shreffin, S., & Perez, S. (2017). *Microeconomics: Principles, applications, and tools* (9th ed.). Pearson Publishing.

Periyasamy, S. (2016). A case analysis on demand and supply of gold in India. https://symbiosiscollege.edu.in/assets/pdf/e-learning/syba/Economics/Article-for-SYBA-Special-Economics1.pdf

Schiller, B. R. (2016). *The micro economy today* (14th ed.). McGraw-Hill Education.

CREDIT

CHAPTER 5

Equilibrium and Market Failure

Concept Highlight

Chapter 5 examines what occurs at equilibrium as well as forces that move the economy away from equilibrium.

Real Life Example: What Does This Mean to You?

The market doesn't always operate perfectly. Therefore, understanding market failure becomes important to recognize its effect on daily economic activity. An example of such recognition lies in the dairy industry. In this industry, the U.S. government incentivizes farmers to produce by paying subsidies. These subsidies lower production cost, which leads to lower prices, thereby, providing a method for U.S. farmers to compete in the global market. However, they also motivate the farmers to produce greater quantities of product than what consumers buy. As a result, the subsidy payments lead to overproduction (excess supply) and market failure.

Introduction

We begin by reviewing demand, supply, and equilibrium, as these concepts are important in setting the foundation for examining market failure. Market failure explains what occurs when the economy moves away from equilibrium. In doing so, market failure occurs through public goods, externalities, market power, and inequities.

OBJECTIVES

While reading this chapter, readers should be able to

LO 5.1. identify demand, supply, and equilibrium

LO 5.2. define the optimal mix of output

LO 5.2. define market failure

LO 5.2. define market mechanisms

LO 5.3. explain the four sources of market failure

LO 5.3. explain the three beliefs about how taxes are paid

OUTCOMES

After completing this chapter, readers will be able to do the following:

- Illustrate the optimal mix of output on a graph.
- Explain how market failure moves the economy away from equilibrium.
- Explain how market mechanisms move the economy away from equilibrium.
- Illustrate and explain how removing tax revenues from a public good affect the economy.
- Illustrate and explain how negative externalities affect the economy.
- Illustrate and explain how monopolies affect the economy.
- Illustrate and explain how inequities affect the economy.
- Explain the three beliefs about how taxes are paid.

Key Terms

The following key terms are discussed in this chapter:

- optimal mix of output
- market failure
- market mechanisms
- public good
- free-rider problem
- externality

- market power
- monopoly
- anti-trust
- equity
- inequity
- progressive tax system
- proportional tax system
- regressive tax system

5.1 Review: Demand, Supply, and Equilibrium

In Chapter 4, we learned that demand (D) refers to the number of a particular product consumers are willing and able to buy at various prices, ceteris paribus. This definition implies that demand focuses on buying. As such, we learned that demand can be seen on a demand curve. A demand curve shows the relationship between price and the number of a particular product that consumers are willing to buy, ceteris paribus. This curve is both negatively sloped and upward sloped because of the law of demand. The law of demand assumes that as price rises, consumer purchases fewer products, due to it becoming more expensive. Figure 5.1 shows an example of a demand curve.

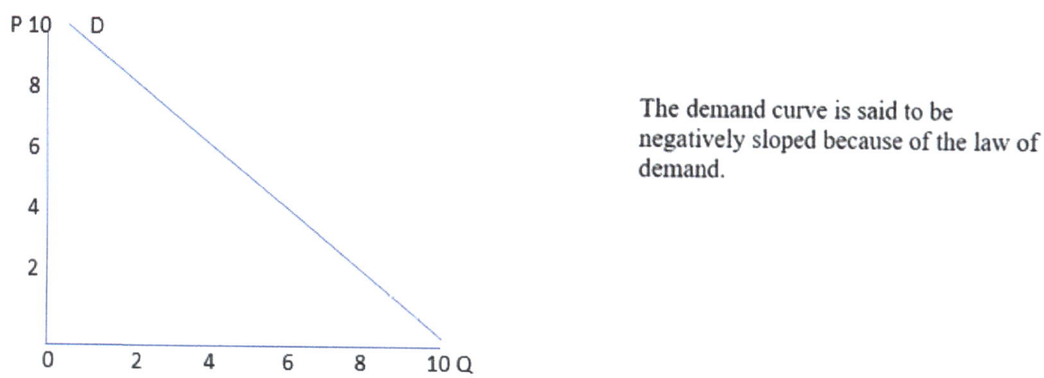

FIGURE 5.1 A Demand Curve

We also learned that supply (S) refers to the number of a particular product producers are willing to sell at a given price, ceteris paribus. This definition implies that supply focuses on selling. As such, we learned that supply can be seen on a supply curve. This curve shows the relationship between price and the number of a particular product producers are willing to sell. This curve is both positively sloped and upward sloped because of the law of supply. The law of supply assumes that as price rises, producers will supply a greater number of products because they can earn more money. Figure 5.2 shows an example of a supply curve.

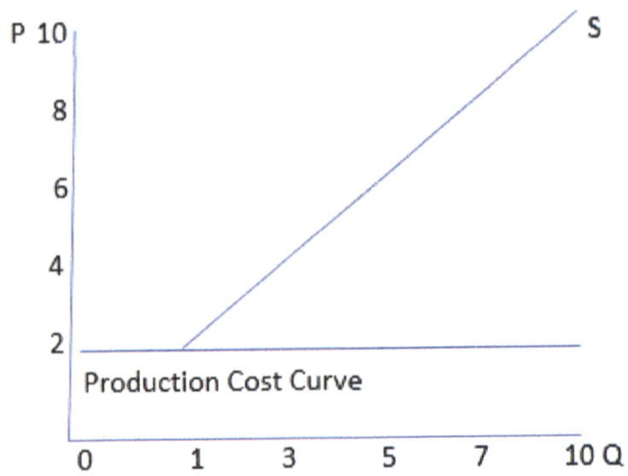

The supply curve is said to be positively sloped because of the law of supply.

FIGURE 5.2 A Supply Curve

In addition, we learned that equilibrium (E) refers to the point at which the number of a particular product consumers are willing to buy equals the number of a particular product that producers are willing to sell. At this point, the market is said to be "efficient." Efficiency refers to having the ability to maximize resources in production by selling to customers. In doing so, at equilibrium, producers sell to the greatest number of consumers and, thereby, earn the greatest profits. Figure 5.3 shows an example of equilibrium.

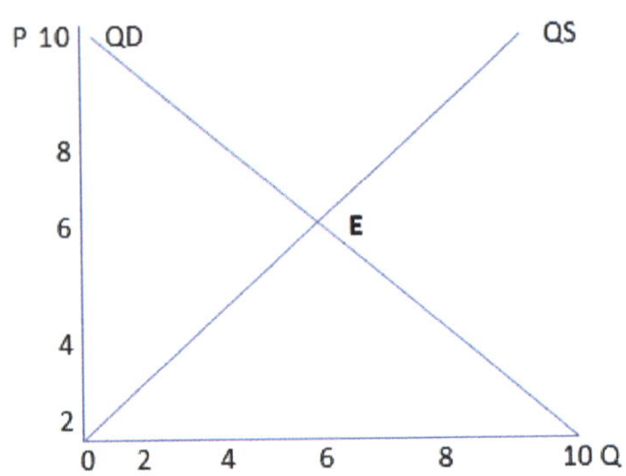

Equilibrium refers to the point where QD equals QS.

FIGURE 5.3 Equilibrium

5.2 What is the Optimal Mix of Output?

The economy isn't always at equilibrium. When it reaches equilibrium, the optimal mix of output also occurs. The **optimal mix of output** is defined as a situation in which the greatest variety of output is produced based on available resources. In other words, when the economy reaches equilibrium, there will be the greatest number of producers who produce the greatest variety of goods and services. Figure 5.4 provides an illustration of the optimal mix of output.

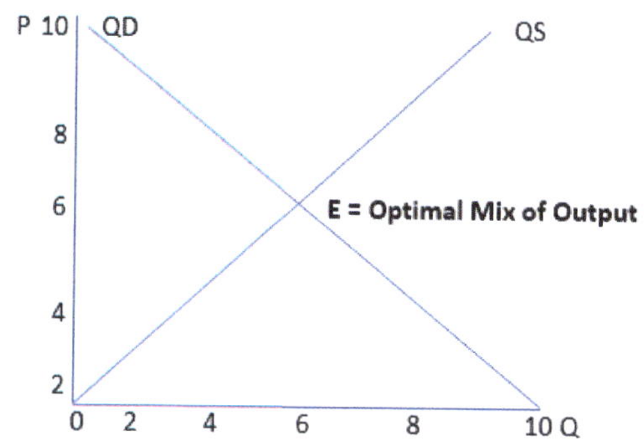

The optimal mix of output occurs at equilibrium.

FIGURE 5.4 The Optimal Mix of Output

How do economists know when the economy has reached equilibrium and, thereby, the optimal mix of output? The answer to this question is that they do not know. In other words, economists cannot use any GDP number to signal equilibrium for the economy. However, they do know that market failure will move the economy away from equilibrium and market mechanisms will move the economy towards equilibrium. **Market failure** refers to forces in the economy that prevent it from performing perfectly. Perfection occurs when the economy reaches equilibrium because producers sell to the greatest number of consumers and, thereby, earn the greatest profits. Understanding this, market failure implies that these forces cause either excess demand or excess supply, which, in turn, leads to fewer consumers and profits. Figures 5.5 and 5.6 show an example of market failure.

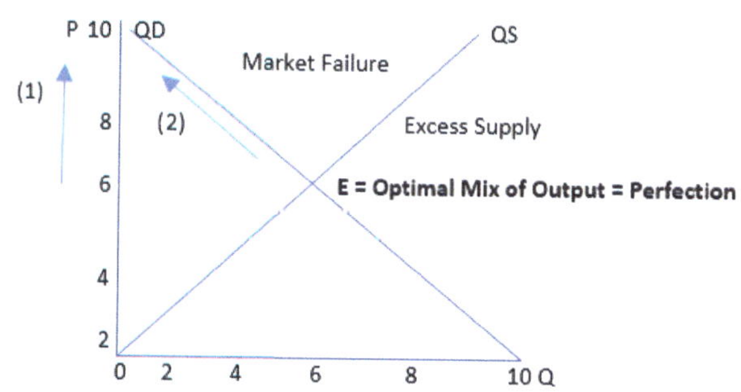

A rise in price causes a decline in quantity demanded. This causes excess supply.

FIGURE 5.5 Market Failure (Excess Supply)

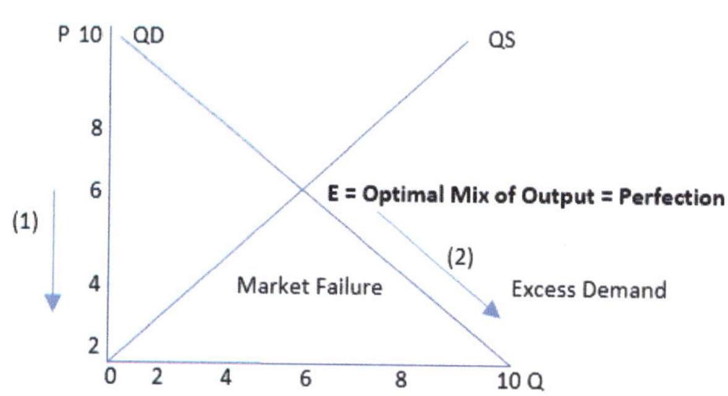

A decline in price causes a rise in quantity demanded. This causes excess demand.

FIGURE 5.6 Market Failure (Excess Demand)

optimal mix of output: a situation in which the greatest variety of output is produced based on available resources

market failure: forces in the economy that prevent it from performing perfectly

market mechanisms: the combination of prices and sales to motivate purchases

By comparison, **market mechanisms** refer to the combination of prices and sales to motivate purchases. In other words, market mechanisms involve having the right products at the right price to move consumers to buy. As purchases increase, the economy moves closer to equilibrium. Figure 5.7 depicts market mechanisms.

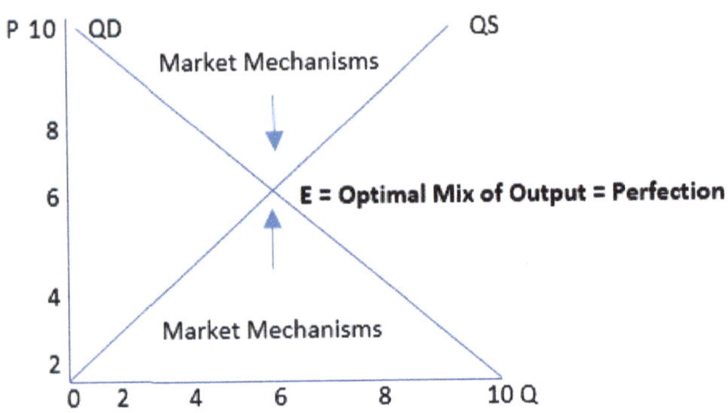

FIGURE 5.7 Market Mechanisms

Market mechanisms move the economy towards equilibrium.

5.3 Sources of Market Failure

Market failure consists of forces that move the economy away from equilibrium. These forces come from four sources. The four sources of market failure are (a) public goods, (b) externalities, (c) market power, and (d) inequities. These sources cause market failure because they will either cause excess demand or excess supply due to prices being too high or too low.

A **public good** is a good that can be consumed by all, regardless of who pays. Examples of these include roads, parks, and public education. As such, these goods are paid for through tax collection. So the question becomes, "What would happen if the government decided to remove the tax to pay for the good?" If the government removed the tax to pay the good, it would create the free-rider problem. The **free-rider problem** refers to a situation in which people will attempt to use a good without paying for it. In other words, if the government removes the tax to pay for the good, the financing of that good falls to individuals. In such instances, people use the good without providing financing. Eventually, the good will be eliminated due to not having enough operational funds. This, in turn, creates market failure due to excess demand, as overall supply falls while there is still a demand. However, this decline in supply is caused by factors other than price (removal of tax revenues), which causes the supply curve to shift to the left. Figure 5.8 shows an example of this effect.

public good: a good that can be consumed by all regardless of who pays

free-rider problem: a situation in which people attempt to use a good without paying for it

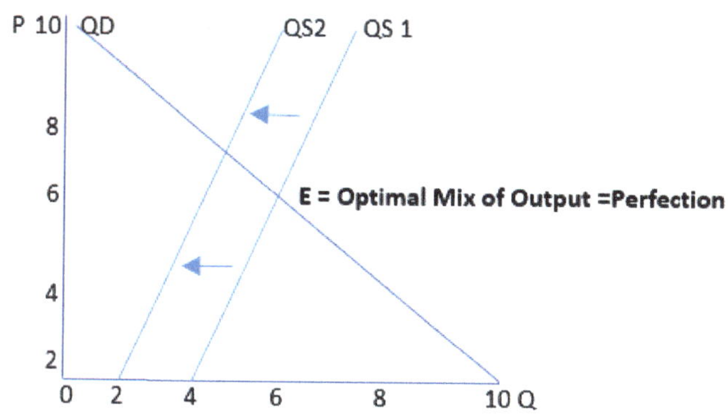

Removal of tax revenues causes supply to fall while demand remains constant.

FIGURE 5.8 Excess Demand Caused by the Free-Rider Problem

externality: a situation in the cost and benefits of an action that affects those who were not involved in the decision-making process

An **externality** is defined as a situation in which the cost and benefits of an action affect those who were not involved in the decision-making process. In the business world, this occurs when management makes a decision that affects greater society. If this decision affects society in a good way, it will be promoted. An example of this includes management deciding to build a park for the community to enjoy. However, if this decision affects society in a negative way, the community may protest. An example of this would be management deciding to allow the spread of their pollution from production through the air into the community. Such actions cause market failure due to excess supply, as fewer consumers choose to buy in protest against management's decision. This, in turn, causes the demand curve to shift to the left to indicate a decline in buying. Figure 5.9 shows an example of this effect.

Market power refers to a situation in which a business has the ability to alter market prices on goods and services. This occurs through monopolies. A **monopoly** is a market that is served by one business. Although there may be competition, the monopoly is the dominant business and, therefore, can alter market prices as well as control production output. This type of arrangement often forces the government

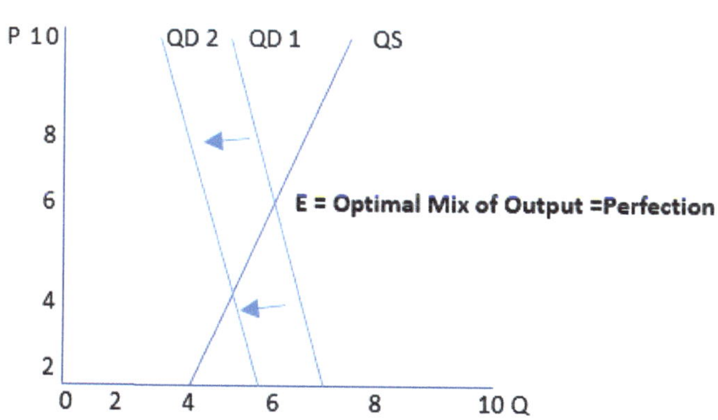

A negative externality causes demand to fall while supply remains constant.

FIGURE 5.9 Excess Supply Caused by a Negative Externality

to intervene in the market by enacting anti-trust laws. **Anti-trust** laws prohibit the formation of monopolies. The goal of anti-trust laws is to encourage competition, which leads to lower prices and greater choice. However, when monopolies occur, it leads to market failure, as it reduces competition and increases prices. Initially, as competition reduces, prices rise and demand falls, thereby causing upward movement along the demand curve. As demand falls, the monopoly reduces supply, which leaves the market with less supply. Figure 5.10 provides an example of this effect.

market power: a situation in which a business has the ability to alter market prices on goods and services

monopoly: a market served by one business

anti-trust: laws that prohibit the formation of monopolies

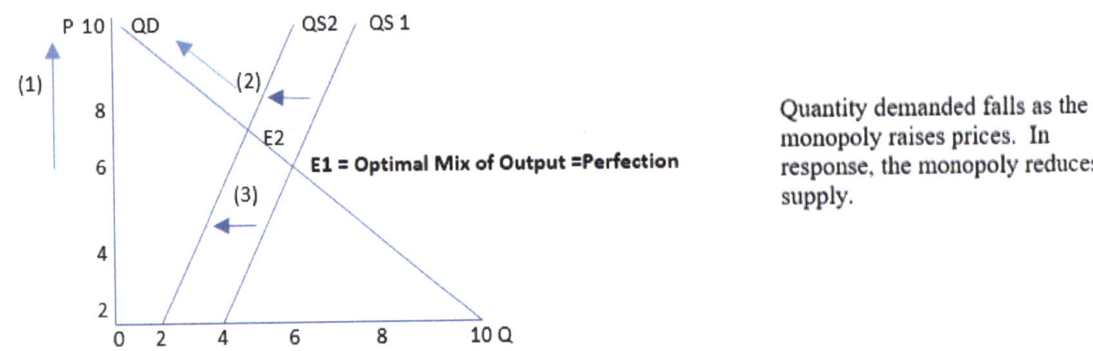

FIGURE 5.10 Excess Demand Caused by the Free-Rider Problem

Equity refers to the equal distribution of resources. When resources are not equally distributed, an **inequity** occurs. This creates market failure, as some people acquire more than others. This, in turn, causes excess supply, as demand falls. Therefore, the demand curve shifts to the left. Figure 5.11 shows an example of this effect.

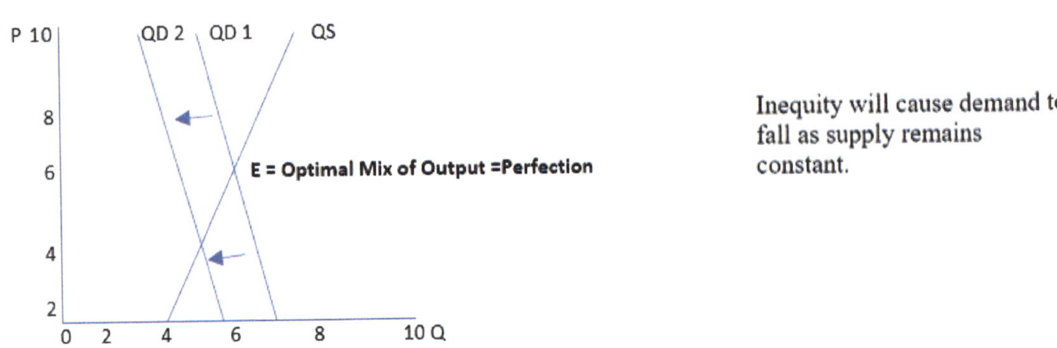

FIGURE 5.11 Excess Supply Caused by Inequity

equity: the equal distribution of resources

inequity: the unequal distribution of resources

progressive tax system: a system in which the tax amount levied increases as income increases

proportional tax system: a system in which the tax amount levied is the same for every dollar of income earned

regressive tax system: a system in which the tax amount levied decreases as income increases

Examples of an inequity that exist in the U.S. economy include a process through which taxes are paid and transfer payments are received. In these examples, both taxes and transfer payments are determined based on income. As such, the purpose of such a system is to redistribute money to those who have less of it. However, this process of redistributing money has raised the question of how taxes should be paid in the country. From this question, a number of beliefs have emerged to explain the tax payment system in the country. Those beliefs include the use of a (a) progressive tax system, (b) proportional tax system, and (c) regressive tax system. A **progressive tax system** is one in which the tax amount levied increases as income increases. A **proportional tax system** is a system in which the tax amount levied is the same for every dollar of income earned. A **regressive tax system** is a system in which the tax amount levied decreases as income increases.

SUMMARY

- A review of demand, supply, and equilibrium provides a foundation into the exploration of market failure. (LO 5.1)
- The optimal mix of output occurs at equilibrium. (LO 5.2)
- Market failure moves the economy away from equilibrium. (LO 5.2)
- Market mechanisms move the economy toward equilibrium. (LO 5.2)
- The free-rider problem occurs when tax revenues are eliminated to pay for public goods. (LO 5.3)
- Externalities occur in the business world when management makes a decision that affects the greater society. (LO 5.3)
- Market power occurs through monopolies. (LO 5.3)
- The government enacts anti-trust laws to intervene in the market. (LO 5.3)
- Inequities occur through unequal distribution of resources. (LO 5.3)
- People believe taxes are paid through a progressive tax system, proportional tax system, and a regressive tax system. (LO 5.3)

END-OF-CHAPTER APPLICATION

Comprehension Questions

Directions: Refer to the chapter to correctly respond to the following questions and prompts.

1. Why does the optimal mix of output occur at equilibrium? What would happen to the optimal mix of output if price rose above equilibrium? What would happen to the optimal mix of output if price declined below equilibrium? (LO 5.2)
2. Provide an example of a current monopoly. State the type of industry in which it operates. Explain how it uses its market power to maintain its monopoly status. (LO 5.3)
3. Suppose local government officials in your hometown decided to eliminate tax revenues for a favorite rest area. What would be some strategies you would use to avoid the free-rider problem? (LO 5.3)
4. Suppose your local town officials approved a measure to build a semi-public charter school in your town. Suppose the officials agreed to allow the school to charge tuition based on the income of town residents. Explain how this could create market failure. Illustrate its effect. (LO 5.3)
5. In the United States, there are three beliefs about how taxes are paid. Which do you believe to be true about how taxes are paid? Provide a rationale for your belief. (LO 5.3)

Case Scenario: An Analysis of the Housing Market Equilibrium

Directions: Use what you learned in the chapter to respond to the following scenario.

Suppose the housing market is at equilibrium when rent prices are at $500 per month. Assume that at this price, the economy experiences the greatest number of rental units of 20,000 rentals. Answer the following questions:

1. Illustrate equilibrium on a graph using these numbers.
2. Suppose this market experiences a vacancy rate of 5% when it's at equilibrium. Provide a rationale for this discrepancy.
3. Suppose the government gave a tax credit to 5,000 landlords to transition their rental units into Airbnbs. Explain the effect this would have on equilibrium. Illustrate this effect on a graph.
4. Suppose 3,000 new renters entered the market. Explain the effect this would have on equilibrium. Illustrate this effect on a graph.

BIBLIOGRAPHY

O'Sullivan, A., Shreffin, S., & Perez, S. (2017). *Microeconomics: Principles, applications, and tools* (9th ed.). Pearson Publishing.

Press Books. (n.d.). *Solutions: Case study—The housing market.* British Columbia/Yukon Open Authoring Platform. https://pressbooks.bccampus.ca/uvicecon103/chapter/case-study-solution-the-housing-market/

Schiller, B. R. (2016). *The micro economy today* (14th ed.). McGraw-Hill Education.

CREDIT

CHAPTER 6

The Causes of Demand and Supply and How it Is Measured

Concept Highlight

Chapter 6 examines the concepts of price elasticity of demand and price elasticity of supply.

Real Life Example: What Does This Mean to You?

Consumers engage in a decision-making process daily to make decide on purchases. An example of this includes consumers making a decision on purchasing products, such as coffee or tea. In examining this decision, economists seek to determine how a change in the price or a variable other than price in one of these products affect the buying decision of the other product. Such a measure allows economists to understand the number of purchases made in one product when there are changes in the factors associated with the other products.

Introduction

Price elasticity of demand is an important concept to understand because it is used to measure buying habits when there is a change in price. However, there are variables other than price that affect buying habits. Price elasticity of supply is an equally important concept to understand because it is used to measure supply habits of producers when there is a change in price. Likewise, there are variables other than price that affect supply habits.

OBJECTIVES

While reading this chapter, readers learn about

LO 6.1. elasticity

LO 6.2. price elasticity of demand

LO 6.2. types of consumer responses to price elasticity of demand

LO 6.2. price elasticity of demand divides products into three groups

LO 6.3. cross-price elasticity of demand

LO 6.3. substitute goods versus complementary goods

LO 6.4. the effect of time on the price elasticity of demand

LO 6.5. income elasticity of demand

LO 6.5. normal goods versus inferior goods

LO 6.6. price elasticity of supply

LO 6.6. types of producer responses to price elasticity of supply

LO 6.7. the effect of time on the price elasticity of supply

OUTCOMES

After completing this chapter, readers will be able to do the following:

- Define elasticity.
- Define price elasticity of demand.
- Explain the two consumer responses to price elasticity of demand.

- Calculate price elasticity of demand.
- Use the three groups in which price elasticity of demand divides products to determine if it is elastic, inelastic, or unitary.
- Calculate cross-price elasticity of demand.
- Use cross-price elasticity of demand to determine whether products are substitute goods or complementary goods.
- Explain how time affects price elasticity of demand.
- Calculate income elasticity of demand.
- Use income elasticity of demand to determine if a product is a normal good or inferior good.
- Define price elasticity of supply.
- Explain the two producer responses to price elasticity of supply.
- Calculate the price elasticity of supply.
- Determine whether price elasticity of supply is elastic, inelastic, or unitary.
- Explain how time affects the price elasticity of supply.

Key Terms

The following key terms are discussed in this chapter:

- elasticity
- price elasticity
- price elasticity of demand (E_d)
- elastic demand
- inelastic demand
- unitary demand
- cross-price elasticity of demand
- substitute goods
- complementary goods
- income (I) elasticity of demand
- normal good
- inferior good
- price elasticity of supply (E_s)
- elastic supply
- inelastic supply

6.1 Determinants of Demand and Elasticity

"Demand," as discussed in previous chapters, refers to the number of a particular product that consumers are willing and able to buy at various prices, ceteris paribus. The definition of demand implies that it focuses on buying. As such, there are several factors affect buying, (i.e., demand). Those factors include (a) the price of the product in question, (b) the price of its substitute and complement, and (c) one's taste

FIGURE 6.1 Decision-Making

or preference at that time. These factors imply that consumers go through a decision-making process when making buying decisions.

Economists seek to determine the amount of a particular product consumers are willing to buy based on factors such as price, substitutes, complements, tastes, and preferences. One tool they can use for this measure is elasticity. **Elasticity** refers to a measure of how much one variable changes when there is a change in another variable. As such, economists are concerned with price elasticity. **Price elasticity** refers to a measure of how much a variable changes when there is a change in price. As such, there are two types of price elasticity: price elasticity of demand (E_d) and price elasticity of supply (E_s).

Elasticity: A measure of how much one variable change when there is a change in another variable

Price elasticity: A measure of how much a variable changes when there is a change in price

6.2 Price Elasticity of Demand

Price elasticity of demand (E_d) is defined as a measure of how much demand changes for a particular product when there is a change in its price. Within this, price elasticity of demand causes either an elastic or an inelastic response from consumers. **Elastic demand** refers to a situation in which a small change in price causes a larger change in quantity demanded. By comparison, **inelastic demand** refers to a situation in which a small change in price causes either a small change in quantity demanded or no change in quantity demanded. To determine whether consumers' response to a change in price is elastic or inelastic, one can use the following formula:

$$\text{(price elasticity of demand) } E_d = \text{\% change in QD / \% change in price}$$

An example of price elasticity of demand includes the price of a gallon of milk rising from $2.00 to $2.20. In response, the quantity demanded for a gallon of milk declines from 100 million to 85 million. In this example, economists use the price elasticity of demand formula to determine if demand is elastic or inelastic. In doing so, the equation looks as follows:

$$\{(100 - 85) / 100\} / \{(\$2.00 - \$2.20) / \$2.00\}$$

In examining this equation, we are seeking to determine the percentage change in quantity demanded and the percentage change in price. To determine the percentage change in each variable, we must begin each half of the equation with the base number. As we begin to work this equation beginning with the base number, we can move through the equation as follows:

1. (15/100) / (–$0.20/$2.00)
2. .15 / –.10
3. –1.5

As shown, the resulting number is −1.5. In determining whether demand is elastic or inelastic, we ignore the negative sign for two reasons. First, for consumers, although quantity demanded for a gallon of milk decline from 100 million to 85 million represents a negative, a price increase from $2.00 to $2.20 also represents a negative because they must pay an additional $0.20 to price milk. This implies that both price and demand move in the same direction, which is incorrect because of the law of demand, which tells us that price and demand will always move in opposite directions. Second, it's easier to understand the number by ignoring the negative sign. This results in the final number being 1.5. To determine if this number signifies quantity demanded being elastic or inelastic, we must understand that the price elasticity of demand divides products into three groups. Those groups are (a) elastic demand, (b) inelastic demand, and (c) unitary demand. **Elastic demand** refers to price elasticity of demand being greater than 1.0. This means that a small change in price creates a large change in quantity demanded. **Inelastic demand** refers to price elasticity of demand being less than 1.0. This means a small change in price creates a small change or no change in quantity demanded. **Unitary demand** refers to price elasticity of demand being equal to 1.0. This means the percentage change in price creates the same percentage change in quantity demanded. Therefore, when applying these three groups to the example, we can say that demand is elastic because it's greater than 1.0. As a result, the change in price will cause upward movement along the demand curve. Figure 6.2 depicts this effect.

Price elasticity of demand (E_d): A measure of how much demand changes for a particular product when there is a change in a price

Elastic demand: A situation in which a small change in price causes a large change in quantity demanded; the change is greater than 1

Inelastic demand: A situation in which a small change in price causes either a small change in quantity demanded or no change in quantity demanded; the change is less than 1

Unitary demand: A situation in which the percentage change in price creates the same percentage change in quantity demanded; equal to 1

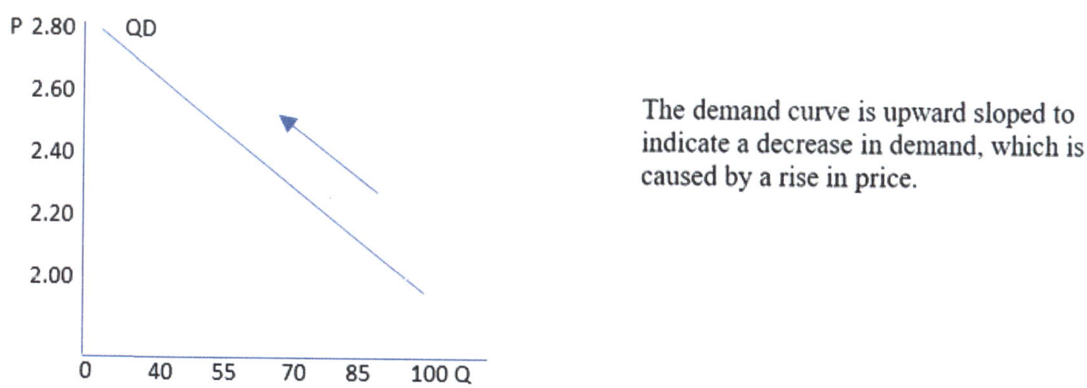

FIGURE 6.2 Price Elasticity of Demand on a Demand Curve

When analyzing price's effect on quantity demanded, economists are concerned with luxury goods and necessity goods. In this analysis, luxury products such as jewelry and high-end vehicles make price elasticity of demand elastic as quantity demand changes when price changes. In contrast, necessity products, such as food and housing, make price elasticity of demand inelastic because they are essential to living, which means consumers will pay for them, regardless of price.

6.3 Cross-Price Elasticity of Demand: Substitute Goods vs. Complementary Goods

However, price is not the only factor that affects the change in the number of a particular product consumers purchase. In fact, three factors other than price affect the price elasticity of demand. Those factors include (a) substitutes versus complementary goods, (b) time, and (c) budgets. Because of this, substitutes make price elasticity of demand elastic as it provides consumers with purchase options as price changes. As such, economists seek to understand how the change in the price of one good affect the quantity demanded of another good. This measurement is known as **cross-price elasticity of demand**. When they use this measure, they can determine if the products are substitutes or complementary. **Substitute goods** refer to goods that replace each other and, therefore, act as substitutes. An example of substitute goods includes butter and margarine. By comparison, **complementary goods** refer to goods that go together and, therefore, act as a pair. An example of complementary goods includes peanut butter and jelly. Therefore, the formula for determining cross-price elasticity of demand is as follows:

cross-price elasticity of demand = % change in quantity demanded of a good / % change in price of another good

An example of cross-price elasticity of demand includes McDonald's deciding to reduce the price of its burgers from $5.99 to $3.99. In response, Burger King experiences a 10% decline in the demand for its burgers. In this example, economists want to know the cross-price elasticity of demand for Burger King's burgers, the meaning of the number, as well as whether McDonald's and Burger King act as substitute or complementary goods. In addition, economists want to illustrate this effect on demand curves. To determine cross-price of elasticity, prior to setting up the formula, we must recognize a few facts within example. First, the example provides the percentage change in demand for Burger King's burgers (.10). However, this percentage will be negative due to Burger King experiencing a decline in its demand for its burgers (–.10). Second, the example did not specify a specific burger type, and therefore, we must determine the average price for a McDonald's burger. The formula for determining the average price is as follows:

base price + price change / the number of data sets

($5.99 + $3.99) / 2 = $4.99

Once the average price for McDonald's burgers is determined, we can determine the percentage change in McDonald's burgers. The formula for determining the percentage change is as follows:

% change in McDonald's burger price = change in price / average price

($5.99 - $3.99) / $4.99 = .40

In examining this percentage change, we must take notice that the price decrease for McDonalds represents a decline in revenues; therefore, the resulting number will be negative (−.40).

Now, we are ready to set up the formula to determine the cross-price elasticity of demand. This setup looks as follows:

cross-price elasticity of demand = −.10 / −.40 = +.25

In determining the meaning of the resulting number, we must use the three product groups in which the elasticity of demand divide goods (elastic, inelastic, or unitary). When employing these three groups, cross-price elasticity of demand for Burger King is inelastic due to the resulting number being less than 1.0. In addition, this means Burger King will lose .25 customers for every percentage point McDonald's burgers decline in price.

In examining the number, we can also determine if the products act as substitutes or complementary goods. Within this examination, the general rule is that the goods are substitutes if the resulting number is positive, and they are complements if the resulting number is negative. Using this, we can conclude that these two goods are substitutes because the resulting number is positive. Figure 6.3 shows the effect of the price change for McDonald's burgers on the demand for both McDonald's and Burger King.

cross-price elasticity of demand: a measure of how a change in the price of one good affects the quantity demanded of another good

substitute goods: goods that replace each other and, therefore, act as substitutes

complementary goods: goods that go together and, therefore, act as a pair

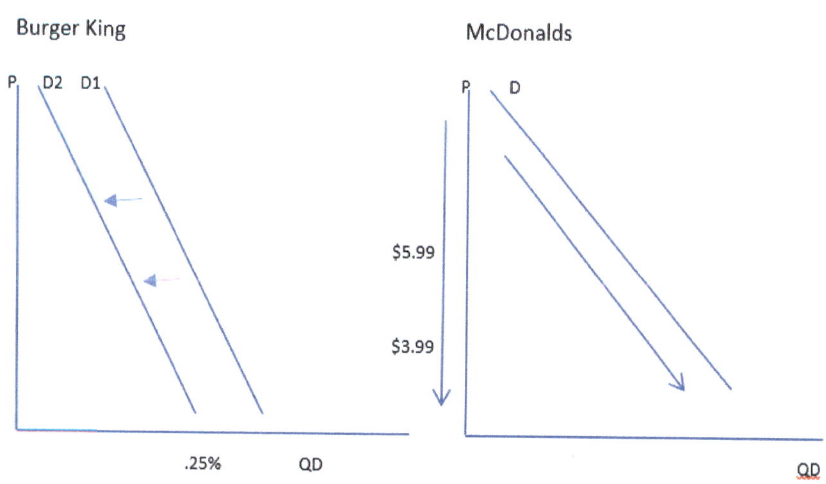

FIGURE 6.3 Cross-Price Elasticity of Demand

In this figure, Burger King experiences .25 decline in demand for its burgers due to McDonald's decision to lower its price from $5.99 to $3.99. As a result, Burger King's demand curve shifts to the left by .25 (change in demand). However, McDonald's demand moves downward along the demand curve due to its decision to lower its price (change in quantity demanded).

6.4 The Effect of Time on Price Elasticity of Demand

Time makes price elasticity of demand elastic, as it gives consumers time to adjust to changes in price. In other words, when the price of a good changes, over time, consumers will adjust their buying habits accordingly. An example of this includes increased fuel prices. In this example as fuel prices rise, over time, consumers will adjust their buying habits by driving less, buying fuel-efficient vehicles, carpooling, walking, or riding bicycles. In either case, they will reduce their fuel demand. This, in turn, will cause the demand curve for fuel to shift to the left. Figure 6.4 shows this effect in this example.

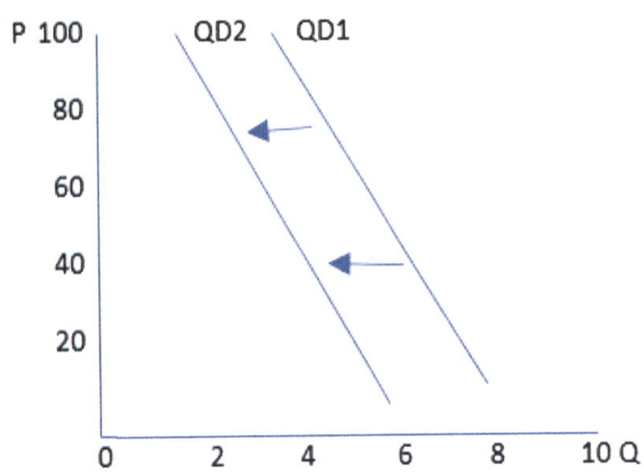

Time causes the demand curve to shift because it is a factor other than price.

FIGURE 6.4 The Effect of Time on Price Elasticity of Demand

6.5 The Effect of Budgets on Price Elasticity of Demand: Income

Budgets make price elasticity of demand elastic, as demand is affected by income. As such, economists are concerned with how income effects demand. So they attempt to measure this effect through income elasticity of demand. **Income** (*i*) **elasticity of demand** measures how much demand changes when income changes. The formula for determining income elasticity of demand is as follows:

income elasticity of demand = % change in quantity demanded / % change in income

In using this formula, economists can also determine if the product is a normal or inferior good. A **normal good** is defined as a good whose demand increases when income rises. An example of a normal good would be a name brand product, such as Nike shoes. By comparison, an **inferior good** is defined as a good whose demand decreases when income increases. An example of an inferior good would be a no-name brand product, such as the store brand. An example in using the income elasticity of demand to determine if demand is elastic or inelastic as well as to determine if the product is a normal good or an inferior good would be a salesperson receiving a pay raise from $10 per hour to $20 per hour. As a result of this increase, the salesperson increases their number of purchases of a name brand dress shoe company, Brand Leather, from two to eight. Within this example, economists seek to determine if the demand for Brand Leather is elastic or inelastic due to an income increase. In addition, they seek to know if Brand Leather is a normal good or inferior good. To determine this, they set up the formula as follows:

$$\{(2 - 8) / 2\} / \{(10 - 20) / 10\}$$

As they begin to work this equation beginning with the base number, they can move through the equation as follows:

1. (-6 / 2) / (-10 / 10)
2. -3 / -1
3. 3

Using the three product groups in which the elasticity of demand divide goods (elastic, inelastic, or unitary), they can determine that the income elastic of demand for Brand Leather is elastic. Within this examination, to determine if Brand Leather is a normal good or inferior, the general rule is that the good is a normal good if income and demand moves in the same direction and is an inferior good if income and demand moves in opposite direction. Therefore, when employing the general rule, Brand Leather is identified as a normal good because both income and demand increase (move in the same direction). Figure 6.5 shows the effect of income on demand in this example. In this figure, an increase in income causes demand to increase by three

income elasticity of demand: a measure of how much demand changes when income changes

normal good: a good whose demand increases when income rises

inferior good: a good whose demand decreases when income increases

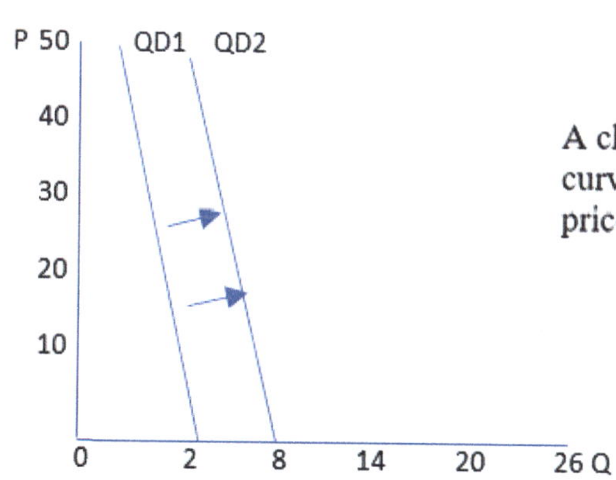

A change in income will cause the demand curve to shift because it is a factor other than price.

FIGURE 6.5 Income Elasticity of Demand

times. As a result, the increase in income causes the demand curve for Brand Leather to shift to the right (change in demand).

6.6 Price Elasticity of Supply

Price elasticity of supply (E_s) is defined as a measure of how much supply changes for a particular product when there is a change in a price. Within this, price elasticity of supply causes either an elastic or an inelastic response from producers. **Elastic supply** refers to a situation in which a small change in price causes a large change in quantity supplied. By comparison, **inelastic supply** refers to a situation in which a small change in price causes either a small change in quantity supplied or no change in quantity supplied. To determine if producers' response to a change in price is elastic or inelastic, one can use the following formula:

$$E_s = \% \text{ change in QS} / \% \text{ change in price}$$

An example of price elasticity of supply would be the price of a gallon of milk rising from \$2.00 to \$2.20. In response, the quantity supplied of milk increases from 100 million to 120 million. In this example, economists use the price elasticity of supply formula to determine if demand is elastic or inelastic. In doing so, the equation looks as follows:

$$\{(100 - 120) / 1\ 00\} / \{(\$2.00 - \$2.20)/\$2.00\}$$

From this equation, we are seeking to determine the percentage change in quantity supplied and the percentage change in price. To determine the percentage change in each variable, we must begin each half of the equation with the base number. As we start to work this equation beginning with the base number, we can move through the equation as follows:

1. (–20 / 100) / (–\$0.20 / \$2.00)
2. –.20 / –.10
3. 2

To understand if supply is elastic or inelastic because of price change in milk, one must use the three groups in which price elasticity of demand divides products. Therefore, when applying these three groups to the example, we can say that supply is elastic because the resulting number greater than 1. As a result, the change in price will cause upward movement along the supply curve. Figure 6.6 depicts this effect in this example.

price elasticity of supply (E_s): a measure of how much supply changes for a particular product when there is a change in a price

elastic supply: a situation in which a small change in price causes a large change in quantity supplied

inelastic supply: a situation in which a small change in price causes either a small change in quantity supplied or no change in quantity supplied

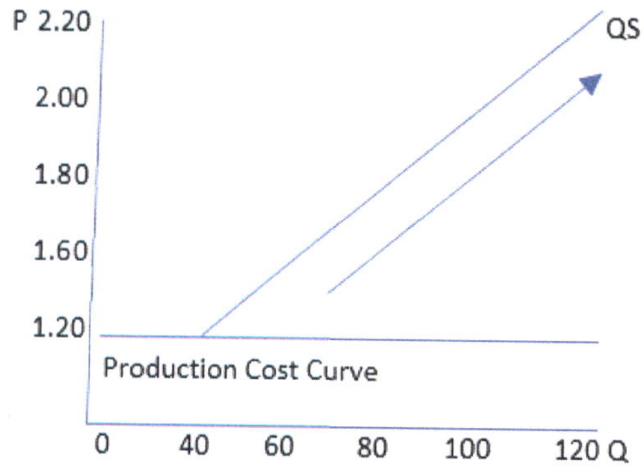

The supply curve is upward sloped to indicate an increase in supply which is caused by a rise in price.

FIGURE 6.6 Price Elasticity of Supply

6.7 The Effect of Time on Price Elasticity of Supply

Price is not the only factor that affects the change in the number of a particular product that producers supply. Another factor that affects price elasticity of supply is time. Time makes price elasticity of supply elastic. Now, the question becomes, "How does time make price elasticity of supply elastic?" The answer to this question involves both the short run and long run. In the short run, when price increases, the immediate response from producers is to increase production (law of supply). However, during this period, as price continues to rise, production increase is limited by capacity, as businesses do not have the ability to change their factors of productions, nor can they modify or build facilities. But over time, as price continues to rise, existing producers will move into the long run, and new producers will enter the market. At this time, additional labor will be hired, facilities will be built and modified, and supply will increase. As a result, time makes supply elastic as the supply curve shifts to the right. Figure 6.7 shows the effect of time on supply in this explanation.

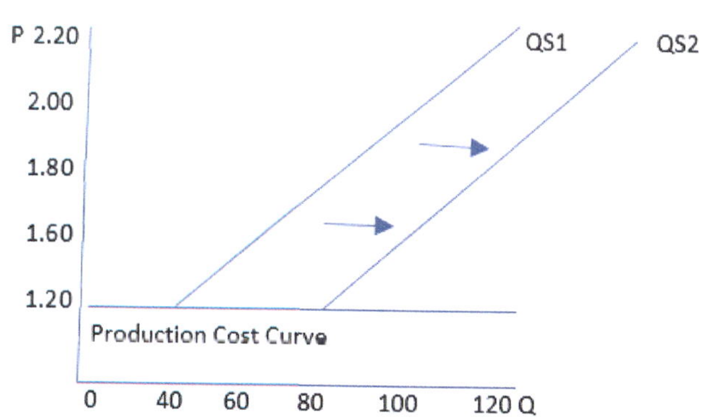

A right shift of the supply curve indicates an increase in supply. This shift is caused by a change in variables other than price.

FIGURE 6.7 The Effect of Time on Supply

SUMMARY

- Elasticity measures how much a variable changes when there is a change in another variable. (LO 6.1)
- Price elasticity measures how much a variable changes when there is a change in price. (LO 6.1)
- Price elasticity of demand measures how much demand changes when there is a change in price. (LO 6.2)
- Price elasticity of demand causes either an elastic or inelastic response from consumers. (LO 6.2)
- Price elasticity of demand divides products into elastic demand, inelastic demand, and unitary demand. (LO 6.2)
- Cross-price elasticity of demand measures how much demand changes in one good when there is a change in the price of another related good. (LO 6.3)
- Cross-price elasticity of demand is used to determine if products are substitute goods or complementary goods. (LO 6.3)
- Time makes the price elasticity of demand elastic. (LO 6.4)
- Income elasticity of demand measures how much demand changes when there is a change in income. (LO 6.5)
- Income elasticity of demand is used to determine whether a product is a normal good or inferior good. (LO 6.5)
- Price elasticity of supply measures how much supply changes when there is a change in price. (LO 6.6)
- Price elasticity of supply causes either an elastic or inelastic response from producers. (LO 6.6)
- Time makes price elasticity of supply elastic. (LO 6.7)

END OF CHAPTER APPLICATION

Comprehension Questions

Directions: Refer to the chapter to correctly respond to the following questions and prompts.

1. Is demand for smart watches elastic or inelastic? Explain. (LO 6.2)
2. Suppose the price of electric vehicles declines to match the price of traditional vehicles. How would consumption of (a) traditional vehicles, (b) home electricity, and (c) gasoline be affected? (LO 6.3)

3. Suppose that there is an increase in amount of optical-based quartz crystals needed to produce products, such as telescopes. How would this affect price over time? How will consumers respond to the change in price over time? (LO 6.4)
4. Why would the income elasticity of demand for a cruise vacation differ between college students and adults? Would you consider a cruise vacation to be a normal good or inferior good? Explain. (LO 6.5)
5. Suppose the price of wearable devices increased $100 to $125. In response, suppose supply for these products increased from 200 million to 220 million. Calculate the price elasticity of supply. Is the price elasticity of supply elastic or inelastic? Illustrate this on a supply curve. (LO 6.6)
6. How does time effect the price elasticity of supply? Explain what would occur to supply over time as price continues to rise. (LO 6.7)

Case Scenario: An Analysis of the Effect of Rising Fuel-Efficiency Standards on Tax Revenues

Directions: Use what you learned in the chapter to respond to the following scenario.

Automotive manufacturers are faced with growing government regulation that requires them to meet increased fuel efficiency standards in new vehicles. Explain how such a policy affects the following:

1. the price of vehicles
2. the supply of vehicles
3. tax revenues
4. the demand for vehicles

Would such government policy cause price elasticity of demand to be elastic or inelastic? Would it cause price elasticity of supply to be elastic or inelastic? Explain your answers.

BIBLIOGRAPHY

O'Sullivan, A., Shreffin, S., & Perez, S. (2017). *Microeconomics: Principles, applications, and tools* (9th ed.). Pearson Publishing.

Schiller, B. R. (2016). *The micro economy today* (14th ed.). McGraw-Hill Education.

CREDITS

CHAPTER 7

Market Surpluses

Concept Highlight

Chapter 7 examines the concepts of utilitarianism, consumer surplus, and producer surplus.

Real Life Example: What Does This Mean to You?

Utilitarianism is a concept used in both the consumer and seller decision-making process. An example of utilitarianism would be consumers shopping at the mall for a pair of jeans and a shirt at the lowest possible price. In response, sellers will offer jeans and shirts at the lowest possible price. In turn, such actions ensure everyone receives the products at the lowest price. Due to this, economists seek to understand the role utilitarianism plays in the market.

Introduction

Utilitarianism is an important concept to understand because it explains how the free market system operates. In this explanation, utilitarianism explains how self-interest in market promotes society's interest. Both consumer and producer surpluses are driven by self-interest. Consumers seek to buy goods and services at the lowest possible price. However, producers seek to earn the greatest profit from the sale of their goods and services.

OBJECTIVES

While reading this chapter, readers learn about

LO 7.1. rationality

LO 7.1. utility

LO 7.1. measuring utility

LO 7.1. two types of utility

LO 7.1. law of diminishing marginal utility

LO 7.1. utility maximizing rule

LO 7.2. utilitarianism

LO 7.2. consumer surplus

LO 7.2. producer surplus

LO 7.2. total surplus

OUTCOMES

After completing this chapter, readers will be able to do the following:

- Explain the relationship between rational choice and the marginal principle.
- Explain the difference between total utility and marginal utility.
- Measure consumer surplus on a demand curve.
- Measure producer surplus on a supply curve.
- Explain total surplus at equilibrium.

Key Terms

The following key terms are discussed in this chapter:

- rationality
- marginal principle
- utility
- util
- total utility
- marginal utility
- law of diminishing marginal utility
- utility maximizing rule
- utilitarianism
- consumer surplus
- producer surplus
- total surplus

7.1 Review: Determinants of Demand

In Chapter 6, we learned that there are a few factors affecting buying (i.e., demand). Those factors include (a) the price of the product in question and (b) the price of its substitute, complement, and one's taste or preference at that time. These factors imply that consumers go through a decision-making process when making buying decisions. As they go through process, they seek to make a rational choice. **Rationality** refers to the process of making a buying decision based on assessing the benefits and the costs associated with that decision and making the decision when the benefits are greater than the cost. An example of this would be Bob, the construction worker, who likes to eat either burgers or tacos for lunch. In this example, his decision to buy burgers or tacos is based on (a) the price of burgers, (b) the price of tacos, and (c) his taste or preference at the time. Suppose the price of a burger is \$2 or \$3. As such, suppose that Bob decides to buy 11 burgers when the price is \$2 and 8 burgers when the price is \$3. From this example, we can see Bob's decision on a demand curve. Table 7.1 depicts Bob's buying decisions on a demand table. Figure 7.1 depicts Bob's buying decisions on a demand curve.

TABLE 7.1 An Example of Bob's Burger Buying Decision on a Demand Schedule

Price	Quantity
2	11
3	8

Each point on this demand curve represents a rational choice by Bob. In other words, Bob's decision of the number of burgers he will buy is based on his assessment of the benefits of buying in relation to the costs. In doing so, he only buys if the benefits of buying are greater than the cost of buying. Because of this, we can say that his rational decision-making is based on the marginal principle. This principle has two definitions. The first definition of the **marginal principle** is the belief that a small change in one variable will cause a change in another variable (small $\Delta V \rightarrow$ large ΔV). The second definition of the marginal principle is the

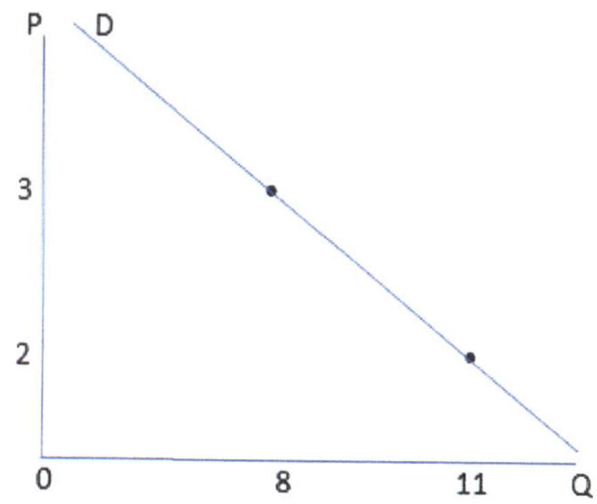

Each point on the demand curve represents a rational choice by Bob.

FIGURE 7.1 Bob's Burger Buying Decision on a Demand Curve

belief that one should increase an activity if one's marginal benefits (MB) are greater than its marginal costs (MC), decrease an activity if the marginal costs (MC) are greater than the marginal benefits (MB), and choose the level of activity where the marginal benefits (MB) equal the marginal costs (MC). As such, rationality is based on the second definition. To understand the relationship between rationality and the marginal principle, we need to understand the marginal benefits and marginal costs associated with buying.

Marginal benefits refer to the additional benefits received from a small increase in an activity. The marginal benefits received from buying goods and services is utility. **Utility** is defined as the satisfaction or pleasure consumers receive when consuming a good. Economists use a unit called a "util" to measure the level of satisfaction or pleasure consumers receive from consuming a good. A **util** refers to a unit of satisfaction or pleasure.

There are two types of utility consumers receive when consuming a good. Those two types of utility include total utility and marginal utility. **Total utility** refers to the level of satisfaction or pleasure consumers

rationality: the process of making a buying decision based on assessing the benefits and the costs associated with that decision and making the decision when the benefits are greater than the cost

marginal principle: the belief that a small change in one variable will cause a change in another variable; the belief that one should increase an activity if one's marginal benefits are greater than its marginal costs, decrease an activity if the marginal costs are greater than the marginal benefits, and choose the level of activity where the marginal benefits equal the marginal costs.

utility: the satisfaction or pleasure consumers receive when consuming a good

util: a unit of satisfaction or pleasure

total utility: the level of satisfaction or pleasure consumers receive from whatever quantity of a product consumed; total satisfaction or pleasure

marginal utility: the change in satisfaction or pleasure consumers receive from each unit of a product consumed

law of diminishing marginal utility: the belief that marginal utility decreases as consumption of a good increases

utility maximizing rule: the belief that when consumers seek to consume two or more goods, they will seek to consume the marginal utility per dollar spent on one good equal the marginal utility per dollar spent on the other good receive from whatever quantity of a product consumed. Therefore, total utility represents total satisfaction or pleasure consumers receive from consuming a good. By comparison, **marginal utility** refers to the change in satisfaction or pleasure consumers receive from each unit of a product consumed. To explain these concepts, we return to Bob, the construction worker. In this example, suppose Bob decides to eat at an all-you-can-eat burger buffet for lunch. While at lunch, Bob eats burgers until he is full. At this point, he has reached total utility. However, as he gets closer to becoming full, he gets less satisfaction from eating each additional burger. This represents marginal utility. This example illustrates the law of diminishing marginal utility. The **law of diminishing marginal utility** is the idea that marginal utility decreases as consumption increases. In other words, the law of diminishing marginal utility assumes satisfaction or pleasure decreases as consumption of a good increases.

The law of diminishing marginal utility explains what occurs when a consumer consumes one good. However, the utility maximizing rule explains what occurs when a consumer seeks to consume two or more goods. The **utility maximizing rule** is the belief that when consumers seek to consume two or more goods, they will seek to consume the marginal utility per dollar spent on one good equal the marginal utility per dollar spent on the other good. In other words, when consuming two or more goods, consumers seek to create the greatest "bang for their buck" by consuming the amounts of each good that brings the same change in satisfaction per dollar.

7.2 Utilitarianism

The free market system was modeled after the invisible hand theory, created by Adam Smith. However, the invisible hand theory is based on the belief that society's interest is promoted when people act in their own self-interest. Such a belief is based on utilitarianism. **Utilitarianism** is defined as the best decision being the one that produces the greatest good for the greatest number of people. Therefore, in a free market, when consumers seek products at the lowest possible price, they are acting in their own self-interest. This ensures that sellers sell at the lowest possible price, which, then, ensures greater society benefits from these actions by being able to also purchase products at the lowest possible price.

When consumers act in their own self-interest, they create consumer surplus. **Consumer surplus** refers to the difference between the maximum price consumers are willing to pay for a product and the actual price paid. In other words, consumer surplus implies consumers are willing to pay more for a product than they actually do and, therefore, receive a discount for buying. So if a consumer is willing to pay $21 to stream a new album from their favorite music band but only pay $10, then the consumer receives a consumer surplus of $11. As such, we can see consumer surplus on a demand curve. Suppose that in the same example, five other consumers were asked how much they would be willing to pay to stream the new album of the same band. In doing so, suppose that they, along with the first consumer, provided the following pricing information, which is seen on a demand schedule in Table 7.2.

We can measure the consumer surplus each consumer received on a demand curve. Figure 7.2 shows this measurement.

In this illustration, the market price (MP) of $10 for a new album is designated by a horizontal line. At this price, we can see the amount of consumer surplus (CS) each consumer receives. As we move from the first consumer to the fifth, the amount of consumer surplus reduces until it falls to zero. For all five consumers, the benefits of buying are at least equal to or greater than the costs of buying, and therefore,

TABLE 7.2 A Demand Schedule for Consumers Willing to Pay to Stream Music

Consumer number	Price
1	21
2	19
3	16
4	14
5	10
6	7

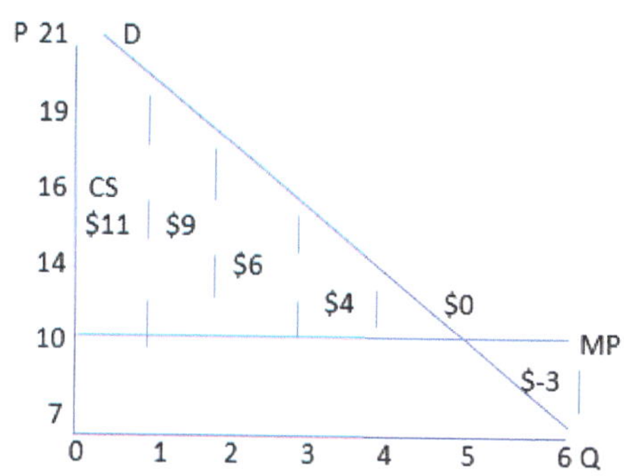

Consumer surplus can be measured on a demand curve.

FIGURE 7.2 A Consumer of Surplus for Consumers Willing to Pay to Stream Music Shown on a Demand Curve

they would buy. However, the sixth consumer would incur a loss of $3, which means they would not receive a consumer surplus. Therefore, for this consumer, the costs of buying would be greater than the benefits of buying, which would lead the consumer to decide not to buy.

Producers also act in their own self-interest. When they do, they create producer surplus. **Producer surplus** refers to the difference between the minimum amount of money producers are willing to accept and the actual amount of money they receive. In other words, producer surplus implies producers are willing to accept less than what they actually receive, and therefore, the additional amount received represents a surplus (profits). So if the producer of a music band is willing to accept $4 as a minimum for a new album but actually receives $10 in the market for the album, the producer surplus is $6. In this example, producer surplus is based on the marginal principle. Therefore, the marginal benefits received by the producer are the revenues earned and these revenues increase by the market price for each unit sold. By comparison, the marginal costs incurred by the producer are the costs associated with producing the product. These costs represent the producer's production cost, and therefore, they rise for each unit produced. This, in turn, is known as "marginal cost."

Another example would be six lawn cutting producers. In this example, suppose the minimum accepted price is different for each producer because each has a different opportunity cost associated with their resources. Therefore, the minimum price they are willing to accept to cut lawn is as provided in Table 7.3.

TABLE 7.3 Minimum Accepted Price for Lawn Cutting Producers

Producers	Minimum accepted price
1	2
2	4
3	6
4	8
5	10
6	12

Suppose that in this example, the market price for cutting lawns is $10. From this, we can measure producer surplus received by each producer on a supply curve. Figure 7.3 shows this measurement.

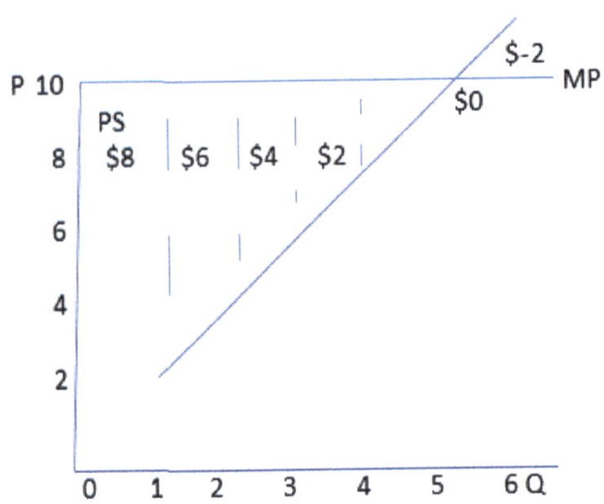

Producer surplus can be measured on a supply curve.

FIGURE 7.3 Producer Surplus Shown on a Supply Curve

utilitarianism: the idea that the best decision is the one that produces the greatest good for the greatest number of people

consumer surplus: the difference between the maximum price consumers are willing to pay for a product and the actual price paid

producer surplus: the difference between the minimum amount of money producers are willing to accept and the actual amount of money they receive

total surplus: the combined quantity of consumer surplus and producer surplus

In this illustration, the market price (MP) of $10 for lawn cutting is designated by a horizontal line. At this price, we can see the amount of producer surplus (CS) each producer receives. As we move from the first producer to the fifth, the amount of producer surplus reduces until it falls to zero. For all five producers, the benefits of producing are at least equal to or greater than the costs of production; therefore, they would cut lawns. However, the sixth producer would incur a loss of $2, which means they would not receive a producer surplus because their production cost is greater than the market price. Therefore, this would lead the producer to decide not to cut lawns.

Total surplus occurs at the point where quantity demanded equals quantity supplied. **Total surplus** is defined as the combined quantity of consumer surplus and producer surplus. In other words, at this point (equilibrium), the highest possible surplus is created. This, in turn, creates efficiency in the market. The question becomes, "How do we know that total surplus creates efficiency?" If price rises above equilibrium, it will create excess supply, as a greater number of consumers will choose not to buy, which moves the market away from total surplus. In addition, if price falls below equilibrium, it will create excess demand, as a greater number of producers will choose not to produce, which also moves the market away from total surplus. In both cases, the market becomes inefficient. Therefore, total surplus creates efficiency. Figure 7.4 depicts total surplus.

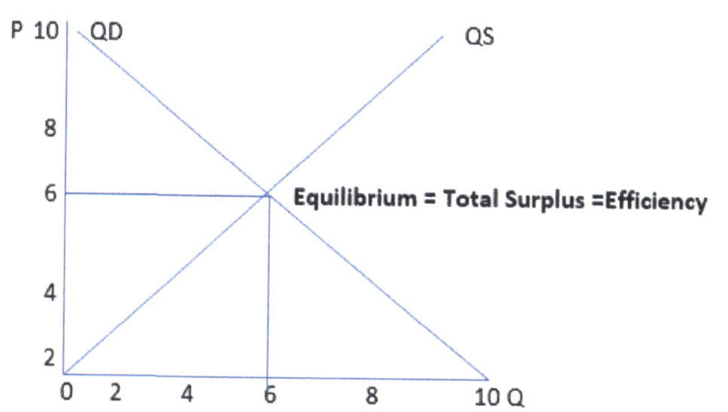

Total surplus creates efficiency in the market.

FIGURE 7.4 Total Surplus

SUMMARY

- Each point on a demand curve represents a rational choice. (LO 7.1)
- A consumer's rational choice is based on the marginal principle. (LO 7.1)
- The marginal benefits received from consumption is known as utility. (LO 7.1)
- A util is the unit used to measure utility. (LO 7.1)
- One reaches total utility as they increase consumption. However, the amount of utility becomes less as one gets closer to reaching total utility. (LO 7.1)
- The law of diminishing marginal utility explains the relationship between total utility and marginal utility. (LO 7.1)
- The utility maximizing rule explains what occurs when one seeks to consume two or more products. (LO 7.1)
- Acting in one's own self-interest in the market is based on utilitarianism. (LO 7.2)

- Acting in one's own self-interest creates both consumer surplus and producer surplus. (LO 7.2)
- Total surplus creates efficiency in the market. (LO 7.2)

END-OF-CHAPTER APPLICATION

Comprehension Questions

Directions: Refer to the chapter to correctly respond to the following questions and prompts.

1. Keith is a college student who likes to purchase video games or clothes with the money he earns from his part-time job. Suppose Keith purchases 2 video games per month when prices are at $50 each and 4 video games per month when the games are offered at a discounted price of $40 per month. Use the concept of rationality to explain his decision. Illustrate his rational choices on a demand curve. (LO 7.1)
2. Suppose you and your friends went to dinner at a favorite restaurant. Use total utility and marginal utility to explain your consumption habits. (LO 7.1)
3. How does utilitarianism support self-interest in the market? Explain. (LO 7.2)
4. Explain the difference between consumer surplus and producer surplus. (LO 7.2)
5. Why does efficiency occur when the market reaches total surplus? Explain. (LO 7.2)

Case Scenario: Calculating Consumer Surplus and Producer Surplus in the Fast-Food Industry

Directions: Use what you learned in the chapter to respond to the following scenario.

The demand and supply curve for the fast-food industry is as follows:

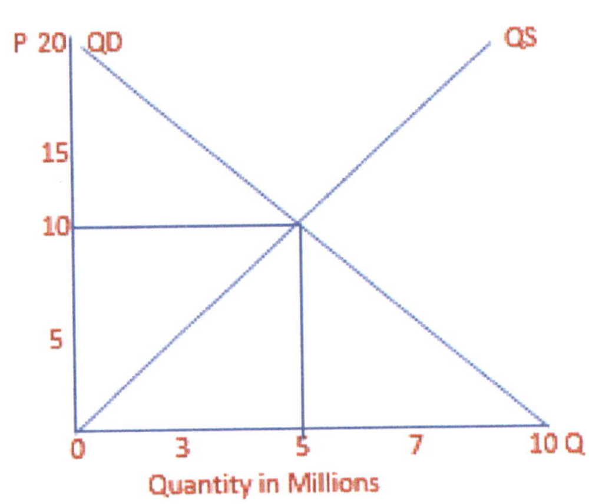

The formula for determining consumer surplus is as follows:

(maximum price – market price) × equilibrium quantity / 2

The formula for determining producer surplus is as follows:

(market price – minimum accepted price) × equilibrium quantity / 2

The formula for determining market surplus is as follows:

consumer surplus + producer surplus

If equilibrium occurs as \$10 (E_P) and 5 million (E_Q), complete the following:

1. Calculate consumer surplus.
2. Calculate producer surplus.
3. Calculate total surplus

BIBLIOGRAPHY

BC Campus. (n.d.). *Solutions: Case study—Automation in fast food. British Columbia/Yukon Open Authoring Platform.* https://pressbooks.bccampus.ca/uvicecon103/chapter/solutions-case-study-automation-in-fast-food/

O'Sullivan, A., Shreffin, S., & Perez, S. (2017). *Microeconomics: Principles, applications, and tools* (9th ed.). Pearson Publishing.

Schiller, B. R. (2016). *The micro economy today* (14th ed.). McGraw-Hill Education.

CREDIT

Part III
Production Cost and Markets

Source: Jerome C. Baysmore/U.S. Air Force, https://commons.wikimedia.org/wiki/File:Cookies_production_in_Bishkek,_Kyrgyzstan_(2).JPG, U.S. Air Force, 2011.

A Business' Production Cost

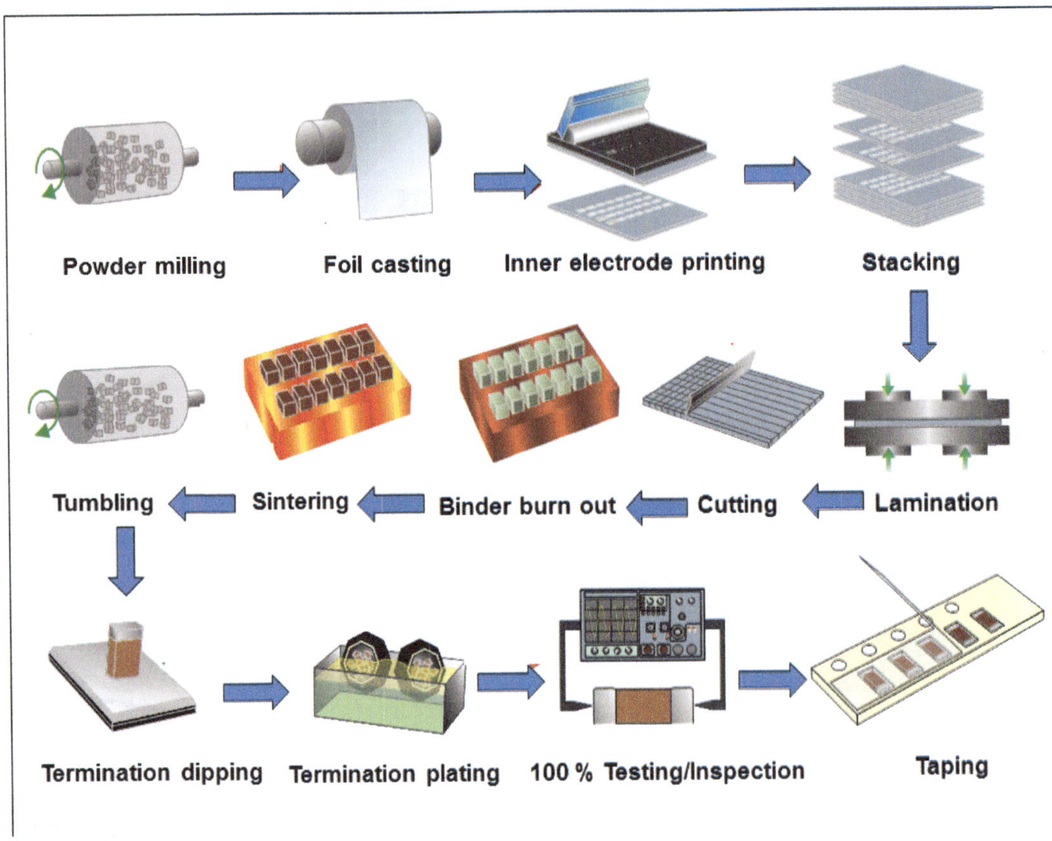

Concept Highlight

Chapter 8 examines the components of a business's production costs.

Real Life Example: What Does This Mean to You?

Businesses produce products and services in response to demand. However, the business owner will incur costs associated with providing products and services to meet demand. An example of this includes a manufacturer who produces toys. In this example, the business owner must determine all costs associated with producing each toy. These costs will affect the business owner's production decision.

Introduction

Production cost is an important concept to understand because it is what a business incurs in exchange for producing products and services. In doing so, understanding the concept of economic cost as a source of production cost becomes important. However, as one considers economic cost, one also learns of explicit cost and implicit cost.

A business produces in both the short run and long run. Therefore, examining these concepts allows for understanding the production decisions made during these periods as well as the impact of those decisions on production cost. As one begins to understand the impact of production decisions on production costs during these periods, one begins to also understand the difference between the short run and the long run.

OBJECTIVES

While reading this chapter, readers learn about

LO 8.1. economic cost

LO 8.1. explicit cost

LO 8.1. implicit cost

LO 8.1. principle of opportunity cost

LO 8.2. short run

LO 8.2. principle of diminishing returns

LO 8.2. total product curve

LO 8.2. marginal product of labor

LO 8.2. types of production costs incurred in the short run

LO 8.2. short run total cost

LO 8.2. short run marginal cost

LO 8.2. types of average production costs expressed in the short run

LO 8.2. production cost graph

LO 8.2. types of curves on the production cost graph in the short run

LO 8.3. long run

LO 8.3. types of production costs incurred in the long run

LO 8.3. long run total cost

LO 8.3. types of average production costs expressed in the long run

LO 8.3. types of curves on the production cost graph in the long run

LO 8.4. difference between the short run and long run in the production process

LO 8.4. indivisible inputs

OUTCOMES

After completing this chapter, readers will be able to do the following:

- Relate production cost to the principle of opportunity cost.
- Relate the short run to the principle of diminishing returns.
- Illustrate the total product curve.
- Illustrate the marginal product of labor.
- Explain the types of production cost incurred in the short run.
- Illustrate and explain the types of curves on a production cost graph in the short run.
- Explain why the short run average fixed cost curve is said to be relatively flat.
- Explain why the short run average variable cost curve is said to be upward sloped.
- Explain why the short run average total cost curve is said to be U-shaped.
- Explain the options a business owner has in responding to an increase in demand in the long run.
- Illustrate the types of production cost incurred in the long run.
- Illustrate and explain the types of curves on a production cost graph in the long run.
- Explain why the long-run average fixed cost curve is said to be relatively flat.
- Explain why the long-run average variable cost curve is said to be upward sloped.
- Explain why the long-run average total cost curve is said to be L-shaped.
- Explain the difference between the short run and the long run.
- Explain indivisible inputs.

Key Terms

The following key terms are discussed in this chapter:

- economic cost
- explicit cost
- implicit cost
- principle of opportunity cost
- short run
- principle of diminishing returns
- total product curve
- marginal product of labor

- fixed cost
- variable cost
- total cost
- short run total cost
- short run marginal cost
- average fixed cost
- average variable cost
- average total cost
- production cost graph
- long run
- long-run total cost
- economies of scale
- minimum efficient scale
- diseconomies of scale
- indivisible inputs

8.1 What is Economic Cost?

A business owner's production cost consists of all costs associated with producing a product or service. At the most basic level, these costs are based on the concept of economic cost. **Economic cost** is the combination of explicit cost and implicit cost. **Explicit cost** refers to the actual cash payments for inputs. Such costs are also known as accounting costs because they are recorded in an account ledger. By comparison, **implicit cost** refers to the costs incurred due to the loss of the business owner's time, energy, or similar measure in exchange for producing products and services. Although such costs are not purchased, they still represent an expense to the business owner. As a result of these costs, we can say that a business owner's economic costs are based on the principle of opportunity cost. The **principle of opportunity cost** is the belief that for one to obtain something, something else must be given up in return. Therefore, the business owner must give up monetary and nonmonetary expenses to produce.

economic cost: the combination of explicit cost and implicit cost

explicit cost: actual cash payments for inputs; also known as accounting cost

implicit cost: the costs incurred due to loss of the business owner's time, energy, or similar measure in exchange for producing products and services

principle of opportunity cost: the belief that for one to obtain something, something else must be given up in return

8.2 A Business's Production Cost in the Short Run

A business produces in the short run. The **short run** has two definitions. The first is a period of time in which one or more factors of production remains fixed. The "short run" is also defined as a period of time in which a business can't build new facilities or modify existing ones. So during this period, the business is incapable of changing many of its factors of production, including facilities. As such, the business owner's production decision will be based on the principle of diminishing returns. The **principle of diminishing returns** is the belief that output will increase at a decreasing rate when one input increases while all other inputs remain at a constant rate. In other words, during the short run, if the business owner seeks to increase production, the only option it has when changing inputs is to hire additional labor, as this is the only input that will not incur an immediate expense. If the business owner hires additional labor while keeping all inputs at its current level, production will increase slowly for each increment, until the production can no longer increase.

We can see the relationship between labor and output on a total product curve. A **total product curve** is a curve that shows the relationship between labor (L) and output (Y). This curve also includes the marginal product of labor. The **marginal product of labor** refers to a curve that shows the change in output for each additional worker employed. In doing so, the marginal product of labor shows diminishing returns. In other words, the marginal product of labor shows *an increase at a decreasing rate.*

An example of the total product curve and marginal product of labor would be the pizza shop owner who has one employee, who we discussed in Chapter 2. This employee can produce 12 pizzas. The pizza shop owner decides to hire a second employee with the hopes of increasing pizza production from 12 to 24 pizzas. However, total production between the two employees only increases to 18. In response, the pizza shop owner hires a third employee with the hopes of increasing pizza production to 24. Yet pizza production between the three employees only increases to 21. Table 8.1 provides a chart that shows the relationship between labor and pizza production. Figure 8.1 depicts this relationship on the total product curve. Figure 8.2 shows the change in output for each additional work (marginal product of labor).

TABLE 8.1 An Example of a Chart Showing the Relationship Between Labor and Output

Number of Employees	Pizza Production (Output)	Change in Pizza Production (Output)
1	12	–
2	18	6
3	21	3

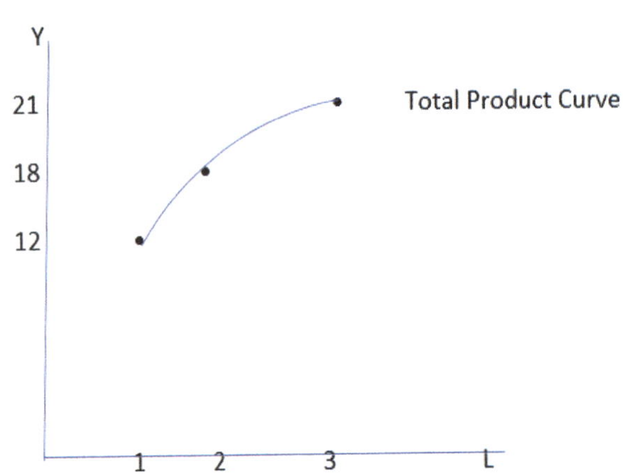

FIGURE 8.1 A Total Product Curve

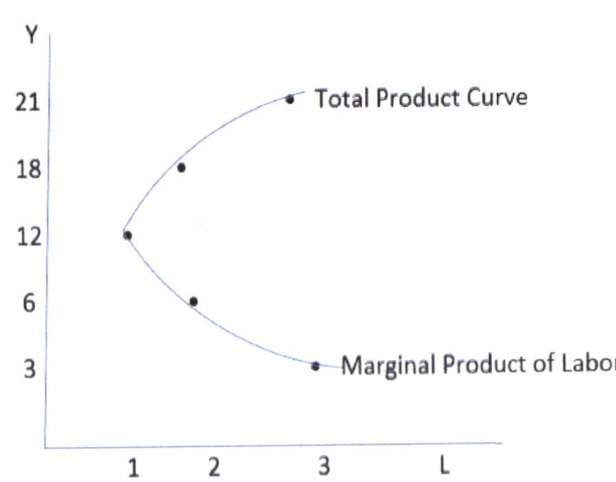

FIGURE 8.2 The Marginal Product of Labor

In the short run, a business's production cost consists of fixed cost (FC) and variable cost (VC). **Fixed cost** (FC) refers to cost that doesn't change when output is changed. Therefore, these costs remain the same, regardless of the number of units produced. Examples of such costs include rent, loan payments, and insurance premiums. By comparison, **variable cost** (VC) refers to cost that change when output changes. In other words, these costs change as the number of products change. Examples of variable cost include raw materials and wages.

The combination of fixed cost and variable cost yields **total cost** (TC). In the short run, this combination creates short-run total cost. **Short-run total cost** (SRTC) is defined as the sum of fixed cost and variable cost in the short run. In the short run, a change in the SRTC is caused by a change in variable cost. This, in turn, creates short run marginal cost. **Short-run marginal cost** (SRMC) refers to a change in SRTC due to a change in units produced.

Business owners express their costs in averages. Therefore, there is an average fixed cost (AFC), average variable cost (AVC), and average total cost (ATC). **Average fixed cost** (AFC) is defined as the fixed cost divided by the number of units produced. **Average variable cost** (AVC) is defined as variable cost divided by the number of units produced. **Average total cost** (ATC) is defined as the total cost divided by the number of units produced. In the short run, these costs are further expressed as "short-run average fixed cost" (SRAFC), "short-run average variable cost" (SRAVC) production cost graph. A **production cost graph** is a graph that shows various production cost for each unit produced. Figure 8.3 shows a production cost graph in the short run.

Examining the production graph, the SRAFC curve always lies at the bottom of the graph. As such, this curve is said to be relatively flat (with a slight downward slope) to represent such costs not varying much as output changes. The SRAVC curve lies above this curve. This curve is said to be upward sloped to represent rises in variable

short run: a period of time in which one or more factors of production remain fixed; a period of time in which a business can't build new facilities or modify existing ones

principle of diminishing returns: the belief that output will increase at a decreasing rate when one input increases and all other inputs remain at a constant rate

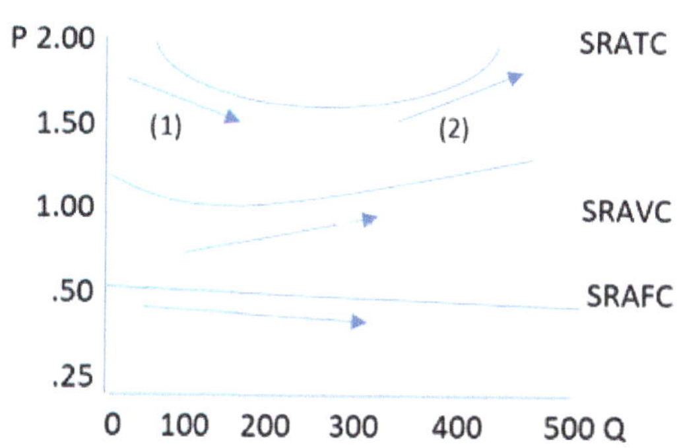

The SRATC is said to be U-shaped because of the spread of labor specialization (1), which leads to lower cost and the rise of variable cost (2) due to the exhausting of labor specialization as production increases.

FIGURE 8.3 A Production Cost Graph in the Short Run

total product curve: a curve that shows the relationship between labor (L) and output (Y)

marginal product of labor: a curve that shows the change in output for each additional worker employed

fixed cost: cost that doesn't change when output changes; such costs are not dependent on the number of units produced

variable cost: cost that changes when output changes; such costs are dependent on the number of units produced

total cost: the combination of fixed cost and variable cost

short-run total cost: the sum of fixed cost and variable cost in the short run

short-run marginal cost: a change in short run total cost due to a change in units produced

average fixed cost: fixed cost divided by the number of units produced

average variable cost: variable cost divided by the number of units produced

average total cost: total cost divided by the number of units produced

production cost graph: a graph that shows various production cost for each unit produced

cost as output rises. The "short run average total cost" (SRATC) curve always lies at the top of the graph. This curve lies above the SRAVC curve and the SRAFC curve because it is the sum of those two. As such, the SRATC curve is said to be U-shaped.

The SRATC curve is said to be U-shaped for two reasons. First, at the beginning of the curve (as designated by [1]), the curve is negatively sloped due to (a) fixed cost being spread across an increasing number of units being produced as well as (b) labor specialization being employed as the number of united produced increases. In other words, as the business increases production, SRATC declines initially, due to the decline in the SRAFC as well as an increase in labor productivity. However, at some point, while using current resources, the business will reach a point where its fixed cost can't decline further and its current labor specialization becomes exhausted. When this occurs, if the business seeks to increase production, its only option is to increase labor, which will lead to an increase in its variable cost (as designated by [2]). At this point, diminishing returns occur. As a result, the U shape of the SRATC curve is caused by a tug of war between two forces, which includes the spreading of fixed costs and labor specialization pulling curve downward, while rising variable costs pull the curve upward.

8.3 A Business's Production Cost in the Long Run

A business also produces in the long run. The **long run** has two definitions. The first refers to a period of time in which the factors of production can be changed. The "long run" is also defined as a period of time in which a business can build new facilities or modify existing ones. So during this period, the business can change its factors of production, including facilities. As such, the question becomes, "What is the difference between the long run and the short?" The answer is diminishing returns. In other words, in the short run diminishing returns occur because the business can only change its labor to respond to an increase in demand. However, in the long run, diminishing returns do not occur because the business can change all other factors of production along with changes in labor as demand increases, thereby allowing its workforce to remain productive.

During the short run, as demand increases, the business owner can only hire additional labor, which leads to diminishing returns. However, in the long run, the business owner can respond to an increase in demand by either modification or replication. "Modification" refers to expanding existing facilities. This allows the business owner to produce at a targeted level, thereby allowing production cost to rise to a targeted level. By comparison, "replication" refers to building an identical facility to the original facility. This allows the business owner to double their production while, also doubling their production cost. In either case, the business owner will incur fixed cost, variable cost, and total cost. In the long run, the combination of fixed cost and variable cost creates long-run total cost (LRTC). **Long-run total cost** (LRTC) is defined as the sum of fixed cost and variable cost in the long run.

Like the short run, in the long run, a business owner expresses their cost in averages. Therefore, "average fixed cost" (AFC), "average variable cost" (AVC), and "average total cost" (ATC) are used. In the long run, these costs are further expressed as "long-run average fixed cost" (LRAFC), "long-run average variable cost" (LRAVC), and "long-run average total cost" (LRATC). These averages can be illustrated on a production cost graph. Figure 8.4 shows a production cost graph in the long run.

Like the short run, the LRAFC curve always lies at the bottom of the graph. As such, this curve is said to be relatively flat (with a slight downward slope) to represent such cost not varying much as output changes. The LRATC curve lies above this curve. This curve is said to be upward sloped to represent rises in variable cost as output rises. The long-run average total cost curve always lies at the top of the graph. The curve lies above the LRAVC curve and the LRAFC curve because it is the sum of the those two. As such, the LRATC curve is said to be L-shaped.

The LRATC curve is said to be L-shaped for three reasons, including economies of scale, minimum efficient scale, and diseconomies of scale. First, the curve slopes downward due to economies of scale. **Economies of scale** are situations in which the average total cost falls as production increases. In other words, during the initial phase of production in the long run, it costs less to produce, on average, as total cost is spread over a greater number of units. This is designated as 1 on the graph in Figure 8.4. However, at some point, the business reaches maximum cost-savings capacity with current resources. At this point,

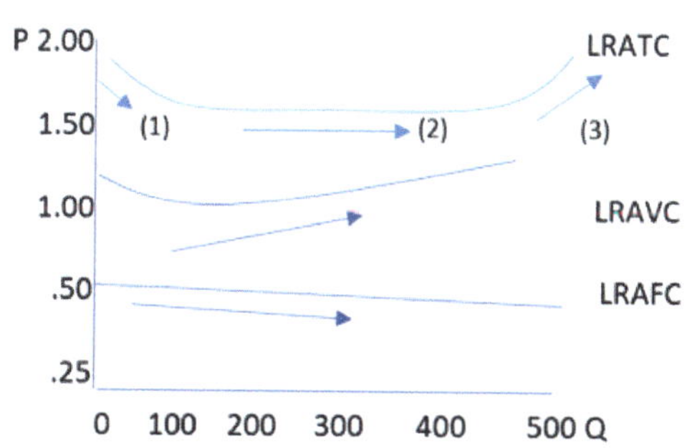

The LRATC is said to be L-shaped because of economies of scale, minimum efficient scale, and diseconomies of scale.

FIGURE 8.4 A Production Cost Graph in the Long Run

long run: a period of time in which the factors of production can be changed; a period of time in which businesses can build new facilities or modify existing ones.

long run total cost: the sum of fixed cost and variable cost in the long run

economies of scale: a situation in which average total cost falls as production increases

minimum efficient scale: a situation in which economies of scale becomes exhausted

diseconomies of scale: a situation in which average total costs rise as production increases

production reaches the minimum efficient scale. The **minimum efficient scale** is a situation in which an economy of scale becomes exhausted. This is designated as 2 on the graph. From here, businesses will incur additional variable costs as they increas production. This, in turn, creates diseconomies of scale. **Diseconomies of scale** are when average total costs rise as production increases. Diseconomies of scale occur for to two reasons: The first is when the business is required to increase its workforce to increase production and the new workforce is less skilled than the existing workforce. The second is when the business incurs higher cost for some inputs as demand for those inputs increases. This is designed as 3 on the graph.

8.4 The Short Run vs. the Long Run in Production: A Review

There are differences in the production process for the short run and the long run. One such difference lies in diminishing returns. In the short run, a business's only response to a rise in demand is to increase labor. If labor is increased while all other resources remain constant, production will increase at a decreasing rate. This is what we mean by "diminishing returns." However, in the long run, a business has a few options in response to a rise in demand. Those options are modification or replication. In either option, the business will increase its other resources as it increases labor, thereby avoiding diminishing returns.

However, what happens in both the short run and long run if demand falls? In the short run, a decline in demand will cause the business to reduce its workforce to produce a smaller number of units of product while all other resources remain the same, since the business does not make any changes to those. But in the long run, a decline in demand could create indivisible inputs. **Indivisible inputs** refer to a situation in which inputs (resources) can't be reduced to produce a smaller number of units. An example of this would be a business owner deciding to expand production with the use of a certain type of material. If the demand declines after the expansion, theoretically, the business owner will not be able to reduce the material cost used in production. In this case, the material cost becomes an indivisible input, and as a result, the business's long run total cost would not decline to match the reduced production.

indivisible inputs: a situation in which inputs (resources) can't be reduced to produce a smaller number of units

SUMMARY

- Production cost is based on the concept of economic cost. (LO 8.1)
- Economic cost consists of explicit cost and implicit cost. (LO 8.1)
- Production decisions in the short run are based on the principles of diminishing returns. (LO 8.2)
- The principle of diminishing returns uses the total product curve to show the relationship between labor and production. (LO 8.2)
- The principle of diminishing returns uses the marginal product of labor to illustrate diminishing returns. (LO 8.2)
- A business's production cost in the short run consists of both fixed cost and variable cost. (LO 8.2)
- Total cost is the sum of fixed cost and variable cost. (LO 8.2)
- The short run creates the short run total cost. (LO 8.2)
- During the short run, a change in total cost creates short run marginal cost. (LO 8.2)
- A business owner uses average fixed cost, average variable cost, and average total cost to express their production cost in the short run. (LO 8.2)
- A production cost graph illustrates the short-run average fixed cost, short-run average variable cost, and short-run average total cost curves. (LO 8.2)
- A business owner can modify or replicate facilities in response to an increase in demand in the long run. (LO 8.3)
- The sum of fixed cost and variable cost in the long run creates long run total cost. (LO 8.3)
- A business owner uses average fixed cost, average variable cost, and average total cost to express their production cost in the long run. (LO 8.3)
- A production cost graph illustrates the long-run average fixed cost, long-run average variable cost, and long-run average total cost curves. (LO 8.3)
- Diminishing returns represent the difference between the short run and the long run. (LO 8.4)
- A business owner may be challenged with indivisible inputs if demand decreases in the long run. (LO 8.4)

END OF CHAPTER APPLICATION

Comprehension Questions

Directions: Refer to the chapter to correctly respond to the following questions and prompts.

1. Eric is the owner of a bicycle manufacturing operation. Provide examples of his explicit cost. Provide examples of his implicit cost. Use the principle of opportunity cost to explain the relationship between his production and production cost. (LO 8.1)
2. How would a business owner respond to an increase in demand in the short run? What production option(s) does the business owner have in this response? How would diminishing returns affect the production decision? (LO 8.2)
3. Provide an example of a current business. Give examples of that business's fixed cost. Give examples of its variable cost. What type of cost would affect the business's total cost? (LO 8.2)
4. Explain why a business's short run average fixed cost curve is flat. Explain why its short run average variable cost curve is upward sloped. Explain why its short run average total cost curve is U-shaped. (LO 8.2)
5. Kim is the owner of a pizzeria. What facility options would she have in the long run if demand increases? How would each affect her production cost? Explain. (LO 8.3)
6. Explain why a business's long run average fixed cost curve is flat. Explain why its long run average variable cost curve is upward sloped. Explain why its long run average total cost curve is L-shaped. (LO 8.3)
7. Explain the difference between the short run and the long run in the production process. (LO 8.4)
8. Kim is the owner of a pizzeria. She expands her operations. Explain what will occur to her operations if demand declines while the business is in the long run. (LO 8.4)

Case Scenario: Analyzing the Business Practices of Microsoft

Directions: Use what you learned in the chapter to respond to the following scenario.

Farmer Joe produces corn on an acre of land. His production cost consists of both explicit and implicit cost. These costs occur in both the short run and the long run. During these times, there are many variables that make up both his fixed cost and variable in producing corn. Perform an analysis of his production cost by answering the following questions:

1. Provide examples of Farmer Joe's explicit cost and implicit cost.
2. Provide examples of Farmer Joe's fixed cost and variable costs.
3. How would Farmer Joe respond to an increase in demand in the short run? How would this affect his corn yield?

4. How would Farmer Joe respond to an increase in demand in the long run? What options would he have in his response? How would each option affect his production and his production cost?

REFERENCES

O'Sullivan, A., Shreffin, S., & Perez, S. (2017). *Microeconomics: Principles, applications, and tools* (9th ed.). Pearson Publishing.

Schiller, B. R. (2016). *The micro economy today* (14th ed.). McGraw-Hill Education.

CREDIT

IMG 8.1: Elcap, https://commons.wikimedia.org/wiki/File:MLCC-Manufacturing-Process.png, 2012.

CHAPTER 9

Types of Markets

Perfectly Competitive Markets

Concept Highlight

Chapter 9 examines the concepts of a perfectly competitive market.

Real Life Example: What Does This Mean to You?

One type of market, a "perfectly competitive market," demonstrates the behavior of businesses who sell the same standardized products. An example of this type of market consists of orange producers within the agricultural industry. Within this industry, farmers must decide how they will compete and determine a strategy for earning profit.

Introduction

A perfectly competitive market is an important concept to understand because it explains behavior between competing businesses who sell the same standardized products. In such a market, it becomes important to know how the businesses compete and the strategies used to achieve profit. In addition, it becomes important to understand what occurs when businesses in this market transition from the short run to the long run.

OBJECTIVES

While reading this chapter, readers learn about

LO 9.1. market

LO 9.1. perfectly competitive market

LO 9.1. competitive business

LO 9.1. price taker

LO 9.2. profit

LO 9.2. economic profit

LO 9.2. strategies used to achieve economic profit

LO 9.2. marginal principle

LO 9.2. components associated with marginal benefits in selling

LO 9.2. marginal revenues

LO 9.2. components associate with marginal costs in selling

LO 9.3. shut down decision

LO 9.3. shut down price

LO 9.3. using the marginal principle in the shutdown decision

LO 9.4. short run supply curve

LO 9.4. long run supply curve

LO 9.4. the differences between the short run and long run for businesses in a perfectly competitive market

LO 9.4. increasing-cost industry

LO 9.4. constant-cost industry

OUTCOMES

After completing this chapter, readers will be able to do the following:

- Define "perfectly competitive market."
- Explain the characteristics of a perfectly competitive market.
- Explain how a competitive business and price taker relate to businesses in a perfectly competitive market.
- Define "economic profit."
- Explain the strategies used by businesses in a perfectly competitive market to achieve economic profit.
- Explain the marginal benefits and marginal costs associated with selling in a perfectly competitive market.
- Explain "the profit maximization rule."
- Define "the shutdown decision."
- Explain how businesses in a perfectly competitive market use the marginal principle to determine to either continue operations or close operations.
- Relate the shutdown price in making the decision to continue operations or close operations.
- Explain why a business will continue to operate when it is losing money.
- Illustrate and explain both the short run supply curve and the long run supply curve.
- Explain the differences between the short run and the long run for businesses in a perfectly competitive market.
- Define "increasing-cost industry."
- Define "constant-cost industry."

Key Terms

The following key terms are discussed in this chapter:

- market
- perfectly competitive market
- competitive business
- price taker
- profit
- economic profit
- marginal principle
- marginal benefits (MB)
- marginal revenues
- marginal costs (MC)
- profit maximization rule
- shutdown decision

- shutdown price
- sunk costs
- short run supply curve
- long run supply curve
- increasing cost industry
- constant cost industry

9.1 What Is a Perfectly Competitive Market?

A "market" is defined as a place where buyers and sellers engage in exchanges (buy and sell). From an economics perspective, four types of markets exist. These types are a "perfectly competitive market," a "monopoly," an "oligopoly," and a "monopolistic competitive market." This chapter focuses on the perfectly competitive market.

A **perfectly competitive market** is a market that consists of many sellers, whereby the sellers sell the same standardized product and no one seller is large enough to control price nor product. In other words, a perfectly competitive market consists of many sellers who sell basically the same product. In doing so, each seller is small and, therefore, doesn't have the ability to dominate the market over its competitors. As such, because all sellers are selling the same basic product, they are forced to compete on price. This forces all sellers to sell at the lowest possible price, which means they all charge a similar low price and earn similar revenues per unit sold. Because of this, this type of market is described by three characteristics, which include (a) having many sellers (b) offering standardized products, and (c) facing intense competition. An example of this type of market would be carrot farmers. In this market, all the farmers are competing for the same customers and, therefore, will compete in price with the goal of having the lowest price. In doing so, they will all charge similar low prices.

Each seller within a perfectly competitive market is known as a competitive business. A **competitive business** is a business that doesn't have market power. This means that due to the small size of each seller, they do not control or dominate the market. This fact also leads to each seller being a price taker. A **price taker** refers to having to accept the market price as given. In other words, each seller is forced to compete with all other sellers for the same customers, and this competition is based on charging the lowest price. This, in turn, means each seller will be forced to accept the lowest price set in the market if the seller wishes to sell the product.

market: a place where buyers and sellers engage in exchanges (buy and sell)

perfectly competitive market: a market that consists of many sellers, whereby the sellers sell the same standardized product and no one seller is large enough to control price nor product

competitive business: a business that doesn't have market power

price taker: having to accept the market price as given

9.2 What is Economic Profit?

Sellers in a perfectly competitive market seek to earn profit. **Profit** is defined as revenues minus expenses. However, although competitors within this market may charge the same price and, therefore, earn the same revenues, they do not incur the same expenses. Therefore, some sellers will seek economic profit.

Economic profit is defined as total revenues minus total economic cost. In other words, economic profit refers to subtracting all costs associated with selling the product from the total revenues received. In doing so, the seller is seeking profit over and beyond what should be earned, which means that the seller is maximizing profits.

Sellers in a perfectly competitive market can use three strategies to earn economic profit, thereby maximizing profits. Those three strategies are as follows:

- They can subtract total cost from total revenues for each unit that they sell until they find the level of sales at which the greatest distance lies.
- They can use the marginal principle to produce at a level where their marginal benefits equal their marginal costs.
- They can use the economic profit formula.

The first strategy used to achieve economic profit entails calculating total revenues each unit produced as well as calculating the total costs incurred. Once calculated, the seller simply subtracts the total cost incurred from the total revenues earned for each unit sold until they reach the level where the greatest profits are earned. An example would be a company that sells rakes. Figure 9.1 shows the sellers production table. This table provides the number of rakes sold, the market price for selling, the total revenues earned for each rake, the total cost incurred for each rake, the profit earned for each rake, the marginal revenues received for each rake, and the marginal cost incurred for each rake. On this table, as the seller moves from selling 0 to 9 rakes, total revenues increase by the market price, and total costs incurred increase as well due to the changing business variable costs. In this example, as the business increases sales, the seller sees the greatest distance between total revenues and total costs occurring at 9 rake sales. Therefore, selling nine rakes is where the seller earns the greatest profit. However, if the seller sells a 10th rake, there will be a greater increase in total cost due to a rise in variable cost (hiring more labor and incurring other variable costs) to sell the additional rakes, and therefore, profits decline. So truly, the seller maximizes profit when 9 rakes are sold.

TABLE 9.1 A Production Table
Production Table for a Rake Producing Company

Output	Price	TR	TC	Profit	Marginal revenue	Marginal cost
0	25	0	36	−36	25	0
1	25	25	44	−19	25	8
2	25	50	48	2	25	4
9	**25**	**225**	**126**	**99**	**25**	**25**
10	25	250	166	84	25	40

The second strategy used to achieve economic profit involves using the marginal principle. The **marginal principle** is the belief that a small change in one variable will cause a change in another variable (small $\Delta V \rightarrow$ large ΔV). It is also defined as the belief that one should increase an activity if one's marginal benefits are greater than its marginal costs, decrease an activity if the marginal costs are greater than the marginal benefits, and choose the level of activity where the marginal benefits equal the marginal costs. This strategy employs the latter definition. In using this definition, we must understand both the marginal benefits and marginal costs to selling products. **Marginal benefits** (MB) refer to the additional benefits received from a small increase in an activity. In selling goods and services, these benefits represent the revenues earned. As the number of units sold increases, the benefits received increases by the market price. This creates marginal revenues. **Marginal revenues** are the additional revenues received for each additional unit sold. Therefore, we can say that the marginal benefits are equal to the market price (MP), total revenues received (TR), the profits earned, and marginal revenues (MR).

Marginal costs (MC) are defined as the additional costs incurred from a small increase in an activity. In selling products and services, these costs represent the production cost incurred by the seller. As the number of units sold increases, these costs also increase. This, in turn, creates marginal cost. As such, we can say that the seller's marginal costs are equal to the change in total production cost incurred (TC) divided by the change in total production for each unit sold ($MC = \Delta TC / \Delta Q$).

Once the seller understands the marginal benefits and marginal costs associated with selling, they can use the marginal principle to achieve maximum economic profit. In doing so, this principle implies that one should continue to sell products and services if their marginal benefits are greater than its marginal cost. The seller should discontinue selling when the marginal costs are greater than the marginal benefits. However, the seller should sell the level where marginal benefits equal marginal cost because this is where the seller will earn the greatest profits. Figure 9.1 provides an example of this principle. In this table, as the seller moves from 0 to 9 rakes, they would compare the marginal revenues (marginal benefits) to marginal costs for unit until he/she finds the level where the two equals. As this occurs, the seller would recognize economic profit occurring at 9 rakes because this is where the marginal benefits equal the marginal cost. At this point, the seller is employing the profit maximization rule. The **profit maximization rule** is the belief that products and services will be produced and sold at a level where the marginal benefits equal the marginal costs. Note that as the seller moves from 9 rakes to 10 rakes, the marginal cost becomes greater than the marginal benefits. This occurs because the seller will incur additional production costs due to a rise in variable costs (labor cost and other variable costs) to sell the 10th rake. As such, the seller would not sell the 10th rake because profits would fall.

The third strategy used to achieve economic profit entails applying the economic profit formula. The economic profit formula is as follows:

$$\text{economic profit} = (\text{market price} - \text{average total production cost}) \times \text{the units produced or sold}$$

The seller would apply this formula for each unit sold until it reaches the level of units sold that produced the greatest profits. In the rake example, the seller is selling rakes for $25 each. Assume that the average total production cost for producing and selling 0 to 9 rakes is $14. The seller can determine economic profit by using the previous information for each unit sold. Table 9.2 provides an example of this formula.

TABLE 9.2 The Economic Profit Formula Applied to Rake Sales

Output	Formula	Economic Profit
0	(\$25 – \$14) x 0	\$ 0
1	(\$25 – \$14) x 1	\$11
2	(\$25 – \$14) x 2	\$22
9	(\$25 – \$14) x 9	\$99
10	(\$25 – \$16) x 10	\$90

Assume the average production cost increased to \$16 to sell the 10th unit due to the rise in labor cost and other variable costs. As a result, the seller would see profit decline as illustrated in Table 9.2. Therefore, in using this formula, the seller would determine the maximum economic profit at 9 rakes.

profit: revenues minus expenses

economic profit: total revenues minus total economic cost

marginal principle: 1. the belief that a small change in one variable will cause a change in another variable. 2. the belief that one should increase an activity if one's marginal benefits are greater than its marginal costs, decrease an activity if the marginal costs are greater than the marginal benefits, and choose the level of activity at which the marginal benefits equal the marginal costs.

marginal benefits (mb): the additional benefits received from a small increase in an activity

marginal revenues: the additional revenues received for each unit sold

profit maximization rule: the belief that products and services will be produced and sold at a level where the marginal benefits equal the marginal costs

9.3 The Shutdown Decision

As discussed earlier in the chapter businesses in a perfectly competitive market all earn similar same revenues. However, they do not all have the same expenses incurred in selling products. This means that at the low market price, some businesses will earn profit, while others will lose money. Those businesses that are losing money will be forced to decide to continue operations or close operations. This decision will be based on the marginal principle. In using the marginal principle, the business will continue to sell as long as its marginal benefits are greater than its marginal costs and will discontinue selling when the marginal costs become greater than the marginal benefits. However, one must choose to either continue to operate or close operations when the marginal benefits equal the marginal costs. As such, this decision requires understanding the marginal benefits and marginal costs associated with deciding to continue operations or close operations.

The marginal benefits associated with continuing operations or closing operations are the total revenues received. These revenues derive from the market price multiplied by the number of units sold. By comparison, the marginal cost associated with continuing operations or closing operations is the production costs incurred. A business's production costs consist of both fixed cost and variable cost. From these two types of costs, the business owner is only concerned with variable costs because these are used to pay wages and purchase raw materials. Therefore, when using the marginal principle, the business will relate total revenues to total variable costs in making its decision to either continue or close operations.

To understand this, we continue to use the previous example of a business that sells rakes. In this example, assume the company sells rakes for $10 each. At this price, assume the company sells 10 rakes. The total revenue earned is $100. Now, assume the average variable cost for producing the rake is $8. This means the total variable cost incurred for production is $80. Using this information, the business is seeking to determine whether to continue operations or close operations. In making this determination, the business would continue to operate because its total revenues ($100) are greater than its total variable costs ($80); therefore it can pay labor and purchase raw materials. The business will continue to operate until the market price declines to $8. At this point, the business is faced with the shutdown decision.

The **shutdown decision** is the decision that the business must make regarding continuing operations or closing operations. In other words, when the market price equals average variable cost, the business is faced with the decision to continue to operate or close operations. This price point is known as the shutdown price. The **shutdown price** is the price at which it doesn't matter if the business continues to operate or closes operation. However, once the price falls below average variable cost, the business will be forced to close operations because it can't pay labor nor purchase raw materials. Table 9.3 shows the application of the marginal principle in this decision.

TABLE 9.3 An Example of the Shutdown Decision

Total revenue (market price × units sold)	Total average variable cost	Decision
$100	$80	continue operations
$80	$80	reached the shutdown decision
$60	$80	close operations

shutdown decision: the decision that the business must make regarding continuing operations or closing operations

shutdown price: the price at which it doesn't matter if the business continues to operate or closes operation

sunk costs: costs that have occurred or will occur regardless of production level

When a business applies the marginal principle in its decision to continue to operate or close operations, this decision only considers the variable costs incurred. This means that if the business continues to operate, it will be doing so at a loss, as it is not covering all its production costs. The question becomes, "Why would a business continue to operate when it is losing money?" The business would make this decision because it has sunk costs. **Sunk costs** are costs that have occurred or will occur regardless of production level. In other words, the business has costs that it must pay regardless of whether it continues to operate or closes operations. Such costs include a mortgage or loans. In such cases, the seller will be required to make payments on these expenses even if the business closes operations. Therefore, the seller will choose to continue to operate even if they are losing money to make at least partial payments on these expenses. In doing so, the seller will continue to do this until its total variable cost becomes greater than its total revenues. At this point, the business must close because it isn't earning enough money to pay labor nor purchase raw materials.

9.4 The Short Run and Long Run for Businesses in a Perfectly Competitive Market

Businesses in a perfectly competitive market produce products and services in both the short run and the long run. In the short run, the number of products and services that they offer for sale will be constrained due to their inability to change their factors of production. Therefore, as demand increases, their production decisions in response will be subjected to the principle of diminishing returns. This means the number of units supplied during this period in response to an increase in demand will, in turn, increase at a decreasing rate. However, in this process, the business must also consider its production cost. In doing so, it must ensure it is selling its products and services at a price that at least covers its cost of production to avoid losing money. Therefore, it will supply products and services at or above its production cost. This can be illustrated on a short run supply curve. A **short run supply curve** refers to a curve that shows the relationship between price and the number of a particular product that producers are willing to sell in the short run. Figure 9.1 provides an example of a short run supply curve. As shown, this curve begins at production cost and it slopes upward to indicate in increase in supply as price rises.

In the long run, the number of products and services offered for sale changes without constraint to changes in demand due to the business having the ability to change its factors of production. Therefore, as demand increases, the business's production decisions will change in response by either modification or replication of its facilities as it hires additional labor. This means the number of units supplied during this period will increase in response to an increase in demand without hindrance from the principle of diminishing returns. But, like the short run, the business must also consider its production cost during this period. In doing so, it must ensure it is selling its products and service at a price that at least covers

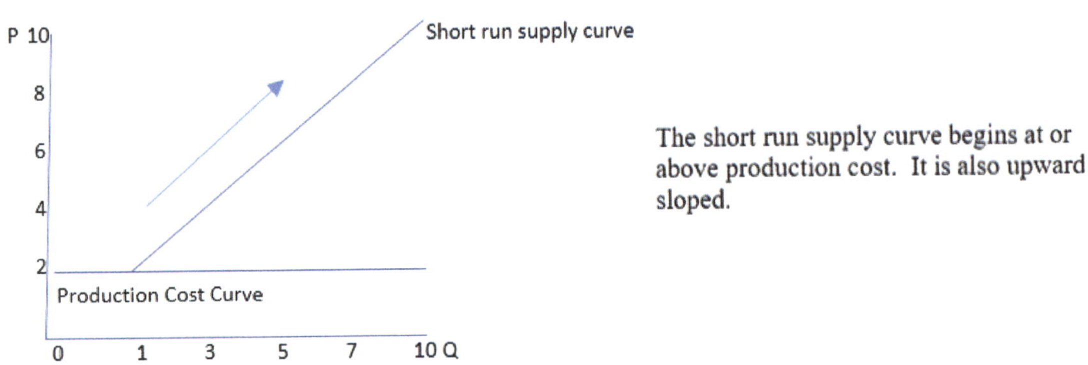

FIGURE 9.1 A Short Run Supply Curve

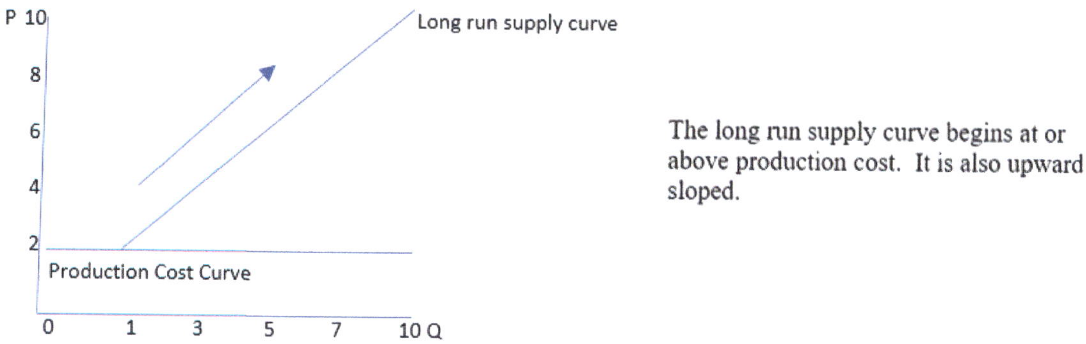

FIGURE 9.2 A Long Run Supply Curve

its cost of production to avoid losing money. Therefore, it will supply products and services at or above its production cost. This can be illustrated on a long run supply curve. A **long run supply curve** refers to a curve that shows the relationship between price and the number of a particular product producers are willing to sell in the long run. Figure 9.2 provides an example of a long run supply curve. Similar to the short run supply curve, this curve begins at production cost, and it slopes upward to indicate in increase in supply as price rises.

There are some differences between the short run and the long run for businesses in a perfectly competitive market. One difference is diminishing returns. Diminishing returns occur in the short run. During this period, businesses do not have the ability to change their resources (raw materials, facilities, equipment, etc.), and therefore, production increases become smaller with each level of output as additional workers are hired. However, diminishing returns do not occur in the long run because businesses are able to change their resources as they hire additional workers. As a result, the additional space created allows each worker to be productive.

Economic profit is the second difference that exists between the short run and the long run for businesses in a perfectly competitive market. Businesses in a perfectly competitive market earn economic profit in the short run and zero economic profit in the long run. In other words, a business's profits are low in the short run as demand is low. However, over time, demand begins to rise, thereby, causing profits to rise. At this point, the business is earning economic profit. This profit moves the business into the long run, as it allows the business to begin expanding its resources and facilities. However, the profits earned also motivate competition to enter into the market. As competition increases, competitors compete on price, which leads to declining prices and less profit earned. As this continues, some businesses will lose money and will be forced to leave the market. As prices continue to fall due to the competition and businesses begin to leave the market, the only remaining companies will be earning zero economic profit. In other words, they are making just enough profit to survive.

The transition from the short run to the long for businesses in a perfectly competitive market creates increasing-cost industries. An **increasing-cost industry** is one in which average production cost increases as overall production increases. In other words, as a business transitions from the short run to the long run due to a rise in both demand and profits, there will initially be a greater need for additional labor, which will lead to higher variable costs. Then, as competition increases, each business will sell fewer units. The short run supply curve: a curve that shows the relationship between price and the number of a particular product that producers are willing to sell in the short run

long run supply curve: a curve that shows the relationship between price and the number of a particular product that producers are willing to sell in the long run

increasing cost industry: An industry in which average production cost increases as overall production increases

constant cost industry: an industry in which average production costs remains fixed as overall production increases

decline in the number of units sold due to an increase in competition will cause a rise in production cost because of the inability to spread the overall cost across a greater number of units. As a result, these factors will lead to a rise in average production cost. An example of this type of industry includes the agricultural industry. In this industry, an increase in demand will lead to a greater need for labor, which causes an increase in labor prices and, therefore, an increase in average production cost. In addition, as competition increases, each farmer's demand will decrease, which also leads to a rise in average production cost.

A constant-cost industry will arise if the prices of the factors of production are not affected as businesses enter and leave the market. A **constant-cost industry** is one in which average production costs remains fixed as overall production increases. An example of this includes the taxi industry where the cost for a license or a gallon of gas remains constant as demand changes.

SUMMARY

- A market is defined a place where buyers and sellers engage in exchanges. (LO 9.1)
- A perfectly competitive market consists of a market that consists of many sellers whereby the sellers sell the same standardized product and no one seller is large enough to control price nor product. (LO 9.1)
- Businesses in a perfectly competitive market are also known as "competitive businesses" and "price takers." (LO 9.1)
- Profit is defined as revenues minus expenses. (LO 9.2)
- Some businesses in a perfectly competitive market seek economic profit. (LO 9.2)
- Economic profit is achieved through subtracting total cost from total revenues for each unit they sell until they find the level of sales where the greatest distance lies, using the marginal principle or through using the economic profit formula. (LO 9.2)
- The marginal benefits associated with selling products is the revenue earned, while the marginal costs are the production costs incurred. (LO 9.2)
- Businesses in a perfectly competitive market employ the profit maximization rule when they earn economic profit. (LO 9.2)
- Some businesses in a perfectly competitive market must engage in the shutdown decision when they are losing money. (LO 9.3)

- Businesses use the marginal principle when determining whether to continue operations or close operations. (LO 9.3)
- The shutdown price represents the price point at which the business must decide to continue to operate or close operations. (LO 9.3)
- Businesses in a perfectly competitive market continue to operate when they are losing money because of sunk costs. (LO 9.3)
- Businesses in a perfectly competitive market operate in both the short run and the long run. (LO 9.4)
- Diminishing returns occur in the short run in a perfectly competitive market. (LO 9.4)
- Economic profit is earned in the short run in a perfectly competitive market. (LO 9.4)
- The short run supply curve and the long run supply curve begin at or above production cost for businesses in a perfectly competitive market. (LO 9.4)
- An increasing-cost industry refers to an industry in which average production costs increase as overall production increases. (LO 9.4)
- A constant-cost industry is an industry in which average production costs remains fixed as overall production increases. (LO 9.4)

END-OF-CHAPTER APPLICATION

Comprehension Questions

Directions: Refer to the chapter to correctly respond to the following questions and prompts.

1. Explain how businesses choose to compete in a perfectly competitive market. (LO 9.1)
2. Why are businesses in a perfectly competitive market known as competitive businesses and price takers? (LO 9.1)
3. Define economic profit. Why do some businesses in a perfectly competitive market seek economic profit? (LO 9.2)
4. Explain the strategies businesses in a perfectly competitive market use to achieve economic profit. (LO 9.2)
5. How would a business owner use the marginal principle in their decision to continue selling and discontinue selling? How would they use the marginal principle to determine the appropriate number of sales to make? (LO 9.2)
6. Tom owns a bottling manufacturing business. He sells the bottles for $2 each. His average production cost is $0.50. He sells 100 bottles. Calculate his economic profit. Show your math. (LO 9.2)

7. How would a business owner use the marginal principle in deciding whether to continue operations or close operations? Explain why the owner would continue operations even when the business is losing money. How long could the owner operate in this manner? (LO 9.3)
8. Explain the transition from the short run to the long run for businesses in a perfectly competitive market. Identify when the businesses will earn economic profit and zero economic profit in this process. (LO 9.4)

Case Scenario: An Analysis of a Business in a Perfectly Competitive Market

Directions: Use what you learned in the chapter to respond to the following scenario.

Whole Farms produces tomatoes. The farm competes in a market in which it is easy for farmers to enter and leave the market. As such, demand and supply forces determine the price of tomatoes. Analyzing this business, answer the following questions:

1. How would Whole Farms choose to compete in this market? How would competition affect this decision?
2. Using the marginal principle, how many tomatoes should Whole Farms produce over a period of a season? How would the concepts of marginal benefits and marginal costs affect this decision? At what point would Whole Farms earn economic profit?
3. Explain what happens to profits as Whole Farms transitions from the short run to the long run. What happens with competition during this transition?
4. As competition increases and price decreases, how would Whole Farms decide to continue or close operations? What determining factors go into this decision? Explain how they would decide to continue operations and how they would decide to close operations.
5. Does Whole Farms operate in an increasing-cost industry or constant-cost industry? Explain your rationale.

BIBLIOGRAPHY

O'Sullivan, A., Shreffin, S., & Perez, S. (2017). *Microeconomics: Principles, applications, and tools* (9th ed.). Pearson Publishing.

Schiller, B. R. (2016). *The micro economy today* (14th ed.). McGraw-Hill Education.

CREDIT

IMG 9.1: Maurits90, https://commons.wikimedia.org/wiki/File:Concurrentei_Mc_Donalds_Burger_King_Subway_FEBo.jpg, 2011.

CHAPTER 10

Types of Markets

Monopolies

Concept Highlight

Chapter 10 examines the concepts of a monopoly.

Real Life Example: What Does This Mean to You?

Monopolies exist in the marketplace, although the government seeks to prevent such businesses from operating by enacting regulation. Within their operational strategy, monopolies reduce competition and keep prices high. Such strategies entice economists to understand how they behave and their effect on the economy as a whole.

Introduction

Monopolies are an important concept to understand, as they represent one of the four types of markets. As such, monopolies behave differently than other types of markets. Therefore, their behavior affects consumer choice as well as the prices paid for products and services.

OBJECTIVES

While reading this chapter, readers learn about

LO 10.1. monopoly

LO 10.1. market power

LO 10.1. antitrust laws

LO 10.1. barrier-to-entry

LO 10.1. patent

LO 10.2. strategies used by a monopoly to earn economic profits (maximize profits)

LO 10.3. societal costs caused by monopolies

LO 10.3. deadweight loss

LO 10.3. regulation

LO 10.3. rent seeking

LO 10.4. natural monopoly

LO 10.4. average-cost pricing policy

LO 10.5. difference between the short run and long run for a monopoly

OUTCOMES

After completing this chapter, readers will be able to do the following:

- Define "monopoly"
- Explain how a patent creates a barrier to entry in a monopolistic market
- Explain the three strategies used by a monopolist to earn economic profit (maximize profit)
- Identify and explain the three societal costs caused by a monopoly
- Define "natural monopoly"
- Explain and illustrate what happens with a competitor entering into a natural monopoly
- Explain how the government regulates natural monopolies
- Explain the difference between the short run and long run for a monopoly

Key Terms

The following key terms are discussed in this chapter:

- monopoly
- market power
- antitrust laws
- barrier to entry
- patent
- deadweight loss
- regulation
- rent seeking
- natural monopoly
- average-cost pricing policy

10.1 What Is a Monopoly?

A **monopoly** is defined as a market that is served by one business. An example of one is U.S. Steel. In such an example, it doesn't mean that there are no other businesses in the market that is providing the service of producing steel, but rather, U.S. Steel dominates the market. In doing so, the dominant business determines how much of the product or service is produced and its selling price. Because of this, the dominant business, such as U.S. Steel, has market power. **Market power** refers to having the ability to control both product and price.

monopoly: a market that is served by one business

market power: having the ability to control both product and price

antitrust laws: laws that seek to prevent the creation of a trust or monopoly

barrier to entry: something that keeps out competition

patent: a document that grants one the exclusive right to produce and sell a good for a period of time, normally 20 years

In the United States, antitrust laws prohibit the formation of monopolies. **Antitrust laws** are laws that seek to prevent the creation of a trust or monopoly. In truth, however, such markets exist because of barriers to entry. A **barrier to entry** refers to something that keeps out competition. In other words, monopolies exist because something exists in the market that prevents competition. An example of such barriers includes patents. A **patent** is a document that grants one the exclusive right to produce and sell a good for a period of time, normally 20 years. Therefore, a patent creates a barrier to the market by granting one business the sole right to produce and sell a product, which, in turn, creates a monopoly.

10.2 Strategies Used by a Monopolist to Earn Economic Profit

One who owns a monopoly is called a "monopolist." Having ownership of the dominant business in the market, the monopolist must determine how much product to produced and its selling price. In doing so, the monopolist is seeking economic profit. In seeking such profit, the monopolists can use any of the following strategies:

- Subtract total cost from total revenues for each unit they sell until they find the level of sales at which the greatest distance lies.
- Use the marginal principle to produce at a level at which their marginal benefits equal their marginal costs.
- Use the economic profit formula.

In using these strategies, the monopolist's goal is to charge the highest possible price. However, the monopolist is faced with the challenge of the law of demand in doing so. This means that demand will fall as price rises. But, on the other hand, if the monopolist lowers price. Although demand will rise, marginal revenues will fall, and if they fall too low, they will turn negative, which means the monopolists will lose money. This, in turn, defeats the purpose of being a monopoly. An example of this reality is provided in Table 10.1.

TABLE 10.1 A Price–Total Revenues Table

Price	Quantity sold	Total revenues	Marginal revenues
16	0	0	–
14	1	14	14
12	2	24	10
10	3	30	6
8	4	32	2
6	5	30	−2
4	6	24	−6

In Table 10.1, marginal revenues decline until they reach negative as price falls, demonstrating the trade-offs associated with lowering price. So the monopolist is challenged with making a choice between charging high prices and losing customers or lowering prices and experiencing a decline in marginal revenues. In making this choice, the monopolist will choose to charge the high price and sell to fewer customers. However, the monopolist understands that it can't charge the highest price because this will lead to seeing its demand fall to an unsatisfactory level. Therefore, the monopolist will find the highest possible price that will attract the most possible customers. In doing so, the monopolist will also choose to reduce production to a level where the marginal benefits equal the marginal costs to maximize profits. Figure 10.1 provides a graphic of this decision. In this illustration, as the monopolist increases price (designated by 1), there is upward movement along the demand curve, as consumers buy less (designated by 2). In response, the supply shifts to the left as the monopolists reduces output (designated by 3). This, in turn, creates a new equilibrium, as the monopolist produces at a level where the marginal benefits equal the marginal costs.

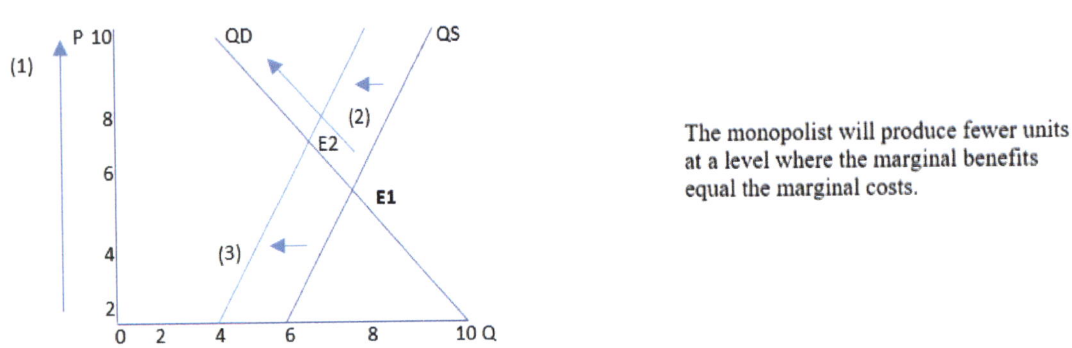

FIGURE 10.1 A Monopolist's Output Decision

10.3 Societal Costs Caused by Monopolies

deadweight loss: a situation in which a monopoly creates inefficiency in the market

regulation: laws

rent seeking: a situation in which the monopoly uses its power to influence government officials to allow it to remain a monopoly

Monopolies are not favored by governments because of the harm that they cause to society. Such harm includes (a) fewer production and higher prices, (b) less consumer choice, and (c) greater governmental influence by the monopoly. As the monopolist gains greater control over the market due to barriers to entry, it has more say in the production output and price. As mentioned earlier, this will encourage the monopolist to decide to sell product at the highest possible price while also limiting supply to ensure prices remain high. In response, consumers will buy fewer units but will also have less choice, as competition in the market has been reduce. This, in turn, creates deadweight loss. **Deadweight loss** is a situation in which a monopoly creates inefficiency in the market. In other words, demand falls as the monopolist raise prices and reduces competition. This moves the economy away from equilibrium, which makes it inefficient.

Rising prices and less competition creates major issues in the market, as it moves the economy away from equilibrium. In response, regulation is used to move the economy closer to equilibrium by influencing price, production, and investment decisions. **Regulation** refers to laws—specifically, antitrust laws, in our case. As stated earlier in the chapter, antitrust laws seek to prevent the creation of a trust or monopoly. In prohibiting the formation of trusts, the goal of antitrust laws is to increase competition, which lowers prices. Therefore, the government uses antitrust laws as a tool to discourage monopolies by encouraging competition in the marketplace. In response to such laws, the monopolist will use rent seeking to influence government officials, ensuring the business maintains its market power. **Rent seeking** refers to a situation in which the monopoly uses its power to influence government officials to allow it to remain a monopoly. This process entails the monopolists using its money and other resources to persuade government officials to support its business operations.

10.4 What Is a Natural Monopoly?

Monopolies occur because of barriers to entry. In other words, monopolies form when something, such as laws, market power, patents, and so on, prevents competition from entering into the market. During such times, the government will use regulation to encourage competitive market entry. However, there are times when a market is free to allow competition to enter but they do not enter. Such times create a natural monopoly. A **natural monopoly** is a market in which the presence of a competitor causes prices to fall below average production, and therefore, the competitor chooses not to enter. This is a market in which one business provides products and services at a high average production cost. In doing so, its customer base is just high enough to cover its cost. This means the business is producing enough product at its price point to meet demand and cover its average production cost. Therefore, if a competitor enters the market, they will compete on price, which means each business will lower price in an attempt to attract customers. This lowering of price will split the customer base, and neither business will sell to enough customers to cover the high cost of production.

Understanding this, a competitor will choose not to enter the market because it will lose money. As a result, although competition is free to enter, they choose not to enter, and the business that serves the market becomes the natural monopolist. An example of such a market includes the U.S. electricity industry. In this industry, the cost of producing electricity is very high and the price charged is just high enough to cover the average production cost. Therefore, competition in this market would create a situation in which neither company could survive. As such, Figure 10.2 demonstrates the effect of a competitor entering the market of a natural monopoly on a demand curve. In this illustration, the amount of product supplied by the natural monopolist at its price point (P1) equals the level of demand (D1) for its products and its average production cost (APC). As competition enters into the market and they begin to compete on price, the customer base will split between them, and both price and demand will fall below average production cost, as illustrated by the shift of the demand curve from D1 to D2. As a result, neither business will have enough customers at the new price line (P2) to cover their average production costs, and therefore, the competition will choose not to enter the market.

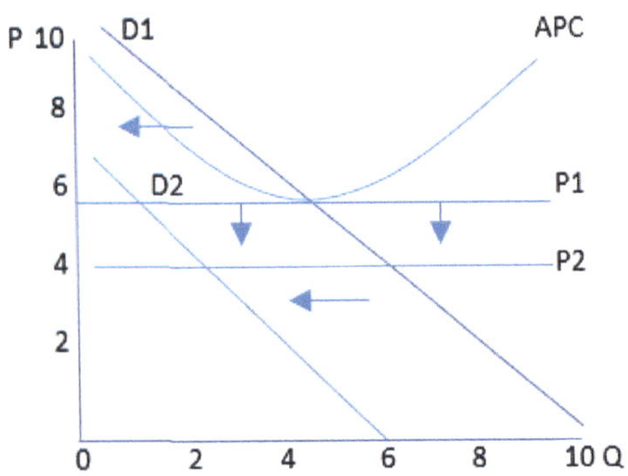

As competition enters into a natural monopoly, demand and price will fall below average production cost.

FIGURE 10.2 The Effect of Competition Entering into a Natural Monopoly

High average production cost is one fact that prevents competition from entering into a natural monopoly. This fact provides a natural monopolist with the opportunity to raise prices to capitalize on nonexistent competition. To prevent the natural monopolist from taking advantage of being the only supplier in the market, the government often implements an average-cost pricing policy. **An average-cost pricing policy** refers to government regulation that sets the market price to the business's average production cost. As such, the government will examine the natural monopolist's average cost to produce and regulate its pricing to match this cost. This ensures the market moves toward equilibrium by preventing prices from rising too high.

natural monopoly: a market in which the presence of a competitor causes prices to fall below average production, and therefore, the competitor chooses not to enter

average-cost pricing policy: government regulation that sets the market price to the business's average production cost

10.5 The Difference Between the Short Run and the Long Run for a Monopoly

A monopoly behaves differently in the marketplace than businesses in a perfectly competitive market. In chapter 9, we learned that businesses in a perfectly competitive market earn economic profit in the short run and zero economic profit in the long run. However, a monopolist may earn zero economic profit in the short run and economic profit in the long run. For a monopoly, in the short run, profits and demand are low, as there is no competition. However, over time, demand begins to rise, thereby causing profits to rise. At this point, the business is earning economic profit. This profit moves the business into the long run, as it allows it to begin expanding its resources and facilities. But unlike businesses in a perfectly competitive market, the monopolist doesn't have competition, and therefore, its profits continue to rise. Table 10.2 shows a comparison of businesses in a perfectly competitive to a monopoly.

TABLE 10.2 Behavior of Businesses in a Perfectly Competitive Market and a Monopoly

Behavior	Perfectly competitive market	Monopoly
competition	many competitors	no competitor
pricing strategy	lowest possible price	highest possible price
short run	economic profit	zero economic profit
long run	zero economic profit	economic profit

SUMMARY

- A monopoly is a market that is served by one business. (LO 10.1)
- Monopolies have market power. (LO 10.1)
- Antitrust laws are used to prevent the formation of monopolies. (LO 10.1)
- Barriers to entry keep competition from entering the market of a monopoly. (LO 10.1)
- Monopolies seek economic profit either by subtracting total cost from total revenues for each unit they sell until they find the level of sells where the greatest distance lies, using the marginal principle, or using the economic profit formula. (LO 10.2)
- Monopolies produce fewer units, charge a higher price, produce less choice, and use rent seeking to maintain their status. (LO 10.3)
- Monopolies create deadweight loss. (LO 10.3)
- A natural monopoly is a market in which the presence of a competitor would cause prices to fall below average production, and therefore, the competitor chooses not to enter. (LO 10.4)

- The government regulates natural monopolies by implementing an average-cost pricing policy. (LO 10.4)
- Monopolies earn zero economic profit in the short run and economic profit in the long run. (LO 10.5)

END-OF-CHAPTER APPLICATION

Comprehension Questions

Directions: Refer to the chapter to correctly respond to the following questions and prompts.

1. How does a monopoly have market power? Explain. (LO 10.1)
2. How does a patent create a barrier to entry for businesses that seek to compete against a monopoly? (LO 10.1)
3. Explain the strategies a monopolist will use to achieve economic profit. (LO 10.2)
4. Explain and illustrate the production and pricing decision a monopolist will make in seeking to achieve economic profit. (LO 10.2)
5. Identify the three societal costs caused by a monopoly. How does this create deadweight loss? Explain. (LO 10.3)
6. Explain and illustrate the effects of competition entering the market of a natural monopoly. (LO 10.4)
7. How would the average-cost pricing strategy move the economy closer to equilibrium in a natural monopoly? (LO 10.4)
8. What is the difference between the short-run and long-run for a monopoly? Explain. (LO 10.5)

Case Scenario: Analyzing the Business Practices of Microsoft

Directions: Use what you learned in the chapter to respond to the following scenario.

Microsoft is the largest computer software manufacturer in the world. Within this industry, the company is diversified and possesses the highest valuations in the world. As a computer software manufacturer, Microsoft produces operating systems for personal computers and servers. Among its product offerings is Windows, which consists of Word, Excel, PowerPoint, Outlook, and Access.

Through the 1990s, Microsoft was investigated by the Federal Trade Commission and the Department of Justice for violating several antitrust laws. During this period, Congressional hearings were held to question the company's business practices. In addition, lawsuits were filed against the company alleging that it engaged in anticompetitive behavior. Answer the following questions:

1. Would you identify Microsoft as a monopoly? Explain the rationale for your answer.
2. How could Microsoft use patents to keep competitors out of the market?
3. What strategies could Microsoft use to achieve economic profits? What decisions would the company make in production and pricing?
4. How does Microsoft's business practices affect consumers?

REFERENCES

Economides, N. (2003). *The Microsoft antitrust case: A case study for MBA students.* New York University. https://neconomides.stern.nyu.edu/networks/homeworks/Microsoft_Case.pdf

O'Sullivan, A., Shreffin, S., & Perez, S. (2017). *Microeconomics: Principles, applications, and tools* (9th ed.). Pearson Publishing.

Schiller, B. R. (2016). *The micro economy today* (14th ed.). McGraw-Hill Education.

CREDIT

IMG 10.1: Parker Brothers, https://commons.wikimedia.org/wiki/File:Monopoly-Logo.svg, 2015.

CHAPTER 11

Types of Markets

Oligopolies

Concept Highlight

Chapter 11 examines the market behavior of oligopolies.

Real Life Example: What Does This Mean to You?

Oligopolies exists in the marketplace; an example of such a market is the wireless telecommunications carrier industry. Although this industry consists of many competitors, it is dominated by only a few businesses. As such, the dominant businesses must decide how they will behave towards customers as well as among the competition. Therefore, economists seek to understand the dynamics of market behavior among the dominant market competitors.

Introduction

Oligopolies are an important concept to understand, as they represent one of the four types of markets. As one of the four types of markets, businesses in an oligopoly are challenged with low barriers to entry as well as consumers who view them as substitutes. This means the dominant businesses in an oligopoly behave like a monopoly. As such, their behavior affects how they respond to customers as well as other competitors in the market.

OBJECTIVES

While reading this chapter, readers learn about

LO 11.1. oligopoly

LO 11.1. concentration ratios

LO 11.2. strategies used by businesses in an oligopoly in acting strategically

LO 11.2. cartel

LO 11.3. duopoly

LO 11.3. strategies used by a duopoly to earn economic profits (maximize profits)

LO 11.3. the choice made by businesses in a duopoly regarding responding to customers who treat them as substitutes

LO 11.4. the game tree

LO 11.4. the components of the game tree

LO 11.4. dominant strategy

LO 11.4. duopolist's dilemma

LO 11.5. strategies used to avoid the duopolist's dilemma

LO 11.5. kinked demand curve

LO 11.6. retaliation strategies against businesses who don't price fix

LO 11.7. insecure monopoly

LO 11.7. contestable market

LO 11.7. strategies used by businesses in an oligopoly to protect their monopoly status

OUTCOMES

After completing this chapter, readers will be able to do the following:

- Define "oligopoly."
- Define "concentration ratios."
- Explain the strategies used by businesses in an oligopoly to respond to customers who treat them as substitutes.
- Define "duopoly."
- Explain the three strategies used by businesses in a duopoly to earn economic profit (maximize profit).
- Explain the decision businesses in a duopoly must make regarding how they will compete.
- Define "game tree."
- Explain the duopolist's dilemma in making a choice about how businesses in an oligopoly will compete against each other.
- Explain the strategies businesses in an oligopoly use to avoid the duopolist's dilemma.
- Explain and illustrate the kinked demand curve.
- Explain the retaliation strategies used by businesses in an oligopoly against businesses who don't price fix.
- Define "insecure monopoly."
- Define "contestable market."
- Explain the strategies used by businesses in an oligopoly to protect their monopoly status.

Key Terms

The following key terms are discussed in this chapter:

- oligopoly
- concentration ratio
- pricing fixing
- cartel
- entry dterrence
- duopoly
- game tree
- dominant strategy
- duopolist's dilemma
- price leadership
- kinked demand curve
- duopoly pricing
- tit-for-tat pricing
- grim trigger pricing
- insecure monopoly
- contestable market
- limit pricing

11.1 What Is an Oligopoly?

An **oligopoly** is a market that consists of a few dominant businesses. In this market, although there may be many competitors, the dominant businesses control both the product and the pricing. An example of such a market is the commercial aircraft manufacturing industry, which consists of Airbus, Boeing, Embraer, and Bombardier. In such markets, the number of products and services produced are expressed based on concentration ratios. A **concentration ratio** refers to a measure of the number of products and services produced and sold by each business in the market. This measure, in turn, describes each business's degree of concentration within the market.

oligopoly: a market that consists of a few dominant businesses

concentration ratios: a measure of the number of products and services produced and sold by each business in the market

11.2 Acting Strategically

An oligopoly consists of a market that has few barriers to entry. As such, competition is allowed to enter and leave the market. As competition enters, they will produce similar products and services. In doing so, customers will perceive the businesses as substitutes and, therefore, will constantly move from one to the other. Therefore, success for businesses in this market is based on acting strategically in determining a way to prevent customers from moving from one competitor to the next. Acting strategically requires businesses in the market to decide to either price fix or engage in entry deterrence. **Pricing fixing** is a strategy whereby competitors conspire to charge the same price. In charging the same price, they behave like a cartel. A **cartel** refers to a situation in which competitors coordinate their pricing. The goal of behaving like a cartel is to charge the highest possible price. As such, this behavior is illegal in the United States because it violates antitrust laws.

pricing fixing: a strategy whereby the competitors conspire to charge the same price

cartel: a situation in which competitors coordinate their pricing

entry deterrence: a situation in which existing businesses within an oligopoly attempt to prevent new competitors from entering into the market

Entry deterrence refers to a situation in which existing businesses within an oligopoly attempt to prevent new competitors from entering into the market. In such an instance, the existing competitors will allow customers to move from one to the next, but they will work to ensure that new competitors remain out of the market. Like price fixing, this behavior is also illegal in the United States because it limits competition.

11.3 What Is a Duopoly?

A major strategic decision facing businesses in an oligopoly is whether to either price fix or engage in entry deterrence. A simple examination of this decision-making process involves discussing a duopoly. A **duopoly** is a market that consists of two dominant competitors. An example of this is the soft drink industry, which consists of Coke and Pepsi. In such a market, each business seeks economic profit. In seeking economic profit, the competitors are like businesses in other markets in that they will use any of the following strategies:

- Subtract total cost from total revenues for each unit they sell until they find the level of sales at which the greatest distance lies.
- Use the marginal principle to produce at a level at which their marginal benefits equal their marginal costs.
- Use the economic profit formula.

However, in choosing one of these strategies, each business in the duopoly is faced with consumers who perceive them as substitutes and, therefore, will constantly move from one to the other. So the success of each business in earning economic profit is based on finding a solution to this problem. The solution is typically to either engage in price fixing or use entry deterrence. If the businesses decide to engage in price fixing, they will agree to coordinate their pricing to charge the same price. In doing so, they will choose to charge a high price, which means they will earn high profits. However, if the businesses choose to use entry deterrence, they will prevent competition from entering into the market and compete against each other. In competing against each other, they will compete on price. In competing on price, they will drive down price, which will lead to low profits. Understanding this, the businesses often choose to price fix to earn high profits. By choosing to price fix, the businesses, in turn, behaves like a cartel. Table 11.1 provides a chart of the choices in this decision-making process.

Duopoly: A market that consists of two dominant competitors

TABLE 11.1 Choices in the Strategic Decision-Making Process for Businesses in an Oligopoly

Strategies	Competitive options	Outcomes
price fix	coordinate pricing and charge the same high price	earn high profits
entry deterrence	keep out competition and compete against each other	earn low profits

11.4 The Game Tree

The game tree ensures businesses in an oligopoly will choose to price fix. The **game tree** is a graphic that shows the consequences of actions taken in the decision-making process. It consists of squares, arrows, and rectangles, with squares representing strategies, arrows pointing to a direction, and rectangles showing outcomes of the decisions taken based on the strategies provided in the squares. Figure 11.1 provides an example of a simple game tree.

In this simplified example, the business has three strategy options, which include charging a high price, charging the average price, or charging the low price. In making this decision, the business seeks the dominant strategy. The **dominant strategy** refers to the strategy that produces the best outcome. Therefore, based on the dominant strategy, the appropriate decision would be to select the strategy involving charging

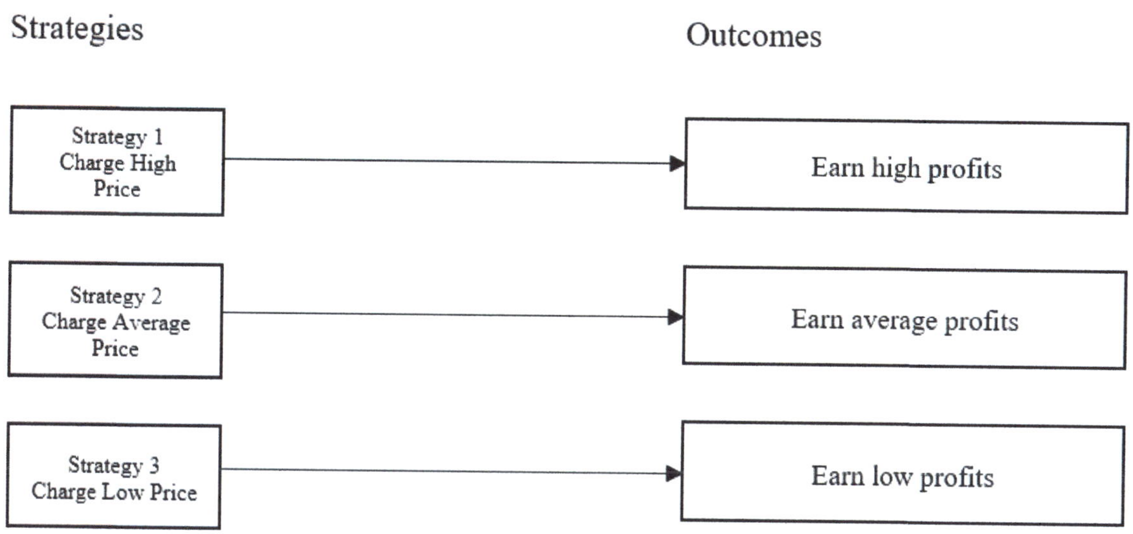

FIGURE 11.1 A Simple Game Tree

the high price because it will produce high profits. However, the business is faced with the problem of having its price undercut by its competitor. So although the business should choose the strategy that produces high profits, it may choose the strategy that produces the low profits. This is known as the duopolist's dilemma. The **duopolist's dilemma** is a situation in which a business would be better off choosing a strategy that produces high profits but, eventually, chooses the strategy that produces low profits. Understanding this, the game tree depicts the consequences of choosing a low strategy due to the fear of being undercut by the competition.

game tree: a graphic that shows the consequences to actions taken in the decision-making process

dominant strategy: the strategy that produces the best outcome

duopolist's dilemma: a situation in which a business would be better off by choosing a strategy that produces high profits but, eventually, chooses the strategy that produces low profits

11.5 Strategies Used to Avoid the Duopolist's Dilemma

The duopolist's dilemma leads businesses in an oligopoly to choose the least desired outcome, which, in turn, generates low profits. This choice selection is demonstrated through the game tree. To avoid this dilemma, businesses can use price matching and price leadership. Price matching refers to businesses in an oligopoly guaranteeing to match the price of the competition. In doing so, this forces the competition to choose between charging a low price or charging a high price. As such, if a business chooses to charge a low price, the competition will also charge the same low price; therefore, all businesses in the market will earn low profit. However, if the business chooses to charge a high price, the competition will charge the same high price, which ensures all businesses earn high profit. Therefore, the market avoids the duopolist's dilemma by choosing to charge the same high price.

price leadership: a situation in which the market chooses a competitor as a price leader and the other competitors follow the pricing set by the price leading competitor

kinked demand curve: a curve that illustrates the competition following the price decrease but not following the price increase

Price leadership is defined as a situation in which the market chooses a competitor as a price leader and the other competitors follow the pricing set by the price leading competitor. An example of this occurs in the commercial airline industry. In this industry, one airline company will announce a change in its pricing, and the competition makes similar announcements soon afterwards. Therefore, if the price leader announces it is lowering its price, the competition follows by announcing that they are doing the same. However, if the price leader announces it will raise price and the competition decides not to follow, this creates a kinked demand curve for the price leader. A **kinked demand curve** is a curve that illustrates the competition following the price decrease but not following the price increase. Figure 11.2 shows this curve. In this illustration, the curve is relatively flat (slightly downward sloped) at the top to demonstrate demand remaining consistent to the business charging a low price and the competition doing the same. However, as the business raises price and the competition doesn't follow, its demand curve steeps downward as demand falls (upward sloped). In response to losing customers, the price-leading business lowers its price to fall back in line with the competition.

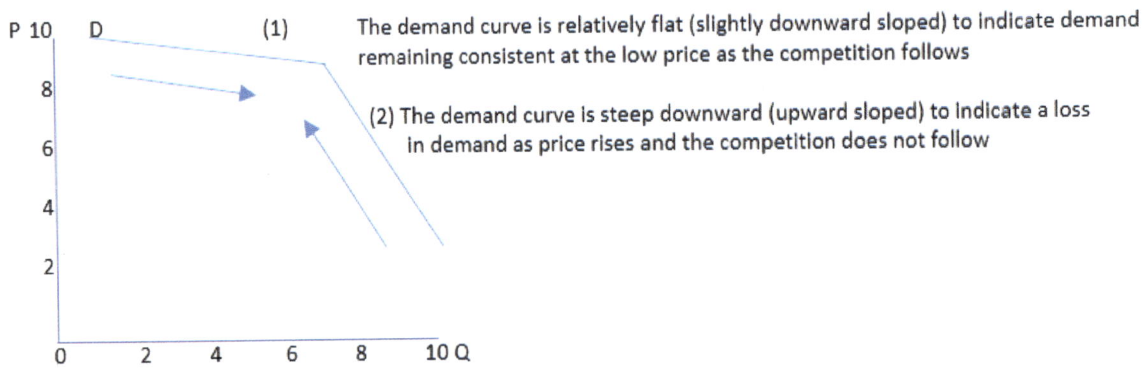

FIGURE 11.2 A Kinked Demand Curve

11.6 Retaliating Against Businesses That Don't Price Fix

Businesses in an oligopoly will choose to price fix to charge high prices and earn high profits. In doing so, they behave like a cartel. In turn, this pricing decision represents an illegal act in the United States. As such, to ensure all competitors in the market engage in this act, businesses will often use a number of punishing strategies. These strategies include employing (a) duopoly pricing, (b) tit-for-tat pricing, and (c) grim trigger pricing.

Duopoly pricing refers to a situation in which the competition charges low prices, thereby ensuring low profits. In doing so, they undercut the pricing of those businesses who decide not to engage in the price fixing behavior, which cause those businesses to sell fewer units and earn lower profit.

Tit-for-tat pricing is a situation in which businesses in the market choose to follow the pricing strategy of the competition. In doing so, they simply price match the competition. This ensures each competitor's market share remains the same, and therefore, no one business will benefit from not following the price fixing behavior.

duopoly pricing: a situation in which the competition charges low prices, thereby ensuring low profits

tit-for-tat pricing: a situation in which businesses in the market choose to follow the pricing strategy of the competition

grim trigger pricing: a situation in which a business lowers its price so much that it drives out the competition from the market

Grim trigger pricing occurs when a business lowers its price so low that it drives out the competition from the market. Under this strategy, when a business lowers its price to a level that is below the competition's production cost, the competition leaves the market because they are losing money. Therefore, those businesses that decide not to engage in the price fixing behavior are forced to leave the market because they cannot survive at the low price point.

11.7 Oligopoly Behavioral Qualities

When businesses in an oligopoly choose to price fix, they behave like a cartel. By acting like a cartel, they, in turn, create a monopoly. However, this monopoly operates in a market that has a low barrier to entry, which means competition can easily enter and leave. Because of this, an oligopoly is also known as an insecure monopoly. An **insecure monopoly** is a monopoly that is challenged by competition entering into the market. Due to the competition entering and leaving the market, the oligopoly is also a contestable market. A **contestable market** refers to a market in which businesses in an oligopoly are constantly under threat from other businesses that enter and leave the market. During such times, the businesses in the oligopoly seek to protect their monopoly status. They do so using two strategies. One strategy entails lowering production quantity and allowing the competition to enter. This means the businesses will compete on price by charging a low price. This strategy makes the market less attractive to competitors, as they will experience low profits.

The second strategy involves using limit pricing. **Limit pricing** is a pricing strategy whereby businesses in an oligopoly discourage the competition by charging a price below monopoly pricing. This means the price is set low enough to make it unprofitable for the competition to enter. Therefore, the competition will choose not to enter the market.

insecure monopoly: a monopoly that is challenged by competition entering into the market

contestable market: a market in which businesses in an oligopoly are constantly under threat from other businesses that enter and leave the market

limit pricing: a pricing strategy whereby businesses in an oligopoly discourage the competition by charging a price below monopoly pricing

11.8 The Difference Between the Short Run and the Long Run for Businesses in an Oligopoly

Businesses in an oligopoly must act strategically in determining a way to prevent customers from moving from one competitor to the next. Acting strategically requires them to choose price fixing by conspiring to charge the same price. In doing so, they behave like a cartel. By acting like a cartel, they, in turn, create a monopoly. When behaving like a monopolist, businesses in an oligopoly earn zero economic profit in the short run and economic profit in the long run. In other words, in the short run, profits and demand are low, as there is no competition. However, over time, demand begins to rise, thereby causing profits to rise. At this point, businesses in the oligopoly are earning economic profit. This profit moves the market into the long run, as it allows them to expand resources and facilities. However, unlike a true monopoly, businesses in an oligopoly are constantly faced with the threat of competition, as the barriers to entry into the market are low. Table 11.2 shows a comparison of businesses in a perfectly competitive market to a monopoly and oligopoly.

TABLE 11.2 Behavior of Businesses in a Perfectly Competitive Market, a Monopoly, and an Oligopoly

Behavior	Perfectly competitive market	Monopoly	Oligopoly
competition	many competitors	no competitor	many competitors
pricing strategy	lowest possible price	highest possible price	acting strategically
short run	economic profit	zero economic profit	zero economic profit
long run	zero economic profit	economic profit	economic profit

SUMMARY

- An oligopoly is a market that consists of a few dominant businesses. (LO 11.1)
- The largest businesses in an oligopoly are characterized by concentration ratios. (LO 11.1)
- Businesses in an oligopoly must act strategically in determining a way to prevent customers from moving from one competitor to the next. (LO 11.2)
- A duopoly is a market that consists of two dominant competitors. (LO 11.3)
- Businesses in a duopoly seek economic profit by subtracting total cost from total revenues for each unit they sell until they find the level of sales where the greatest distance lies, using the marginal principle, or the economic profit formula. (LO 11.3)
- Businesses in a duopoly often choose to price fix, which leads them to behave like a cartel. (LO 11.3)
- The game tree is a graphic that depicts the consequences of choosing a low strategy due to the fear of being undercut by the competition. (LO 11.4)

- A kinked demand curve is a curve that illustrates the competition following the price decrease but not following the price increase. (LO 11.5)
- Businesses use duopoly pricing, tit-for-tat pricing, and grim trigger pricing as strategies to ensure that all competitors in the market engage in price fixing. (LO 11.6)
- An oligopoly is an insecure monopoly as well as a contestable market. (LO 11.7)
- Businesses in an oligopoly earn zero economic profit in the short run and economic profit in the long run. (LO 11.8)

END-OF-CHAPTER APPLICATION

Comprehension Questions

Directions: Refer to the chapter to correctly respond to the following questions and prompts.

1. Explain the ways businesses in an oligopoly respond to consumers who view them as substitutes and, thereby, constantly switch from one business to the other. (LO 11.2)
2. Define a duopoly. Explain the strategies that businesses in a duopoly will use to achieve economic profit. (LO 11.3)
3. Why would businesses in a duopoly choose to price fix? Explain. (LO 11.3)
4. How does the game tree ensure that businesses in an oligopoly will choose to price fix? Explain. (LO 11.4)
5. Identify and explain the strategies businesses in an oligopoly can use to avoid the duopolist's dilemma. (LO 11.5)
6. Explain what will happen to a price leader if it raises prices and the competition doesn't follow. Illustrate this effect on a kinked demand curve. (LO 11.5)
7. Identify and explain the strategies used by businesses in an oligopoly to ensure all competitors in the market engage in price fixing. (LO 11.6)
8. Identify and explain the strategies used by businesses in an oligopoly to protect their monopoly status. (LO 11.7)

Case Scenario: An Examination of the Commercial Airline Industry

Directions: Use what you learned in the chapter to respond to the following scenario.

Oligopolies are present in the commercial airline industry. This industry has a low barrier to entry and represents pricing behavior that is characterized by having a small number of participating businesses who offer standardized products and services. Therefore, in setting pricing for airline tickets, their competing behavior is interconnected, as the decision by one airline carrier affects the pricing decision of all other carriers. In making these decisions, although management seeks to choose a pricing strategy that generates the greatest profit, there is fear that the competition will undercut them. Use this information to answer the following questions:

1. How would concentration ratios describe the largest airline carriers in this industry?
2. How does the entry of a new competitor into this market affect the industry? Explain.
3. What choices do management have regarding price competition in the market?
4. How would businesses in this market benefit from price fixing? Explain.
5. Suppose industry management decided to use price leadership in their price decision. How would competing businesses respond a decline in pricing? What would occur to the price leader if it decided to raise prices and the competition chose not to follow? Illustrate this effect.

BIBLIOGRAPHY

Bartleby Online. (2021). *Oligopoly behavior in the airline industry: Case analysis*. https://www.bartleby.com/essay/Oligopoly-Behavior-in-the-Airline-Industry-Case-FKK29CS57KG4Y

O'Sullivan, A., Shreffin, S., & Perez, S. (2017). *Microeconomics: Principles, applications, and tools* (9th ed.). Pearson Publishing.

Schiller, B. R. (2016). *The micro economy today* (14th ed.). McGraw-Hill Education.

CREDIT

CHAPTER 12

Types of Markets

Monopolistic Competitive Markets

Concept Highlight

Chapter 12 examines the behavior of businesses in a monopolistic competitive market.

Real Life Example: What Does This Mean to You?

Many businesses operate in a monopolistic competitive market. Examples of such a market include hair salons, clothing retailers, and fast-food restaurants. In such a market, competition is intense due to low barriers-to-entry as well as similar product and service offerings. Therefore, businesses must decide how they will compete in search of earning economic profit. As such, economists seek to understand businesses' decision-making strategies for competing in this market as well as their behavior as they transition from the short run to the long run.

Introduction

Most businesses operate in a monopolistic competitive market. This market is characterized as being highly competitive; therefore, this market is an important concept to understand because it explains the competitive strategies used to achieve economic profits. In addition, it becomes important to understand what occurs when businesses in this market transition from the short run to the long run.

OBJECTIVES

While reading this chapter, readers should be able to

LO 12.1. monopolistic competitive market

LO 12.2. strategies used by businesses in a monopolistic competitive market to achieve economic profit

LO 12.2. strategies used by businesses in a monopolistic competitive market to differentiate their products and services

LO 12.2. the meaning of "monopolistic" and "competitive" within the term "monopolistic competition"

LO 12.3. the differences between the short run and long run for businesses in a monopolistic competitive market

OUTCOMES

After completing this chapter, readers will be able to do the following:

- Define "monopolistic competitive market."
- Explain the strategies used by businesses in a monopolistic competitive market to achieve economic profit.
- Explain the ways businesses in a monopolistic competitive market differentiate their products and services.
- Explain the meaning of "monopolistic" and "competitive" within the term "monopolistic competition."
- Explain the differences between the short run and the long run for businesses in a monopolistic competitive market.

Key Terms

The following key term is discussed in this chapter:

- monopolistic competitive market

12.1 What Is a Monopolistic Competitive Market?

Monopolistic competitive market: A market that consists of many competing businesses that sell similar but slightly difference products and services

A **monopolistic competitive market** consists of many competing businesses that sell similar but slightly different products and services. Examples of such a market include the fast-food industry and the sneaker manufacturing industry. These markets consist of many competitors that sell very similar products. As such, these markets are characterized by intense competition, low barriers to entry, and differentiated product and service offerings.

12.2 Differentiating Products and Services

Businesses in a monopolistic competitive market face intense competition because they sell products and services that are similar but slightly different to other products in addition to the market having low barriers to entry. However, in such a market, each business seeks to earn economic profit. In seeking economic profit, the competitors are like businesses in other markets in that they will use any of the following strategies:

- Subtract total cost from total revenues for each unit they sell until they find the level of sales at which the greatest distance lies.
- Use the marginal principle to produce at a level at which their marginal benefits equal their marginal costs.
- Use the economic profit formula.

Due to the nature of the products and services being offered, customers will perceive the businesses' offerings as substitutes. Therefore, success in achieving economic profits for businesses in a monopolistic competitive market is based on differentiating products and services from the competition, meaning these businesses are attempting to make their offerings stand out. To achieve this, businesses in this market use four main techniques: (a) providing offerings with physical characteristics that look different from the competition, (b) offering products and services in locations where the competition isn't present, (c) offering additional services not offered by the competition, and (d) creating an image or reputation that is unmatched by the competition.

The goal of differentiating products and services in a monopolistic competitive market explains the rationale for the term "monopolistic competitive." Within this rationale, "monopolistic" derives from the fact that each business in the market will develop a small loyal customer base through product differentiation. This, in turn, allows them act as a small monopoly, as they become the sole seller of that specific product. However, most consumers perceive the businesses' goods and services as substitutes, since they are similar in nature. Because of this, "competitive" comes from the fact that each business in a monopolistic competitive market must compete for the same customers.

12.3 The Difference Between the Short Run and the Long Run for Businesses in a Monopolistic Competitive Market

Businesses in a perfectly competitive market must differentiate their products from the competition to achieve economic profit. In doing so, they will behave similarly to businesses in a perfectly competitive market. This behavior consists of experiencing diminishing returns in the short run. During this period, businesses do not have the ability to change their resources (raw materials, facilities, equipment, etc.); therefore, production increases become smaller with each level of output as additional workers are hired. However, diminishing returns do not occur in the long run because businesses are able to change their resources as they hire additional workers. As a result, the additional resources allow each worker to be productive.

In addition, businesses in a monopolistic competitive market may earn economic profit in the short run and zero economic profit in the long run. In other words, a business's profits are low in the short run, as demand is low. However, over time, demand begins to rise, thereby causing profits to rise. At this point, the business is earning economic profit. This profit moves the business into the long run, as it allows the business to begin expanding its resources and facilities. However, the profits also motivate competition to enter the market. As competition increases, each business competes on price, which leads to declining prices and less profit earned. As this continues, some businesses will lose money and will be forced to leave the market. As prices continue to fall due to the competition and businesses begin to leave the market, the only remaining companies will be earning zero economic profit. In other words, they will make just enough profits to survive. Table 12.1 shows a comparison of businesses in a monopolistic competitive market with the other markets.

TABLE 12.1 Behavior of Businesses in a Monopolistic Competitive Market and Other Markets

Behavior	Perfectly competitive market	Monopoly	Oligopoly	Monopolistic competitive market
Competition	Many competitors	No competitor	Many competitors	Many competitors
Pricing Strategy	Lowest possible price	Highest possible price	Acting strategically	Differentiated products and services
Short Run	Economic profit	Zero economic profit	Zero economic profit	Economic profit
Long run	Zero economic profit	Economic profit	Economic profit	Zero economic profit

SUMMARY

- A monopolistic competitive market consists of many competing businesses that sell similar but slightly different products and services. (LO 12.1)

- Businesses in a monopolistic competitive market seek economic profit through subtracting total cost from total revenues for each unit that they sell until they find the level of sales at which the greatest distance lies, using the marginal principle, or using the economic profit formula. (LO 12.2)
- Success in achieving economic profits for businesses in a monopolistic competitive market is based on differentiating products and services from the competition. (LO 12.2)
- Businesses in a monopolistic competitive market differentiate their products and services through physical characteristics, location, additional service offerings, and image or reputation. (LO 12.2)
- "Monopolistic" within the term "monopolistic competitive" is derived from the fact that each business in the market will develop a small loyal customer base through product differentiation. (LO 12.2)
- "Competitive" within the term "monopolistic competitive" comes from the fact that each business in a monopolistic competitive market must compete for the same customers. (LO 12.2)
- Diminishing returns occur in the short run in a monopolistic competitive market. (LO 12.3)
- Businesses in a monopolistic competitive market may earn economic profit in the short run and zero economic profit in the long run. (LO 12.3)

END-OF-CHAPTER APPLICATION

Comprehension Questions

Directions: Refer to the chapter to correctly respond to the following questions and prompts.

1. Define monopolistic competitive market. Identify and explain the characteristics of this market. (LO 12.1)
2. Explain the strategies businesses in a monopolistic competitive market use to achieve economic profit. (LO 12.2)
3. Identify and explain the four strategies used by businesses in a monopolistic competitive market to differentiate their products and services. (LO 12.2)
4. Explain why a monopolistic competitive market is called "monopolistic competitive." (LO 12.2)
5. Explain the transition from the short run to the long run for businesses in a monopolistic competitive market. Identify when the businesses will earn economic profit and zero economic profit in this process. (LO 12.3)

Case Scenario: An Analysis of a Monopolistic Competitive Market

Directions: Use what you learned in the chapter to respond to the following scenario.

Taylor opens a convenient store on Main Street in her hometown. Main Street has 6 other convenient stores serving the community. All the convenient stores offer similar products. In analysis, answer the following questions:

1. Identify and explain the strategies that Taylor could use to compete in this market.
2. How would customers treat the convenient stores in this market? Explain your rationale.
3. Explain what happens to profits as each convenience store transitions from the short run to the long run. What happens with competition during this transition?

REFERENCES

O'Sullivan, A., Shreffin, S., & Perez, S. (2017). Microeconomics: Principles, applications, and tools (9th ed.). Pearson Publishing.

Schiller, B. R. (2016). *The micro economy today* (14th ed.). McGraw-Hill Education.

CREDIT

Part IV
Regulation

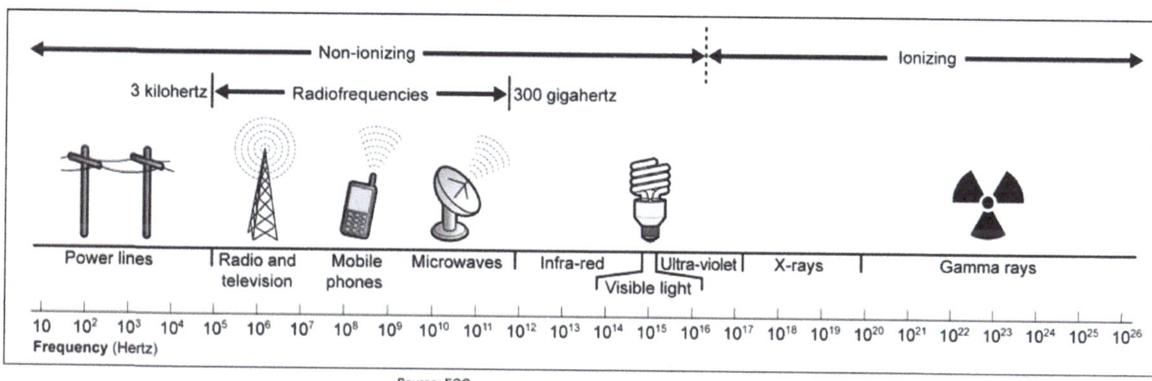

Source: FCC.

Source: U.S. Government Accountability Office, https://commons.wikimedia.org/wiki/File:Figure_1-_The_Electromagnetic_Spectrum_(7801782170)_(2).jpg, 2012.

CHAPTER 13

Business Regulation

Concept Highlight

Chapter 13 examines the effect of regulation on business operations.

Real Life Example: What Does This Mean to You?

One of the ways the government intervenes in the marketplace is through regulation. An example of such actions involves the Occupational Safety and Health Administration (OSHA), mandating safety procedures in the workplace. Such mandates require businesses to comply with safety standards set by OSHA for a safe work environment. When this occurs, economists seek to understand how the regulations or deregulations affect pricing, business investment, and production decisions.

Introduction

Regulation is an important concept to understand because it is used by governments as a policy decision-making tool to intervene in the marketplace. As such, the use of regulation affects business decision-making, as it will either require businesses to comply or provide a measure of relief for businesses in the marketplace.

OBJECTIVES

While reading this chapter, readers learn about

LO 13.1. market

LO 13.1. free market system

LO 13.1. invisible hand theory

LO 13.1. laissez faire

LO 13.1. market failure

LO 13.2. regulation

LO 13.2. anti-trust

LO 13.2. trust

LO 13.2. merger

LO 13.2. price fixing

LO 13.2. tying

LO 13.2. predatory pricing

LO 13.3. natural monopoly

LO 13.3. average-cost pricing policy

LO 13.3. marginal-cost pricing policy

LO 13.3. marginal-cost pricing theory

OUTCOMES

After completing this, chapter readers will be able to do the following:

- Define "market."
- Define "free market system."
- Define "invisible hand theory."
- Define "laissez faire."
- Define and illustrate "market failure."

- Define "regulation," and explain its purpose.
- Define "anti-trust," and explain its purpose.
- Define "trust."
- Define "merger."
- Define "price fixing."
- Define "typing."
- Define "predatory pricing."
- Explain how government regulation affects most businesses.
- Define "natural monopoly."
- Explain how governments regulate a natural monopoly.
- Explain how government regulation of a natural monopoly leads to a downward spiral of average production costs and pricing.
- Define "average-cost pricing policy."
- Define "marginal-cost pricing policy."
- Define "marginal-cost pricing theory."
- Explain how a natural monopoly violates the marginal-cost pricing theory.
- Explain how far a natural monopolist can lower its average production cost.

Key Terms

The following key terms are discussed in this chapter:

- market
- free market system
- invisible hand theory
- laissez faire
- market failure
- regulation
- anti-trust
- trust
- merger
- pricing fixing
- tying
- predatory pricing
- natural monopoly
- average-cost pricing policy
- marginal-cost pricing policy
- marginal-cost pricing theory

13.1 Review: The Free Market System

As we've discussed in earlier chapters, **market** is defined as a place where buyers and sellers engage in exchanges (buy and sell). The U.S. economy was built upon the free market system. The **free market system** is one in which sellers have the freedom to sell their products at any price and buyers have the freedom to buy. Adam Smith is given credit for the creation of this system and, therefore, is known as the father of the free market system. This credit was based on his writings on the invisible hand theory, from which the free market system idea was founded. The **invisible hand theory** is the belief that if the government lets the market be, without intervention, eventually, both the buyer and the seller will agree upon a price at which they are satisfied. In other words, the invisible hand theory indicates that the market would be better if the government allowed the buyer and seller to negotiate on prices of goods and service without intervention.

This concept, in turn, derives from laissez faire. **Laissez faire** is theory based on the belief that the government should not intervene or simply leave it alone. However, from the government's perspective, it must intervene in the marketplace to protect consumers and prevent market failure. **Market failure** refers to forces in the economy that prevent it from performing perfectly. Perfection occurs when the economy reaches equilibrium because producers sell to the greatest number of consumers and, therefore, will earn the greatest profits. Market failure implies that these forces will cause either excess demand or excess supply, which, in turn, leads to fewer consumers and profits. Figures 13.1 and 13.2 show an example of market failure.

market: a place where buyers and sellers engage in exchanges (buy and sell)

free market economy: a system in which sellers have the freedom to sell their products at any price and buyers have the freedom to buy

invisible hand theory: the belief that if the government let the market be, without intervention, eventually, both the buyer and the seller would agree upon a price at which they are satisfied

laissez faire: theory based on the belief that the government should not intervene

market failure: forces in the economy that prevent it from performing perfectly

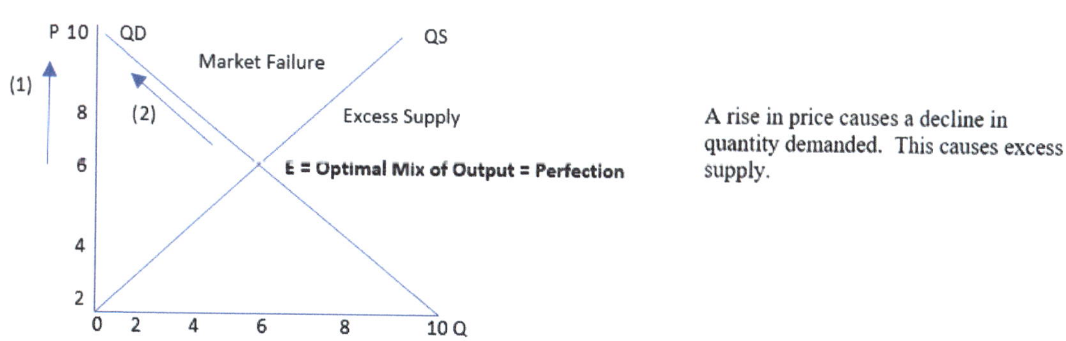

FIGURE 13.1 Market Failure (Excess Supply)

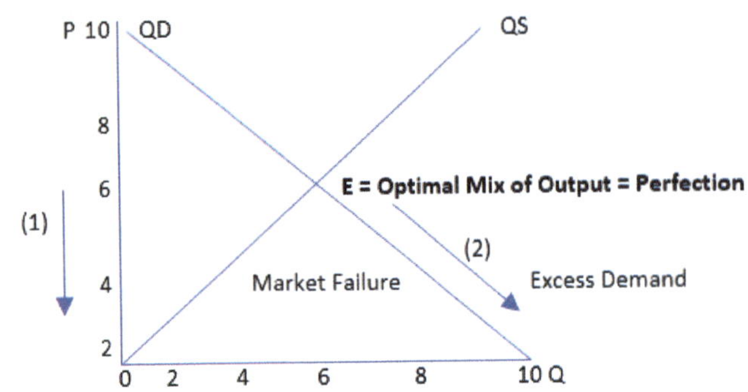

A decline in price causes a rise in quantity demanded. This causes excess demand.

FIGURE 13.2 Market Failure (Excess Demand)

13.2 Regulation: Anti-trust vs. Trust

One government strategy for preventing market failure is to enact regulation. **Regulation** is defined as an official rule or act. The government uses regulation to change business operating behavior by limiting price, production, or investment decisions. In doing so, regulation causes changes in marketplace behavior. One type of regulation used by the government is antitrust. **Anti-trust** laws prohibit the formation of monopolies. The goal of anti-trust laws is to encourage competition, which leads to lower prices and greater choice. Anti-trust laws seek to break up monopolies into several smaller businesses. This, in turn, often creates a trust. A **trust** is an arrangement under which the owners of several companies transfer their decision-making powers to a small group of trustees, who then make decisions for all the businesses in the trust. So all the businesses in a trust act as one single business, thereby creating a kind of monopoly. An example of such a behavior is AT&T, which operated as a legal monopoly by having regional Bell companies throughout the United States in the 1970s. However, responding to lack of competition in the telecommunication industry, the U.S. government filed an anti-trust lawsuit that eventually led to AT&T selling off its regional bell companies to local operators, thereby, creating greater competition in the marketplace.

A second use of anti-trust laws involves blocking corporate mergers, which would reduce competition and lead to higher prices. A **merger** refers to a process in which two or more businesses combine operations. An example of this includes the merger attempt by Direct TV and Dish Network Corporation in 2002.

regulation: an official rule or act

anti-trust: laws that prohibit the formation of monopolies

trust: an arrangement under which the owners of several companies transfer their decision-making powers to a small group of trustees who then make decisions for all the businesses in the trust

merger: a process in which two or more businesses combine operations

pricing fixing: a strategy whereby the competitors conspire to charge the same price

tying: a practice whereby businesses force consumers to buy one product to purchase another product

predatory pricing: a strategy whereby a business charges different prices for the same product or service

In this attempt, the government sued to stop the merger out of concern that it would eliminate an industry competitor and create higher subscription fees.

A third use of anti-trust entails regulating business practices. Such regulation is used to change practices that would allow for greater demand in the market. Therefore, the government will use anti-trust to reduce price fixing, tying, and predatory pricing. **Pricing fixing** is a strategy whereby the competitors conspire to charge the same price. **Tying** refers to a practice whereby businesses force consumers to buy one product to purchase another product. **Predatory pricing** involves a business charging different prices for the same product or service. One example of regulating business practices is the U.S. government prohibiting businesses in cable TV industry from requiring customers to buy internet service and landline phone service to purchase cable TV.

13.3 Regulation's Effect on Businesses vs. a Natural Monopoly

When the government intervenes in the marketplace through regulation, it will cause changes in the operating behavior for most businesses. In other words, the new regulation will force those businesses to either change their pricing, production, or investment decisions to comply. As a result, the new regulation will lead to an increase in production costs. As these production costs rise, eventually, they will be passed on to the customers in higher prices. At the higher prices, the businesses will seek to maximize profit by producing at a level where their marginal benefits equal their marginal costs. However, this concept works differently for a natural monopoly.

A **natural monopoly** is a market in which the presence of a competitor will cause prices to fall below average production, and therefore, the competitor chooses not to enter. In other words, this is a market in which one business provides products and services at a high average production cost. In doing so, its customer base is just high enough to cover its cost. Therefore, if a competitor enters into the market, they will compete on price, which means each business will lower price in an attempt to attract customers. This lowering of price will split the customer base, and neither business will sell to enough customers to cover the high cost of production. Understanding this, a competitor will choose not to enter into the market because it will lose money. As a result, although competition is free to enter, they choose not to enter, and the business that serves the market becomes the natural monopolist. Figure 13.3 demonstrates the effect of a competitor entering into a natural monopoly on a demand curve.

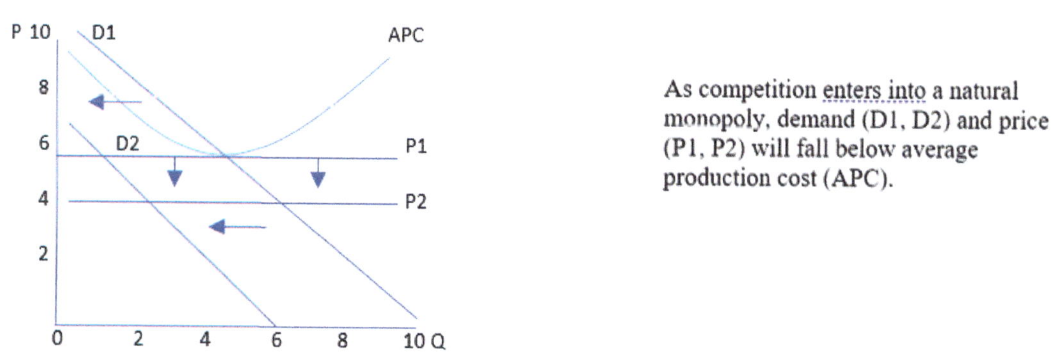

FIGURE 13.3 An Example of the Effect of Competition Entering into a Natural Monopoly

In such a situation, the government often uses regulation to prevent the natural monopolist from taking full advantage of the customers in the market, which could lead to market failure. Such efforts seek to create market efficiencies, which is the preferred outcome of the regulation. These efficiencies are sought by regulating the price charged in the market by the natural monopolist. In doing so, the government regulates price by either (a) using the **average-cost pricing policy**, which refers to the government setting the market price at average production cost; (b) using the **marginal-cost pricing policy**, which means the government sets the market price at the natural monopolist's marginal cost for each additional unit produced; or (c) regulating normal profits, which implies the government will set the market price just high enough to cover all of the natural monopolist's cost. In all cases, the natural monopolist will respond by focusing on lowering its average production costs to maximize profit. This, in turn, will eventually cause the government to lower prices, according to the reduced average production costs. This leads to a downward spiral of production costs and prices, thereby creating efficiency in the market, as it also creates a downward-sloping demand curve for the natural monopolist. Figure 13.4 demonstrates this effect.

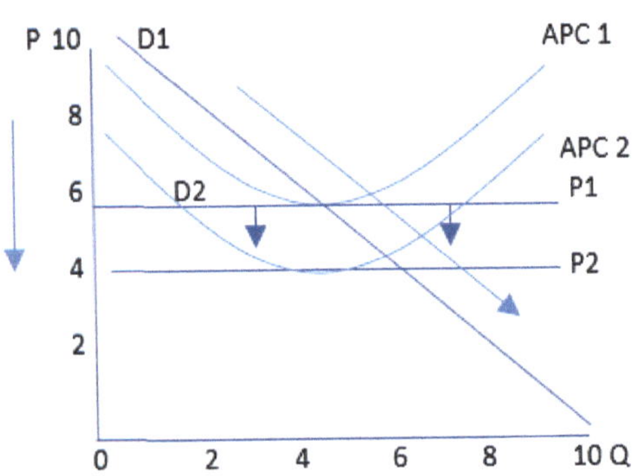

The natural monopolist responds to the government's regulation of price by lowering its average production costs (APC 1 to APC 2). In response, the government lowers price to the new average production cost level (P1 to P2). This causes downward movement along the demand curve.

FIGURE 13.4 An Example of the Downward-sloping Demand Curve caused by the Downward Spiral of Production Costs and Prices

This illustration shows that the natural monopolist behaves differently to government regulation than any other business. For any other business, government regulation will lead to higher production costs and prices. As such, these businesses will seek to maximize profit at the higher price by producing at a level at which their marginal benefits equal their marginal costs. However, government regulation of a natural monopolist prevents it from raising price. Therefore, to maximize profit, the natural monopolist must focus on lowering its average production cost. Doing so means the natural monopolist violates the concept of marginal-cost pricing theory. **Marginal-cost pricing theory** refers to the

natural monopoly: a market in which the presence of a competitor would cause prices to fall below average production, and therefore, the competitor chooses not to enter

average-cost pricing policy: government regulation that sets the market price to the business's average production cost

marginal-cost pricing policy: government regulation that sets the market price to the business' marginal cost for each additional unit produced

marginal-cost pricing theory: the belief that businesses sell products at a level at which their marginal cost equals their price belief that businesses sell products at a level at which their marginal cost equals their price. This means the natural monopolists' price will be higher than its marginal cost for at least a period of time, until the government regulates the price.

But the natural monopolist will not be able to reduce its production cost to zero. In fact, at some point, the natural monopolist will reach production capacity in its efforts to reduce its production costs. In other words, at some point, the natural monopolist will reach a level where it can't lower its production costs any further, and at this point, its costs will rise for each unit produced.

SUMMARY

- A market is a place where buyers and sellers engage in exchanges (buy and sell). (LO 13.1)
- The free market system is one in which sellers have the freedom to sell their products at whatever price and buyers have the freedom to buy. (LO 13.1)
- The invisible hand theory is the belief that if the government let the market be, without intervention, eventually, both the buyer and the seller would agree upon a price at which they are satisfied. (LO 13.1)
- Laissez faire is a theory based on the belief that the government should not intervene. (LO 13.1)
- Market failure prevents the economy from performing perfectly. (LO 13.1)
- The government uses regulation to change business operating behavior by limiting price, production, or investment decisions. (LO 13.2)
- The goal of anti-trust laws is to encourage competition, which leads to lower prices and greater choice. (LO 13.2)
- A trust is an arrangement under which the owners of several companies transfer their decision-making powers to a small group of trustees who then make decisions for all the businesses in the trust. (LO 13.2)
- A merger refers to a process in which two or more businesses combine operations. (LO 13.2)
- The government uses anti-trust laws to reduce price fixing, tying, and predatory pricing. (LO 13.2)
- Government intervention in the marketplace through regulation causes changes to the operating behavior of most businesses. (LO 13.3)
- A natural monopoly is a market in which the presence of a competitor causes prices to fall below average production, and therefore, the competitor chooses not to enter. (LO 13.3)
- The government regulates a natural monopoly price by (a) using the average-cost pricing policy, (b) using the marginal-cost pricing policy, or (c) regulating normal profits. (LO 13.3)
- The government regulation of a natural monopoly leads to a downward spiral of production costs and prices. (LO 13.3)

- A natural monopolist violates the concept of marginal-cost pricing theory in its search for maximizing profits. (LO 13.3)
- A natural monopolist continues to lower its average production cost until it reaches production capacity. (LO 13.3)

END-OF-CHAPTER APPLICATION

Comprehension Questions

Directions: Refer to the chapter to correctly respond to the following questions and prompts.

1. Explain the purpose of government intervention in the marketplace. (LO 13.1)
2. Define "regulation." Explain the purpose of regulation. (LO 13.2)
3. Define "anti-trust." Explain the goal of anti-trust. (LO 13.2)
4. Explain the difference between price fixing, tying, and predatory pricing. (LO 13.2)
5. Explain how government regulation affects most businesses in the market. (LO 13.3)
6. Explain how the government regulates a natural monopoly. Explain how the natural monopolist will respond to government regulation. (LO 13.3)
7. Explain how government regulation of a natural monopoly leads to a downward spiral of average production costs and prices. Illustrate this effect. (LO 13.3)
8. Explain the difference in maximizing profit strategy between most businesses and a natural monopoly when government regulates the market. (LO 13.3)

Case Scenario: Analysis of Government Regulation of Retail Stores vs. a Utility Company

Directions: Use what you learned in the chapter to respond to the following scenario.

Suppose the Federal Regulatory Advising Commission recommends stricter regulation in the sale of certain products to minors in retail stores. Suppose this commission also recommends increased regulation of the local utility company to provide greater access to services in underserved communities. Use this example to answer the following questions:

1. What could the government regulation look like for the retail industry? What could the government regulation look like for the utility company.
2. How would the government regulation affect retail stores? How would it affect the utility company? Explain.

3. How would the retail stores respond to the regulation? How would the utility company respond to the regulation? Explain.

4. What would the maximizing profit strategy for the retail stores be? What would the maximizing profit strategy for the utility company be? Explain.

REFERENCES

BC Online. (n.d.). *Regulating anticompetitive behavior.* https://opentextbc.ca/principlesofeconomics/chapter/11-2-regulating-anticompetitive-behavior/

Britannica. (n.d.). Marginal-cost pricing. In *Britannica online.* https://www.britannica.com/topic/marginal-cost-pricing

Cambridge Dictionary. (2022). Regulation. In *Cambridge Dictionary Online.* https://dictionary.cambridge.org/us/dictionary/english/regulation

Investopedia. (2022, February 7). *Price discrimination.* Investopedia online. https://www.investopedia.com/terms/p/price_discrimination.asp

Lazaroff, L. (2014, May 23). *5 mergers that failed.* (2022). The Street. https://www.thestreet.com/investing/stocks/5-government-blocked-mergers-that-should-worry-comcast-att-12714173

Monopolies and trust. (2019). In *Encyclopedia online.* Retrieved on May 16, 2022 from https://www.encyclopedia.com/history/encyclopedias-almanacs-transcripts-and-maps/monopolies-and-trusts

O'Sullivan, A., Shreffin, S., & Perez, S. (2017). Microeconomics: Principles, applications, and tools (9th ed.). Pearson Publishing.

Schiller, B. R. (2016). *The micro economy today* (14th ed.). McGraw-Hill Education.

CREDIT

IMG 13.1: Daderot, https://commons.wikimedia.org/wiki/File:Guardian_of_Law_by_James_Earle_Fraser,_US_Supreme_Court.jpg, 2008.

CHAPTER 14

Environmental Pollution and Societal Cost

Concept Highlight

Chapter 14 examines the costs associated with business pollution in the production process.

Real Life Example: What Does This Mean to You?

Market incentives drive the level of pollution emitted by businesses. Therefore, the level of pollution emitted by businesses becomes a production decision. An example of this includes a product manufacturer emitting harmful particles into the air to produce its goods. Economists seek to understand the effect of such actions on the environment and society; in addition, they seek to analyze how government environmental regulation affect businesses, including natural monopolies.

Introduction

Pollution is an important concept to understand because it is the negative result of the effects of the production process. This effect leads to market failure as both the environment and society as a whole are affected. Government intervention in the marketplace through regulation seeks to reduce the negative effects of pollution on the environment as well as members of society.

OBJECTIVES

While reading this chapter, readers learn about

LO 14.1. pollution

LO 14.2. the production decision

LO 14.3. external costs

LO 14.3. social costs

LO 14.3. private costs

LO 14.4. the efficiency decision

LO 14.5. emission charges

LO 14.5. permits

OUTCOMES

After completing this chapter, readers will be able to do the following:

- Define "pollution."
- Identify and explain the different types of pollution.
- Explain the production decision in a business' selection of the amount of pollution to emit.
- Explain when external costs occur.
- Explain how external costs lead to market failure.
- Explain how most businesses respond to government regulation requiring them to upgrade to a less polluting production technology.
- Explain how a natural monopolist responds to government regulation requiring it to upgrade to a less polluting production technology.

- Explain the efficiency decision in a natural monopolist's selection of technology used in the production process.
- Explain the regulatory strategies the government uses to protect the environment from pollution.

Key Terms

The following key terms are discussed in this chapter:

- pollution
- production decision
- external costs
- social costs
- private costs
- efficiency decision
- emission charge
- permit

14.1 What Is Pollution?

pollution: waste

FIGURE 14.1 Air Pollution

Businesses produce products and services in response to demand. In meeting this response, the business owner will incur production costs associated with production. These costs include both monetary and nonmonetary expenses related to the actual production process of providing products and services. As the business goes through the production process, it will create pollution. **Pollution** refers to waste. Pollution occurs in air, land, and water. Air pollution occurs when particles are discharged into the air, which causes smog and greenhouse emissions. Land pollution occurs when hazardous materials are spilled and leaks into the soil. Water pollution occurs when chemicals and debris leak into or spill into the water supply.

14.2 Market Incentives' Effect on Business Pollution

Society needs products and services to satisfy needs and wants—but this often comes at the cost of business pollution. It is currently considered impossible for businesses to produce without polluting. So the goal is to determine an appropriate level of pollution in the production process. However, the level of pollution businesses create will be driven by market incentives. In other words, businesses operate to maximize profit; therefore, they will pollute at a level where their marginal benefits equal their marginal costs because this allows them to earn the greatest profits. As a result, the business owner's pollution level becomes a production decision. A **production decision** is a business's decision on the short-run rate of production based on current facilities and equipment.

production decision: A business's decision on the short-run rate of production based on current facilities and equipment

14.3 Costs Associated With Pollution

The production decision implies that the business owner will sacrifice polluting air, land, and water in exchange for maximizing profits. This action, in turn, imposes costs on members of society. Such costs are known as **external costs**. An example of external costs would be town citizens getting sick from drinking water that has been polluted by a local manufacturer.

External costs occur when the social costs of an activity become greater than the private costs. **Social costs** refer to the costs incurred by society as a whole. By comparison, **private costs** refer to costs incurred by one person or business. Therefore, external costs occur when society pays a greater cost than the person or the business that created the activity. This, in turn, creates market failure, as the external cost leads to the market moving away from equilibrium. An example of this would be a business owner deciding to avoid paying $5 million to properly dispose of the waste produced by the business and then this waste leaking into the town's water supply. As a result, the town is forced to pay $100 million in medical bills to cover the illnesses caused by the business owner's decision. An investigation determines that the business's waste is the cause of the town's illnesses. In response, the citizens protest, sue, and stop buying the business's products. This, in turn, leads to market failure as demand falls, thereby creating excess supply.

FIGURE 14.2 External Costs Caused by Smog in a City

external costs: costs incurred by members of society

social costs: costs incurred by society as a whole

private costs: costs incurred by one person or business

14.4 A Business's Response vs. a Natural Monopoly's Response to Pollution Regulation

External costs lead to market failure, as demand for a particular product or service changes due to society bearing a greater cost than the business that created the activity. This forces the government to intervene to move the market towards equilibrium. One of the ways in which the government intervenes is by using regulation to force businesses to upgrade their technology to reduce their pollution. If this occurs, most businesses will be forced to upgrade their production technology to comply with the new regulation. This will cause their production costs to rise. As their costs rise, businesses will raise prices on customers. At the higher prices, the businesses will seek to maximize profit by producing at a level at which their marginal benefits equal their marginal costs.

Natural monopolies behave differently from most businesses. If the government intervenes in a natural monopoly through regulation to force the natural monopolist to upgrade its production technology to reduce its pollution, the natural monopolist will be forced to make a decision. As such, the natural monopolist must decide to either (a) comply with the regulation and upgrade to the new technology or (b) continue production with the current technology. This decision is based on the government setting the market price for the natural monopolists, which means the natural monopolist will not be able to change its price. This creates a horizontal price line for the natural monopolist. So if the natural monopolist decides to comply with the regulation, although it will pollute less, it will experience a rise in production costs due to the investment costs. This will lead to a decline in production and profits. But if the natural monopolist decides to continue production with the current technology, although it will continue to pollute at its current level, it will produce more products and earn greater profits. Understanding this, the natural monopolist chooses to continue to produce with the current technology. This represents an efficiency decision for the natural monopoly. An **efficiency decision** is a decision regarding a production process. In other words, the natural monopolist weighs whether to use the polluting technology in its production process based on its ability to control its costs to maximize profits, since it is not able to change its price.

FIGURE 14.3 Electricity Lines to Depict a Natural Monopoly

efficiency decision: a decision regarding a production process

14.5 A Business's Response vs. a Natural Monopoly's Response to Pollution Regulation

Pollution not only harms societal members, but it also harms the environment. Therefore, the government will use regulation to protect the environment from the harmful waste caused by pollution. In doing so, the government can use two regulatory strategies: (a) change business market incentives that would lead to less pollution and (b) limit the amount of pollution created by businesses. One way to change business market incentives through regulation is to impose emission charges on the polluter. An **emission charge** is a fee charged for pollution. This fee could be imposed each time the business pollutes or as a value of the overall amount of pollution created by the business. As a result, the business will be motivated to pollute less to reduce the amount of fees levied. An example of this includes the carbon tax, in which the government charges emitters for each ton of greenhouse gas emissions they emit.

emission charge: a fee charged for pollution

permit: license

Another way to limit the amount of pollution created by businesses through regulation is to use permits. A **permit** refers to a license. Therefore, the government could limit pollution by selling a limited number of permits to businesses. Each permit would allow a business to emit a certain amount of pollution, and the businesses could sell the permits among each other based on the pollution needs of each business. As a result, the government controls the amount of pollution by controlling the number of businesses allowed to pollute. An example of this includes the Resource Conservation and Recovery Act, which requires businesses to obtain a permit for the disposal of hazardous waste.

OFFICE OF THE GOVERNOR * STATE OF OHIO *

TED STRICKLAND
GOVERNOR
STATE OF OHIO

Executive Order 2010 – 15S

Immediate Adoption of Rules to Adopt USEPA Permitting Thresholds for Stationary Sources Emitting Greenhouse Gases

1. **The United States Environmental Protection Agency ("USEPA") has Adopted Rules under the Federal Clean Air Act for the Issuance of Permits to Sources Emitting Greenhouse Gases.** USEPA, on June 3, 2010, adopted rules under the federal Clean Air Act ("CAA") requiring certain stationary sources of greenhouse gases (defined as carbon dioxide, nitrous oxide, methane, hydrofluorocarbons, perflourocarbons, and sulfur hexafluoride) to obtain CAA permits prior to the installation or modification of the sources, and to obtain operating permits under Title V of the CAA. The rules require CAA permits if the source to be installed or operated, or if the modification of a source, is "major" as defined by laws and regulations. The requirement to obtain CAA permits for the installation or operation of major sources emitting greenhouse gases and for the major modification of sources emitting greenhouse gases takes effect on January 2, 2011.

2. **The USEPA's "Tailoring Rule" Establishes Higher Major Source Emission Thresholds for the Permitting of Sources of Greenhouse Gases than for Sources of Other Regulated Pollutants.** USEPA has established higher emission thresholds for determining whether a source of greenhouses gases is "major" for purposes of the requirement to obtain CAA permits as compared to the thresholds for other pollutants. The rule establishing the higher threshold for establishing "major sources" of greenhouse gas emissions is known as the "Tailoring Rule". When it adopted its Tailoring Rule, USEPA explained that the higher emission thresholds are necessary to avoid imposing major source CAA permitting requirements on a far larger number of sources than would otherwise be required to obtain such permits.

(Page 1 of 3)

TEXTBOX 14.1 A Permit That Allows for the Emission of Greenhouse Gases

Source: Governor Ted Strickland, "Immediate Adoption of Rules to Adopt USEPA Permitting Thresholds for Stationary Sources Emitting Greenhouse Gases," Executive Order 2010 - 15S, State of Ohio, 2010.

SUMMARY

- Pollution occurs in air, land, and water. (LO 14.1)
- The level of pollution businesses create is driven by market incentives. (LO 14.2)
- The business owner's pollution level becomes a production decision. (LO 14.2)
- Business pollution imposes external costs. (LO 14.3)
- External costs occur when the social costs of an activity become greater than the private costs. (LO 14.3)
- External costs lead to market failure. (LO 14.4)
- Government regulation requiring businesses to upgrade their production technology to reduce their pollution cause the business's production cost to rise. (LO 14.4)
- Government regulation requiring a natural monopolist to upgrade its production technology to reduce its production force natural monopolists into a decision. (LO 14.4)
- The government can protect the environment from pollution through emission charges and requiring permits. (LO 14.5)

END-OF-CHAPTER APPLICATION

Comprehension Questions

Directions: Refer to the chapter to correctly respond to the following questions and prompts.

1. List and explain the three types of pollution. (LO 14.1)
2. What market incentives drive business pollution? Explain. (LO 14.2)
3. Explain how external costs create market failure. (LO 14.3)
4. Explain how government pollution regulation affects most businesses in the market. How would the regulation affect price? Explain. (LO 14.4)
5. Explain how government pollution regulation would affect a natural monopoly. Explain how the natural monopolist would respond to the regulation. (LO 14.4)
6. List and explain the two regulatory strategies the government can use to protect the environment. (LO 14.5)

Case Scenario:

Directions: Use what you learned in the chapter to respond to the following scenario.

A mining company operates outside of a small town in Illinois. For years, residents filed complaints of gasoline-type odors in their private water well. These complaints lead to a groundwater investigation by the Illinois Department of Public Health. The department's investigation discovers chemicals found in gasoline in the water wells. In its investigation, the source of the contamination was determined to mostly be from an old gas station.

About 10 years later, residents from the town filed complaints about a gasoline odor in their tap water. Once again, the Illinois Department of Public Health began an investigation and discovered high benzene levels in the water supply. This prompted the department to advise the residents to no longer drink the water. A further investigation determined that the leaking gasoline storage tanks were located on the mining company's property. Furthermore, it was discovered that mining company changed the direction of the ground water. Answer the following questions:

1. Briefly describe the pollution problem. Identify possible external costs that could be created by the problem.
2. Explain the difference between the possible societal costs and private costs associated with this case study.
3. Suppose the mining company is found guilty of contaminating the town's drinking water. What could the possible consequences of the mining company's actions be?
4. How could the government regulate the mining industry to prevent future water supply contamination?

BIBLIOGRAPHY

C2es online. (n.d.). *Carbon tax*. https://www.c2es.org/content/carbon-tax-basics/

EPA online. (2021, May 18). *What is a Resource Conservation and Recovery Act (RCRA) permit?* https://www.epa.gov/hwpermitting/what-hazardous-waste-permit

O'Sullivan, A., Shreffin, S., & Perez, S. (2017). *Microeconomics: Principles, applications, and tools* (9th ed.). Pearson Publishing.

Serc Carleton online (2021, January 27). *Case study 3: My water smells (and tastes) like gasoline*. https://serc.carleton.edu/integrate/teaching_materials/map_sense/student_materials/unit4_3.html

Schiller, B. R. (2016). *The micro economy today* (14th ed.). McGraw-Hill Education.

CREDITS

Part V
Asymmetric Information and Financial Markets

Source:: Copyright © 2019 by Xylem22 (CC BY-SA 4.0) at https://commons.wikimedia.org/wiki/File:Swenson_Financial_Markets_Lab_at_St._Cloud_State_University_(located_in_first_floor_of_Centennial_Hall).jpg.

CHAPTER 15

Knowledgeable and Unknowledgeable Market Players

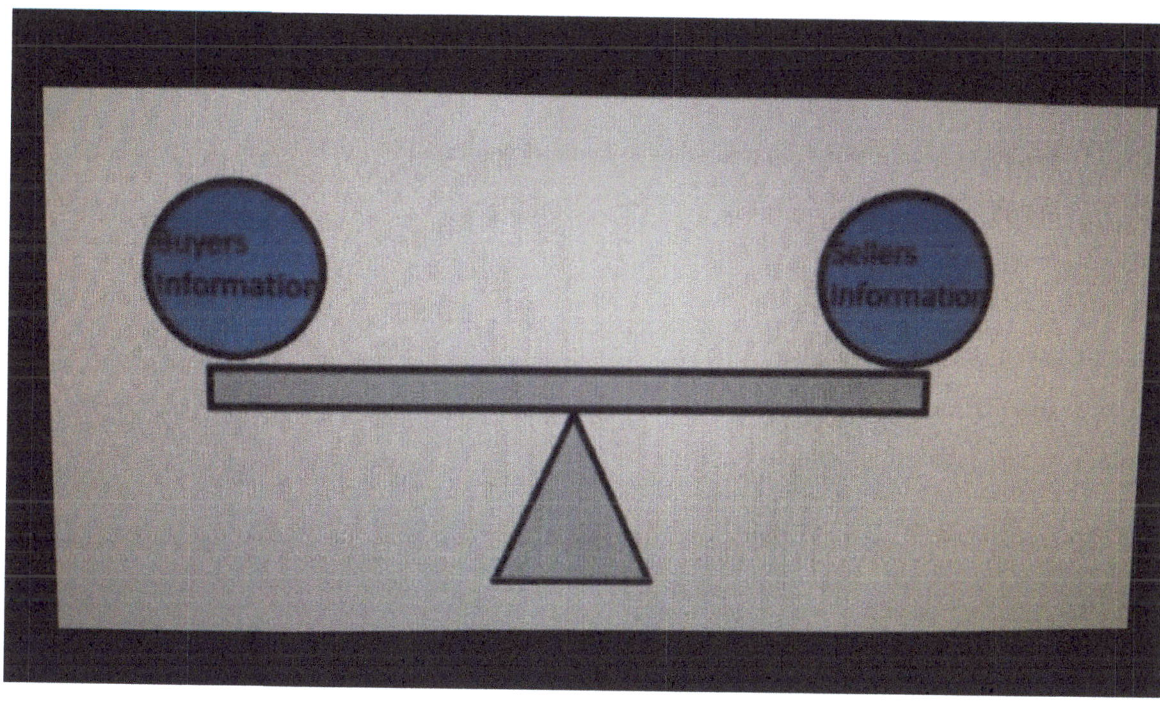

Concept Highlight

Chapter 15 examines the concepts of asymmetric information.

Real Life Example: What Does This Mean to You?

The free market system operates based on both the buyer and seller having the same information. This allows products and services to be sold at the fairest price, thereby moving the economy toward equilibrium. However, the economy moves away from equilibrium when one side of the market has more or better information than the other side. An example of this would be car salespeople having more or better information about the vehicles for sale than buyers. In such a situation, economists seek to understand the pricing decisions made by consumers as well as how these decisions affect the quality of the products being sold.

Introduction

Asymmetric information is an important concept to understand because it provides insights into the behaviors of both the buyers and sellers based on the information each has about products and services being sold. This information leads to the sellers pricing their goods at one price and buyers setting a price they are willing to pay for those products and services. In doing so, their behaviors affect equilibrium.

OBJECTIVES

While reading this chapter, readers learn about

LO 15.1. asymmetric information

LO 15.1. two types of goods that are created by asymmetric information

LO 15.1. lemon

LO 15.1. neutral expectations

LO 15.1. pessimistic expectations

LO 15.2. adverse-selection problem

LO 15.2. thin market

LO 15.2. types of guarantees offered by sellers

OUTCOMES

After completing this chapter, readers will be able to do the following:

- Define "asymmetric information."
- Explain how asymmetric information affects the market.
- Define "lemon."
- Identify and explain the types of expectations consumers form when faced with the chances of buying a lemon.
- Define "the adverse-selection problem."
- Explain how the adverse-selection problem affects prices and the quality of goods.
- Define "thin market."
- Identify and explain the types of guarantees offered by sellers.

Key Terms

The following key terms are discussed in this chapter:

- asymmetric information
- lemon
- neutral expectations
- pessimistic expectations
- adverse-selection problem
- thin market

15.1 What Is the Asymmetric Information Problem?

A market provides a place for buyers and sellers to engage in exchanges. The free market system allows sellers the freedom to sell products at whatever price they choose as well as allows buyers the freedom to buy whatever they choose. This system is built upon the invisible hand theory, which suggests that in the process of freely engaging in exchanges, both the buyer and seller will negotiate what they consider to be a fair price for the products being sold. This negotiation is based on both the buyer and the seller having the same information about the product. However, when one side has more or better information than the other, this becomes known as **asymmetric information**; in such a situation, one side of the market can take advantage of the other side, which leads to market failure. An example of this would be a retailer selling jewelry to the public. As the seller, the retailer has more or better information about the jewelry being sold than the consumer does. This also means the retailer is in a better position to take advantage of the information known than the buyer. Therefore, if the retailer sells fake jewelry at a higher price, the buyer is at a disadvantage due to their lack of knowledge.

Asymmetric information creates a market with two types of goods. Those two types are "high-quality goods" and "low-quality goods." In such a situation, three questions must be addressed. Those questions are as follows:

- How much are consumers willing to pay for high-quality goods?
- How much are consumers willing to pay for low-quality goods?
- What are the chances consumers will buy a lemon?

When a consumer buys a **lemon**, they are buying a product that is unsatisfactory, not of its true value, or disappointing. Understanding this, the market will set a minimum price for high-quality goods and a minimum price for low-quality goods for which goods will be sold. But consumers will also set a price at which they are willing to pay for goods based on the chances of them buying a lemon. The price they set is based on neutral expectations and pessimistic expectations. **Neutral expectations** are consumers' belief that they will purchase a lemon at least half the time. Therefore, they will be willing to pay the average price between the high-quality goods and the low-quality goods. An example of this includes a retailer selling high-quality jewelry for a minimum price of $100 and low-quality jewelry for a minimum of $50. Having neutral expectations, customers will be willing to pay $75. This, in turn, will cause a decline in the supply

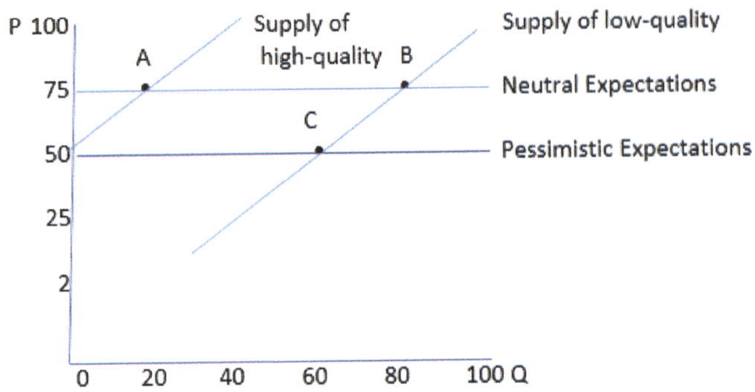

Neutral expectations lead consumers to be willing to pay $75 for jewelry. In response, the retailer is willing to supply 20 high-quality jewelry (A) and 80 low-quality jewelry (B).

Pessimistic expectations lead consumers to be willing to pay $50 for jewelry. In response, the retailer is willing to supply 60 low-quality jewelry (C). Therefore, no high-quality jewelry will be supplied at this price.

FIGURE 15.1 Neutral Expectations and Pessimistic Expectations

asymmetric information: a situation in which one side of the market has more or better information than the other side of the market

lemon: a product that is unsatisfactory, not of its true value, or disappointing

neutral expectations: consumers' belief that they will purchase a lemon at least half the time

pessimistic expectations: consumers' belief that they will purchase a lemon more than half the time

of high-quality jewelry, thereby moving the market away from equilibrium.

Pessimistic expectations are consumers' belief that they will purchase a lemon more than half the time. Therefore, they will be willing to pay the lowest price between the two goods. In the example provided, when consumers have pessimistic expectations, they are willing to pay $50 for jewelry. This will lead to the elimination of the supply of high-quality jewelry, which also moves the market away from equilibrium. Figure 15.1 depicts this example.

15.2 The Adverse-Selection Problem

When consumers believe there is a greater chance of buying a lemon, they will buy fewer goods. This will cause prices to fall and move the market closer to equilibrium. However, as prices continue to fall, sellers will sell a greater quantity of low-quality goods because they will feel that they are not getting fair value for the high-quality goods. This downward spiral of prices and quality goods will cause the adverse-selection problem. The **adverse-selection problem** is a situation in which consumers are forced to choose from an undesirable group of goods. In other words, when consumers are willing to pay low prices due to having pessimistic expectations, most goods provided by the sellers will be low quality. This, in turn, is caused by asymmetric information.

The downward spiral of prices and quality goods do not mean that there will not be any high-quality goods available for sale. Rather, it means that there will be a thin market of high-quality goods for sale. A **thin market** refers to a market in which the quantity of high-quality goods sold is less than what it would be in a market in which the buyer and seller have the same information. So in a thin market, consumers will be forced to shop extensively to find the smaller quantity of high-quality goods being sold because of the low prices.

adverse-selection problem: a situation in which consumers are forced to choose from an undesirable group of goods

thin market: a market in which the quantity of high-quality goods sold is less than what it would be in a market in which the buyer and seller have the same information

The adverse-selection problem creates challenges for both the buyer and the seller. Low prices force the buyer to choose among undesirable goods, while seller earns less in profit. As a result, neither side of the market is satisfied. To correct this problem and close the gap between the higher prices the seller is seeking and the low prices the seller is actually receiving, the seller can provide guarantees to the buyer. In doing so, the seller can offer two types of guarantees, including money back and warranties, that would allow them to charge a higher price while also providing assurances to the buyer of the quality of the good. As such, money back guarantees would provide money back to the buyer should the buyer become dissatisfied with the purchase, while warranties provide promises to repair broken parts. Such guarantees give the buyer incentives to pay a price higher than their preference.

FIGURE 15.2 The Cycle of the Adverse-Selection Problem

SUMMARY

- "Asymmetric information" refers to a situation in which one side of the market has more or better information than the other side of the market. (LO 15.1)
- Asymmetric information creates high-quality goods and low-quality goods. (LO 15.1)
- A "lemon" refers to a product that is unsatisfactory, not of its true value, or is disappointing. (LO 15.1)
- The chances of buying a lemon leads consumers to forming either neutral or pessimistic expectations. (LO 15.1)
- The adverse-selection problem is a situation in which consumers are forced to choose from an undesirable group of goods. (LO 15.2)
- A thin market refers to a market in which the quantity of high-quality goods sold is less than what it would be in a market in which the buyer and seller have the same information. (LO 15.2)
- The seller can offer money back guarantees and warranties that allow them to charge a higher price while also providing assurances to the buyer of the quality of the good. (LO 15.2)

END-OF-CHAPTER APPLICATION

Comprehension Questions

Directions: Refer to the chapter to correctly respond to the following questions and prompts.

1. Define asymmetric information. Explain how this moves the economy away from equilibrium. (LO 15.1)
2. Define a lemon. Identify and explain the two types of expectations formed by consumers when they are faced with the chances of buying a lemon. State the price points formed by consumers based on their expectations. (LO 15.1)
3. Define the adverse-selection problem. Explain how the adverse-selection problem affect prices and the quality of goods. (LO 15.2)
4. Explain how the adverse-selection problem affects the quantity of high-quality goods on the market. (LO 15.2)
5. Explain the types of guarantees sellers can offer to close the gap between the higher prices the seller is seeking and the low prices the seller actually receives. (LO 15.2)

Case Scenario: An Analysis of Asymmetric Information

Directions: Use what you learned in the chapter to respond to the following scenario.

Dan is a dealer of rare diamonds. As a dealer, Dan sells diamonds of various qualities. Most of his customers are people who attend his workshops on diamond quality that he holds in many towns and cities throughout the country. During these workshops, Dan has noticed that most of the attendees have little knowledge about the diamond industry. Although Dan works hard to educate them, he finds his job to be very challenging at times. Answer the following questions:

1. Identify and explain the asymmetric information in this case.
2. If Dan charges $20,000 for a high-quality 1 carat diamond and $2,000 for a low-quality 1 carat diamond, determine the price attendees would be willing to pay with neutral expectations and the price they would be willing to pay with pessimistic expectations.
3. What would happen to the quality of diamonds Dan sells if the price attendees are willing to pay continues to fall? How would this affect the attendees who seek to make a purchase? Should Dan offer high-quality diamonds at the lower price? Explain.
4. What guarantees can Dan offer that would allow him to raise prices while also providing assurances to the attendees?

REFERENCES

Grammarist. (2022). Buy a lemon. https://grammarist.com/idiom/buy-a-lemon/

O'Sullivan, A., Shreffin, S., & Perez, S. (2017). Microeconomics: Principles, applications, and tools (9th ed.). Pearson Publishing.

Schiller, B. R. (2016). *The micro economy today* (14th ed.). McGraw-Hill Education.

CREDITS

CHAPTER 16

The Role of Financial Markets in the Economy

Concept Highlight

Chapter 16 examines the financial market.

Real Life Example: What Does This Mean to You?

The financial market provides a place for lenders and borrowers to engage in a transaction. An example of this would be a person going into a bank in search of a loan. In this context, economists seek to understand the factors that drive the borrower into seeking a loan as well as the factors that drive the lender into lending money.

Introduction

The financial market is an important concept to understand because it is critical in the movement of money from lenders to borrowers. However, there are many factors that affect the demand for money and the supply of money in this process. These factors, in turn, affect the demand for products and services.

OBJECTIVES

While reading this chapter, readers learn about

LO 16.1. financial market

LO 16.1. interest

LO 16.1. loanable funds theory

LO 16.1. demand for money

LO 16.1. supply of money

LO 16.2. interest rates

LO 16.3. types of interest rates

LO 16.3. inflation

LO 16.4. time value of money

LO 16.4. types of values associated with the time value of money

LO 16.4. discounting

LO 16.5. expected return

LO 16.5. cost of borrowing

LO 16.6. assets

LO 16.6. financial assets

LO 16.6. debt instrument

LO 16.6. bond

LO 16.6. principal

LO 16.6. maturity date

LO 16.6. coupon

LO 16.6. equity securities

LO 16.6. stock

LO 16.6. dividends

OUTCOMES

After completing this chapter, readers will be able to do the following:

- Define "financial market."
- Define "interest."
- Define "loanable funds theory."
- Explain and illustrate the relationship between interest, the demand for money, and the supply of money.
- Define "interest rate."
- Explain and illustrate the relationship between an interest rate and the demand for money.
- Define "nominal interest rate."
- Define "real interest rate."
- Calculate the real interest rate, and explain the meaning of the resulting number.
- Define "time value of money."
- Explain the two types of values associated with the time value of money.
- Define "discounting," and use the formula to determine the future value of money.
- Define and calculate "expected return."
- Explain and illustrate the relationship between expected return and the demand for money.
- Calculate the cost of borrowing.
- Explain and illustrate the relationship between the cost of borrowing and the demand for money.
- Define "asset."
- Define "financial asset."
- Define "debt instrument."
- Define "bond."
- Define "principal."
- Define "maturity date."
- Define "coupon."
- Define "equity securities."
- Define "stock."
- Define "dividends."

Key Terms in This Chapter

The following key terms are discussed in this chapter:

- financial market interest
- loanable funds theory
- demand for money (DFM)
- supply of money (SOM)
- interest rate
- nominal interest rate
- real interest rate inflation
- time value of money
- present value
- future value
- discounting
- expected return (ER)
- cost of borrowing
- asset
- financial asset
- debt instrument
- bond
- debt capital
- principal
- maturity date
- coupon equity securities
- stock
- equity capital
- dividend

16.1 What Is a Financial Market?

Demand for products and services are based on income earned by consumers or money borrowed by them. The borrowing of money is depended on financial markets. A **financial market** is a place that allows for the movement of funds from savers to borrowers. Financial markets exist for the purpose of providing a place for borrowing and lending.

Financial markets consist primarily of banks that provide lending to individuals and businesses. In exchange for borrowing money on this market, banks charge interest to these borrowers. **Interest** is defined the charge for borrowing money. Another way of saying this is that interest is the price that borrowers pay for borrowing money. As such, the interest that banks charge for borrowing is based on the loanable funds theory. The **loanable funds theory** is the belief that the interest charged by banks (and other lenders) is based on the demand for and the supply of money. The **demand for money** (DFM) refers the amount of money borrowers are willing to get and hold onto for the purpose of spending. By comparison, the **supply of money** (SOM) refers to the amount of money banks (and

financial market: a place that allows for the movement of funds from savers to borrowers

interest: the charge for borrowing money; the price borrowers pay for borrowing money

loanable funds theory: the belief that the interest charged by banks (and other lenders) is based on the demand for and supply of money demand for money: the amount of money borrowers are willing to get and hold onto for the purpose of spending

supply of money: the amount of money banks (and other lenders) are willing to lend

other lenders) are willing to lend. Therefore, banks will charge higher interest if the DFM is greater than the SOM and lower interest if the DFM is less than the SOM. Table 16.1 provides a chart depicting the relationship between the DFM, SOM, and interest.

TABLE 16.1 The Relationship Between the Demand for Money, Supply of Money, and Interest

demand for money vs. supply of money	interest
demand for money > supply of money	increases
demand for money < supply of money	decreases

Table16.1 shows that the interest that banks charge for lending is based on the relationship between the DFM and the SOM. Within this relationship, the DFM is driven by the desire of individuals and businesses needing to make purchases, while the SOM is driven by the banks' willingness to lend. So there will be an increase in the DFM if there is an increase in the demand for goods, which will put pressure on the SOM. In doing so, this increase will cause a right shift of the DFM curve. Likewise, there will be a decrease in the DFM if there is a decrease in the demand for goods, which will ease pressure on the SOM. As a result, there will be a left shift of the DFM curve. Figure 16.1 depicts the relationship between the demand for goods, the DFM, and the SOM.

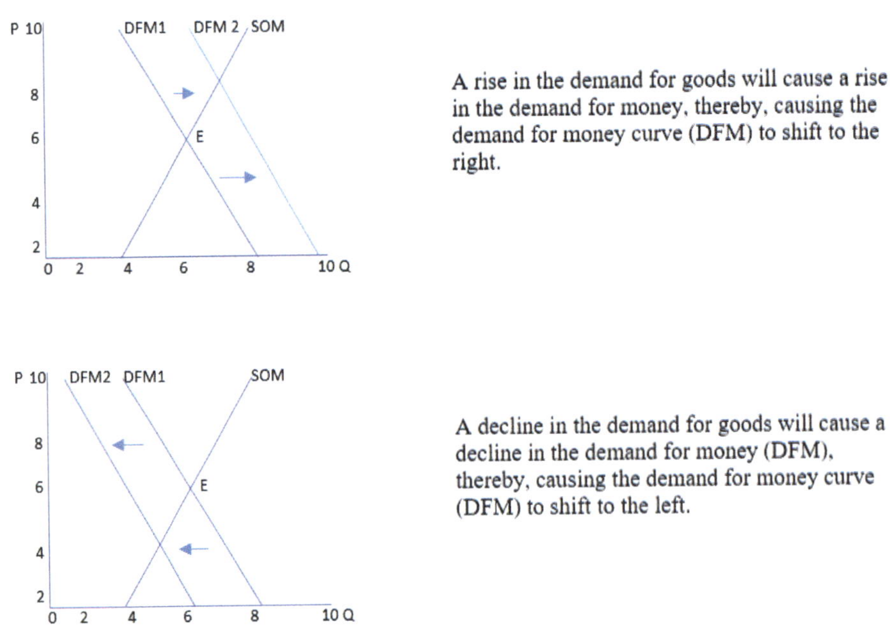

FIGURE 16.1 The Relationship Between the Demand for Goods, Demand for Money, and Supply of Money

16.2 How Changes in Interest Rates Affect the Demand for Money

Banks charge interest in exchange for borrowing money. The interest charged is the price that the borrower pays for borrowing. This interest is expressed as a percentage of the overall amount of money borrowed. This percentage is called the **interest rate**. An example of this would be a bank lending $100 to a borrower and, in return, charging 4% interest. This 4%, which is $4 ($100 x .04), represents the interest rate. Now, the interest rate that banks charge for borrowing affects the amount of borrowing and, thereby, affects the DFM. Therefore, a rise in the interest rates charged by banks will cause a decline in borrowing because it is expensive to do so. This will cause a decline in the quantity demanded for money because spending declines. As a result, there will be upward movement along the DFM curve, which indicates a decrease in the quantity demanded for money. However, a decline in the interest rates charged by banks will cause a rise in borrowing because it is cheaper to do so. This, in turn, will cause a rise in the quantity demanded for money due to there being an increase in spending. Therefore, there will be downward movement along the DFM curve, which indicates an increase in the quantity DFM. Figure 16.2 shows the effect of changing interest rates (*i*) on the quantity DFM.

interest rate: a percentage of the overall amount of money borrowed

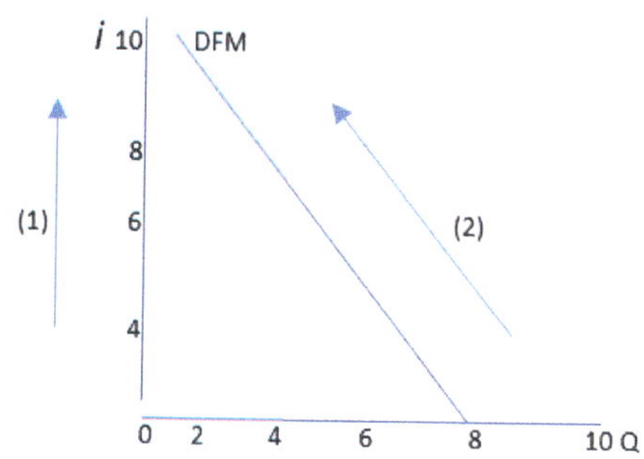

A rise in interest rates (*i*) causes upward movement along the demand for money curve (DFM) as the demand for goods decline.

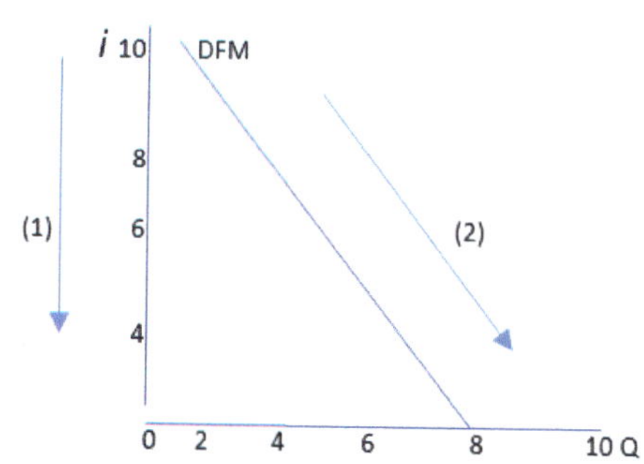

A decline in interest rates (*i*) causes downward movement along the demand for money curve (DFM) as the demand for goods rise.

FIGURE 16.2 The Effect of Changing Interest Rates on the Quantity Demanded for Money

16.3 Types of Interest Rates

The financial market consists of both the nominal interest rates and real interest rates. The **nominal interest rate** refers to the interest rate banks charge for borrowing. Therefore, this rate represents what is offered in the market. By comparison, the **real interest rate** is the interest rate determined when future inflation is not expected. **Inflation** refers to rises in prices. Because this is the case, the real interest rate is adjusted for inflation. In making this adjustment, the nominal rate doesn't include inflation, while the real interest rate includes inflation. By including inflation, investors (borrowers and lenders) use the real interest rate to determine if they are better or worse off borrowing or lending money today. To determine this, investors use the following formula for determining the real interest rate:

real interest rate = nominal interest rate - expected (future) inflation

nominal interest rate: the interest rate that the banks charge for borrowing

real interest rate: the interest rate determined when future inflation is not expected

inflation: rises in prices

An example of nominal and real interest rates would be a bank lending $100 to a borrower and charging 4% with repayment in 1 year. The 4% represents the nominal interest rate because this is what the bank is charging for borrowing. Now, suppose that current inflation is 3%. In this example, the real interest rate is 1% (4% – 3%). This means that although the borrower is paying the bank $4 in interest in one year, due to rises in prices of 3%, this money will only spend like $1. Therefore, the bank loses 3% in buying power.

Suppose inflation rises to 6% before the borrower spends the money. Now, the real interest rate is –2% (4% – 6%). This means that although the borrower borrowed $100, the price increase will cause it to spend like $98. Therefore, the borrower loses 2% in buying power.

By examining the nominal and real interest rates, one can begin to understand their effect on the DFM. In other words, the nominal interest rate provides an investor a picture of the current state of financial market, (i.e., borrowing and lending). However, the real interest rate provides an investor with insight into their buying power based on inflation.

16.4 Time Value of Money

The financial market consists of a number of different lenders. The primary lender on this market is banks. However, individuals and businesses also lend. All three lenders are known as "investors" because they are seeking to earn profit from the money loaned through charging interest. As such, these investors charge interest for two reasons. The first reason for charging interest is to earn profit. The second is to cover, at least in part, the loss of buying power over time due to inflation. Understanding this, these investors utilize the time value of money in their lending policies.

The **time value of money** is defined as a process of earning interest on an investment. Because of this, the time value of money includes present and future value. **The present value** refers the value of money at the time it is invested. As such, present value represents the money that is loaned. In contrast, the **future**

value refers to the value of money at some specific point in the future. Future value consists of the amount loaned in addition to the interest earned. An example of this would be a college student who has saved $1,000 from a part-time job. The student decides to deposit the money into a certificate of deposit (CD) that pays 2% annually. In this example, the student's present value is represented by the $1,000 deposit. On the 1-year anniversary date of the deposit, the student's future value will be represented by $1,020 ($1,000 × .02).

One's decision to invest in the financial market through lending is dependent on understanding the difference between the present value of money and the future value of money. Within this analysis, the investor must recognize that the present value of money worths more than the future value of money because of inflation. Therefore, to understand how much less money will be worth in the future compared to the present, one must engage in discounting. **Discounting** is the process of determining the future value of money by dividing it by the interest. In order words, discounting reduces the future value of money based on the belief that the interest paid has current inflation built into it, at least in part. Therefore, the formula for discounting is as follows:

future payment / (1 + interest)

Using the previous example of the college student who saved $1,000 from a part-time job, the student deposits the money into a CD that pays 2% annually. The student seeks to understand the future value of the money deposited. Using discounting, the student determines that in one year, $1,000 will only be worth $980.39 ($1,000 / 1.02). If the student decides to keep the money in the account for 2 years, the $1,000 will only be worth $961.17 {$1,000 / (1.02)2}. Realizing this, the longer the student waits to receive their money back, the less present value the money has.

time value of money: the process of earning interest on an investment

present value: the value of money at the time that it is invested

future value: the value of money at some specific point in the future

discounting: the process of determining the future value of money by dividing it by the interest

Finding the difference between the present value and future value of money requires examining the interest being paid. In theory, the higher the interest paid on the investment, the greater the decline in the value of the future payment, due to the increase in inflation. Using the previous example, suppose that the bank increases the interest paid to the college student's $1,000 deposit from 2% to 3% annually. This means that at the new rate, in one year, the $1,000 will only be worth $970.87 ($1,000 / 1.03).

16.5 Demand for Loanable Funds

The financial market consists of a number of borrowers. In fact, those parties who lend (banks, businesses, and individuals) also borrow money because they have a demand for loanable funds. This "demand for loanable funds" (DFM) is driven by the fact that banks and businesses will use the borrowed funds to generate profit from the sale of products and services. However, the amount of money that they borrow are dependent on two factors: expected return and the cost of borrowing. **Expected return** (ER) is defined the profits that are expected to be earned from an investment. Because of this, expected return is also known as the **rate of return** (RoR). An example of ER involves a manufacturer borrowing money to create a new product that has a 50% chance of generating a profit of 30% and a 50% chance of losing 20%. Expected return in this example is as follows:

$$\text{expected return} = (.50 \times .30 + .50 \times -.20)$$

$$\text{expected return} = .15 + -.10$$

$$\text{expected return} = 5\%$$

The ER and DFM move in the same direction. In other words, rise in the expected return will cause an increase in the DFM because the investor expects to earn greater profit. By comparison, a decline in the expected return will cause a decline in the DFM because the investor expects to earn less profit. As a result, a change in expected return will cause the DFM curve to shift either to the right or to the left. Figure 16.3 provides an example of this relationship.

Cost of borrowing refers to the interest and other fees charged for borrowing. As such, it represents what the lender charges for the use of the money being loaned. Because of this, the cost of borrowing is also referred to as **finance charges**. An example of would be a person borrowing $3,000 with an interest rate of 5% for a period of one year. In this example, the borrower would pay $150 in interest ($3,000 x .05) along with the amount borrowed. In doing so, $150 represents the cost of borrowing.

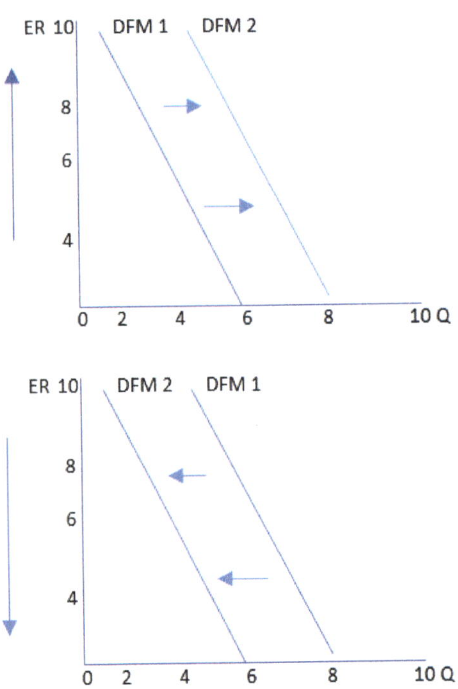

A rise in expected return causes an increase in the demand for money as the demand for money curve (DFM) shifts to the right.

A decline in expected return causes a decline in the demand for money as the demand for money curve (DFM) shifts to the left.

FIGURE 16.3 The Relationship Between Expected Return and the Demand for Money

The cost of borrowing and the DFM move in opposite direction. This means a rise in the cost of borrowing will cause a decline in the DFM because it's more expensive to borrow, while a decline in the cost of borrowing will cause a rise in the DFM because it's less expensive to borrow. As such, a change in the cost of borrowing will cause upward or downward movement along the DFM curve. Figure 16.4 depicts this relationship.

expected return: the profits expected to be earned from an investment

rate of return: see expected return

cost of borrowing: the interest and other fees charged for borrowing

finance charges: see cost of borrowing

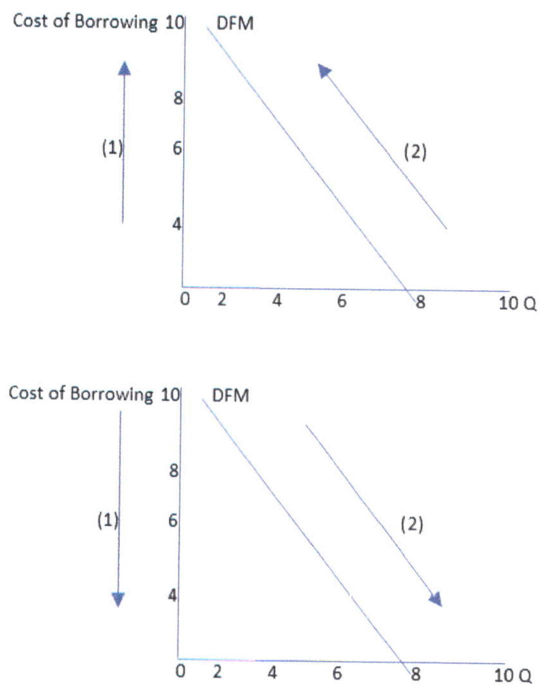

A rise in the cost of borrowing causes upward movement along the demand for money (DFM) curve as the demand for goods declines.

A decline in the cost of borrowing causes downward movement along the demand for money (DFM) curve as the demand for goods rises.

FIGURE 16.4 The Relationship Between the Cost of Borrowing and the Demand for Money

16.6 Types of Financial Securities Offered on the Financial Market

The financial market consists of assets. An **asset** is simply defined as something of value. Examples of assets include land, buildings, and equipment. But there are also financial assets. **Financial assets** are assets in the form of debt instruments and equity securities. A **debt instrument** refers to something that produces debt. A common example of a debt instrument is a bond. A **bond** is a certificate of indebtedness. In other words, when an investor buys a bond, they lends money to either a business or the government, who, in turn, promises to repay the money plus interest. As such, a bond is also called **debt capital** because the business or the government is going into debt to acquire money.

The investor who buys a bond is called the "bondholder," while the business or government who sells the bond is called the "bond issuer." Within this transaction, the bond issuer promises to repay the money borrowed (**principal**) on the day in which payment is due (**maturity date**). Before the maturity date, the bond issuer promises to make interest payments throughout the life of the bond. An interest payment is called a **coupon**. The coupon is paid monthly, quarterly, semi-annually, or annually and represents the profit earned by the bondholder. An example would be an investor buying a $100 bond that offers a coupon of 4% annually and matures in 1 year. In this example, on the maturity date (1 year), the investor will receive $104.

Investors are attracted to bonds based on the coupons offered, which represent the profits earned. This attraction consists of the coupon and the demand for the bond—hence, the DFM—moving in the same direction. Therefore, an increase in the coupon offered on a bond will cause an increase in the DFM due to a rise in the demand for the bond, since the investor will earn more profit. However, a decline in the coupon offered on a bond will cause a decline in the DFM due to a decline in the demand for the bond, since the investor will earn less profit. Figure 16.6 depicts the relationship between bond coupon offerings (profits) and the DFM.

Equity securities refer to securities that provide ownership. The most common example of equity securities are stocks. A **stock** is a certificate of ownership. In other words, when an investor buys a stock, the investor gives money to a corporation, which, in turn, makes the investor a part

asset: something of value

financial assets: assets in the form of debt instruments and equity securities

debt instrument: something that produces debt

bond: certificate of indebtedness

debt capital: the process of acquiring money by going into debt

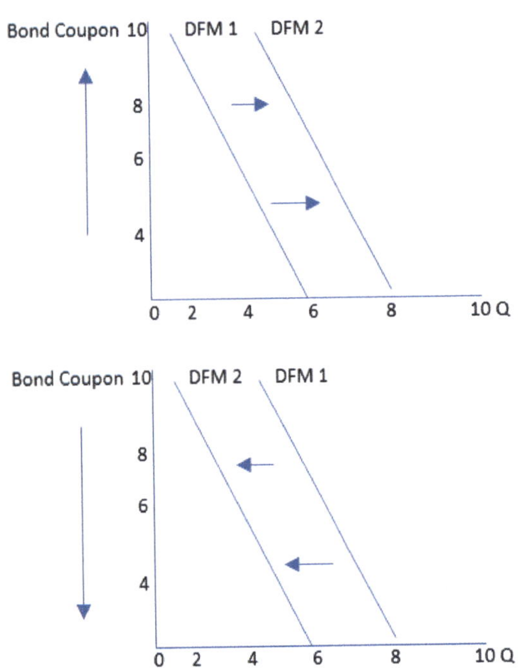

A rise in bond coupon offerings cause an increase in the demand for money as the demand for money curve (DFM) shifts to the right.

A decline in bond coupon offerings cause a decline in the demand for money as the demand for money curve (DFM) shifts to the left.

FIGURE 16.5 Examples of the Relationship Between Bond Coupon Offerings (Profits) and the Demand for Money

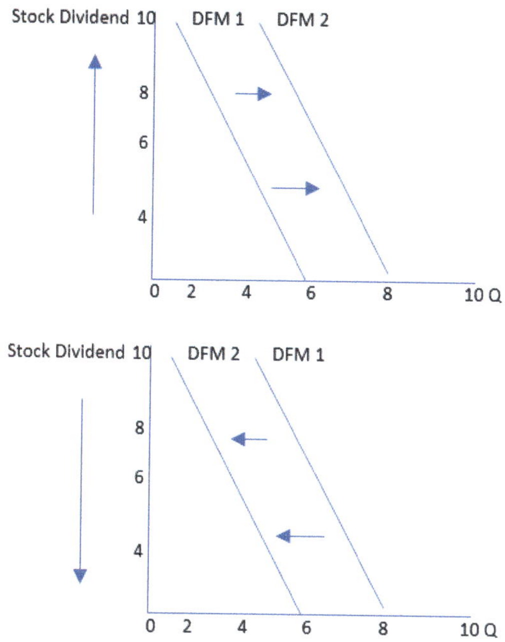

A rise in stock dividend payments cause an increase in the demand for money as the demand for money curve (DFM) shifts to the right.

A decline in stock dividend payments cause a decline in the demand for money as the demand for money curve (DFM) shifts to the left.

FIGURE 16.6 The Relationship Between Stock Dividend Payments (Profits) and the Demand for Money

owner. As such, a stock is also called **equity capital** because the corporation is acquiring money from the owner.

The investor who buys a stock is called the "stockholder," while the corporation that sells the stock is called the "stock issuer." Within this transaction, the stockholder becomes part owner and receives a share of the corporation's profits. The share of profits is called **dividends**. These dividends are paid monthly, quarterly, semi-annually, or annually.

Like bonds, investors are attracted to stocks based on the dividends paid, as this represents the profits earned. This attraction consists of the dividends and the demand for the stock—hence, the DFM—moving in the same direction. Therefore, an increase in the dividends paid on a stock will cause an increase in the DFM due to a rise in the demand for the stock, since the investor will earn more profit. However, a decline in the dividends paid on a stock will cause a decline in the DFM due to a decline in the demand for the stock, since the investor will earn less profit. Figure 16.6 shows relationship between stock dividend payments (profits) and the DFM.

principal: the money loaned

maturity date: the date at which the loan repayment is due

coupon: the interest paid on a bond

equity securities: securities that provide ownership

stock: certificate of ownership

equity capital: the process of acquiring money from its owners

dividends: profits

SUMMARY

- A financial market is a place that allows for the movement of funds from savers to borrowers. (LO 16.1)
- In exchange for borrowing money on this market, banks charge interest to borrowers. (LO 16.1)
- The interest banks charge for borrowing is based on the loanable funds theory. (LO 16.1)
- "Loanable funds theory" is the belief that the interest charged by banks (and other lenders) is based on the demand for and the supply of money. (LO 16.1)
- This interest rate is the percentage charged based on the overall amount of money borrowed. (LO 16.2)
- The financial market consists of both the nominal interest rates and real interest rates. (LO 16.3)
- "Inflation" refers to rises in prices. (LO 16.3)
- The "time value" of money is defined as a process of earning interest on an investment. (LO 16.4)
- The time value of money includes present and future value. (LO 16.4)
- "Discounting" is the process of determining the future value of money by dividing it by the interest. (LO 16.4)
- "Expected return" (ER) is defined as the profits expected to be earned from an investment; also known as the rate of return (RoR). (LO 16.5)
- "Cost of borrowing" refers to the interest and other fees charged for borrowing; also known as "finance charges." (LO 16.5)
- An "asset" is something of value. (LO 16.6)
- "Financial assets" are assets in the form of debt instruments and equity securities. (LO 16.6)
- A "bond" is a certificate of indebtedness. (LO 16.6)
- A "stock" is a certificate of ownership. (LO 16.6)

END-OF-CHAPTER APPLICATION

Comprehension Questions

Directions: Refer to the chapter to correctly respond to the following questions and prompts.

1. Define "loanable funds theory." Explain and illustrate the relationship between the demand for money and the supply of money in determining interest. (LO 16.1)

2. Define "interest rate." Explain and illustrate the relationship between the interest rate and the demand for money. (LO 16.2)
3. Bob, an owner of a construction company, received a bank loan with an interest rate of 2.5% annually. Suppose inflation is currently at 2%. Calculate the real interest rate. Suppose inflation is expected to rise to 4%. Calculate the real interest rate. Explain what the numbers mean. (LO 16.3)
4. Karen invests $200 in a bank CD that pays 1.5% annually. Calculate the future value of her money. Explain what the resulting value means in relation to her investment. (LO 16.4)
5. Explain and illustrate how expected return affects the demand for money. Explain and illustrate how the cost of borrowing affects the demand for money. (LO 16.5)
6. Define "financial assets." Explain why a bond is known as "debt capital." Explain why a stock is known as "equity capital." (LO 16.6)

Case Scenario: Analyzing the Possibilities of a Bank Closure During the Recession of 2008 on the Demand for Money

Directions: Use what you learned in the chapter to respond to the following scenario.

During the recession of 2008, Wells Fargo received $25 billion loan from the U.S. government under the "too-big-to fail" policy. This policy was adopted by the federal government during this period based on the belief that the failure of large financial institutions would create serious economic repercussions. In this context, answer the following questions:

1. How would the closure of Well Fargo affect the relationship between the demand for money and the supply of money? Illustrate this effect.
2. How would the closure of Wells Fargo affect the relationship between interest rates and the demand for money? Illustrate this effect.
3. Suppose Wells Fargo provides lending at very low interest to a business customer on a regular basis. If Wells Fargo then increased the interest rates charged to all borrowing customers to repay the government for the money it borrowed during the recession, how would the increased interest rates affect the future value of the funds received by Wells Fargo? How would the increased interest rates affect the bank's expected returns? How would the increased interest rates affect the cost of borrowing for borrowers?
4. Suppose Wells Fargo decided to sell bonds and stocks to acquire funds to repay the bailout loans. What factors would investors use in their decision to the purchase of the bond? What factors would investors use in their decision to purchase the stock?

BIBLIOGRAPHY

Attkisson, S. (2009, February 9). Following the bailout money to Wells Fargo. *CBS News online.* https://www.cbsnews.com/news/following-the-bailout-money-to-wells-fargo/

Chen, J. (2021). *What is expected return?* Investopedia. https://www.investopedia.com/terms/e/expectedreturn.asp

GSMR online. (2022). *The cost of borrowing.* https://gsmr.org/financial-tips/the-cost-of-borrowing

O'Sullivan, A., Shreffin, S., & Perez, S. (2017). *Microeconomics: Principles, applications, and tools* (9th ed.). Pearson Publishing.

Schiller, B. R. (2016). *The micro economy today* (14th ed.). McGraw-Hill Education.

Wex Definitions Team. (2021). *Too big to fail.* Cornell Law School. https://www.law.cornell.edu/wex/too_big_to_fail

CREDITS

Part VI
Labor and International Trade

CHAPTER 17

The Labor Market Environment

Concept Highlight

Chapter 17 examines the labor market.

Real Life Example: What Does This Mean to You?

The labor market is critical to provide a place for both the demand for and supply of labor. An example of this market includes a manufacturer seeking to hire additional workers. In this example, economists seek to understand how wages affect the demand for and supply of labor. Within this context, economists also seek to understand how wages affect workers' decision to supply labor and seek greater leisure.

Introduction

The labor market is an important concept to understand because it explains the demand that businesses have for labor as well as the willingness of workers to supply their labor. Within this explanation, this concept identifies the factors that affect both the business' hiring decisions and workers' labor decisions.

OBJECTIVES

While reading this chapter, readers should be able to

LO 17.1. labor market

LO 17.1. demand for labor

LO 17.1. supply of labor

LO 17.2. wage

LO 17.2. derived demand

LO 17.2. marginal physical product

LO 17.2. marginal revenue product

LO 17.3. substitution of higher wages effect

LO 17.3. income effect of higher wages

LO 17.4. equilibrium wage

OUTCOMES

After completing this chapter, readers will be able to do the following:

- Define "the labor market."
- Define "the demand for labor," and explain and illustrate the relationship between price and the demand for labor on a demand for labor curve.
- Define "the supply of labor," and explain and illustrate the relationship between the price and the supply of labor on a supply of labor curve.
- Define "wage."
- Explain the relationship between a business's hiring decision and the marginal principle.
- Explain the relationship between a business's hiring decision in the short run and the principle of diminishing returns.
- Illustrate a business's hiring decision in the short run on a total product curve and the marginal product of labor.

- Explain why diminishing returns do not occur in the long run as it pertains to a business's hiring decision.
- Define "derived demand."
- Define "marginal physical product," and then calculate it.
- Define "marginal revenue product," and then calculate it.
- Explain the relationship between the supply of labor and the principle of opportunity cost.
- Explain the substitution effect of higher wages.
- Explain the income effect of higher wages.
- Explain why the labor market is efficient at the equilibrium wage.

Key Terms in This Chapter

The following key terms are discussed in this chapter:

- labor market
- demand for labor (DFL)
- demand for labor curve
- law of demand
- supply of labor (SOL)
- supply of labor curve
- law of supply
- wage
- marginal principle
- short run
- principle of diminishing returns
- total product curve
- marginal product of labor
- long run
- derived demand
- marginal physical product
- marginal revenue product
- principle of opportunity cost
- substitution effect of higher wages
- income effect of higher wages
- equilibrium wage
- excess supply
- excess demand

17.1 What is the Labor Market?

Businesses produce in response to demand. In this response, businesses need facilities, equipment, labor, and raw materials. As such, labor is acquired through the labor market. The **labor market** is defined as a market that consists of the demand for labor and the supply of labor. In other words, the labor market provides a place for businesses to hire labor. The **demand for labor** (DFL) refers to the amount of labor

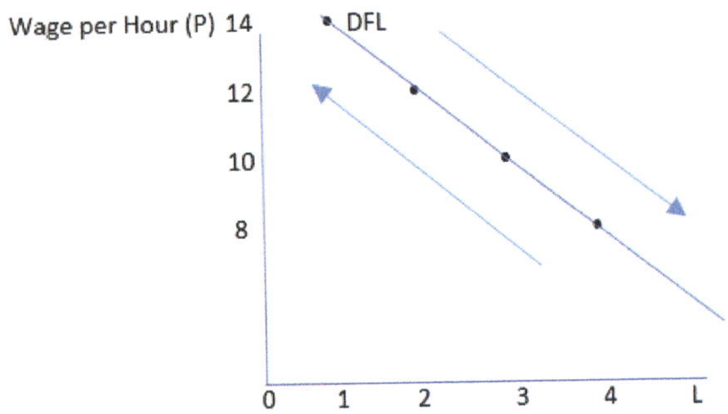

The demand for labor curve (DFL) shows the relationship between wage per hour (P) and the number of workers hired (L).

FIGURE 17.1 A Demand for Labor Curve

that businesses are willing to hire at various prices, ceteris paribus. This definition implies businesses are buying labor based on the various prices labor is willing to accept. As such, the relationship between price and the number of workers businesses hire can be seen on a demand for labor curve. A **demand for labor curve** shows the relationship between price and the number of workers a business is willing to hire at various prices, ceteris paribus. An example of a DFL curve includes a pizza shop owner seeking to hire labor at various wage prices. In this example, Figure 17.1 shows the relationship between the wage prices (P) and the number of workers hired (L).

In this example, the DFL curve is both negatively sloped and upward sloped because of the law of demand. The **law of demand** is the belief that as price rises, the number of a product consumers buy declines. Pertaining to the labor market, the law of demand assumes that as price rises, businesses will hire fewer workers due to it becoming more expensive, and as price falls, businesses will hire additional workers because it becomes less expensive. Because of this, demand for workers *moves up (hiring less)* and *down (hiring more)* along the demand curve (the demand curve remains stationary). Figure 17.1 shows this movement.

The **supply of labor** refers the amount labor individuals are willing to supply at a given price, *ceteris paribus*. This definition implies workers are selling their labor based on a given price they are willing to accept. As such, the relationship between price and the number of workers willing to hire their labor can be seen on a supply for labor curve. A **supply of labor curve** shows the relationship between price and the amount of labor individuals are willing to supply at

labor market: a market that consists of the demand for labor and the supply of labor

demand for labor: the amount of labor businesses are willing to hire at various prices, ceteris paribus

demand for labor curve: a curve that shows the relationship between price and the number of workers a business is willing to hire at various prices, ceteris paribus

law of demand: the belief that as price rises, the amount of a particular product consumers buy declines

supply of labor: the amount labor that individuals are willing to supply at a given price, ceteris paribus

supply of labor curve: a curve that shows the relationship between price and the amount of labor that individuals are willing to supply at a given price, ceteris paribus

law of supply: the belief that as price rises, the amount of a particular product producers supply increases.

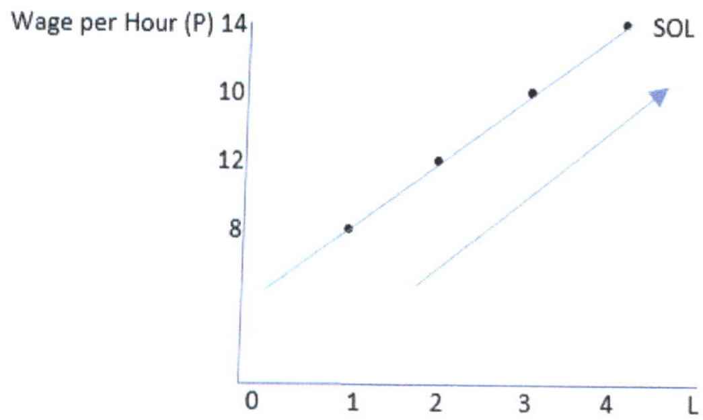

The supply of labor curve (SOL) shows the relationship between wage price (P) and the number of workers who are willing to work (L).

FIGURE 17.2 The Relationship Between the Wage Prices (P) and the Number of Workers Willing to Hire Their Labor (L)

a given price, ceteris paribus. An example of a SOL curve would be the number of people willing to work at a pizza shop based on the wages prices being offered. In this example, Figure 17.2 shows the relationship between the wage prices (P) and the number of workers willing to hire their labor (L).

In this example, the SOL curve is both positively sloped and upward sloped because of the law of supply. The **law of supply** is the belief that as price rises, the number of a particular product producers supply increases. Pertaining to the labor market, the law of supply assumes that as wage price rises, a greater number of workers will supply labor because they can earn more money, and if wage price falls, a fewer number of workers will supply labor because they will earn less money. Because of this, the SOL *moves up (greater number of workers)* and *down (fewer number of workers)* along the SOL curve (the SOL curve remains stationary). Figure 17.2 shows these movements.

17.2 The Demand for Labor

A business's DFL is determined by the wage requirement. A **wage** is defined as the amount of money paid and received for work. As such, wages represent the price that the business pays for labor services. Therefore, the number of workers that a business is willing to hire is dependent on the price (wage) each worker is willing to accept (shown in Figure 17.1). However, within this context, the business seeks to maximize profit. Therefore, the actual number of workers hired at a given price (wage) will occur at the level of production at which its marginal benefits equal its marginal costs. Understanding this, it can be said that a business's decision on the number of workers to hire at a given price is based on the marginal principle. The **marginal principle** is the belief that one should increase an activity if one's marginal benefits are greater than its marginal costs, decrease an activity if the marginal costs are greater than the marginal benefits, and choose the level of activity at which the marginal benefits equal the marginal costs.

Businesses produce in both the short run and the long run. Therefore, businesses will have a demand for labor in both the short run and the long run. The **short run** is defined as a period of time in which one or more factors or production remains fixed. It is also defined as a period of time in which a business can't build new facilities or modify existing ones. During this period, a business's decision on the number of workers to hire will be based on the principle of diminishing returns. The **principle of diminishing returns** is the belief that output will increase at a decreasing rate when one input increases while all other inputs remain at a constant rate. So during this period, businesses do not have the ability to change their resources (raw materials, facilities, equipment, etc.), and therefore, production increases become smaller with each level of output as additional workers are hired.

An example of this would be a pizza shop owner who has one employee. This employee can bake 12 pizzas. The pizza shop owner decides to hire a second employee with the hopes of increasing pizza production from 12 to 24 pizzas. However, total production between the two employees only increases to 18. In response, the pizza shop owner hires a third employee with the hopes of increasing pizza production to 24. Yet pizza production between the three employees only increases to 21. Table 17.1 shows the pizza production output as the number of workers increases. In addition, Table 17.1 shows the change in output for each additional worker.

TABLE 17.1 The Relationship Between Labor and Output

Number of employees	Pizza production (output)	Change in pizza production (output)
1	12	-
2	18	6
3	21	3

Figure 17.3 shows *an increase at a decreasing rate* in the last column, as pizza production changes from 12 to 8 to 3. We can see this change on a total product curve. A **total product curve** is a curve that shows the relationship between labor (L) and output (Y).

The total product curve also includes the marginal product of labor. The **marginal product of labor** refers to a curve that shows the change in output for each additional worker employed. In doing so, the marginal product of labor shows diminishing returns. In other words, the marginal product of labor shows *an increase at a decreasing rate*. Figure 17.4 shows an example of the marginal product of labor. Using the example provided, this illustration shows pizza output changing from 12 to 8 to 3.

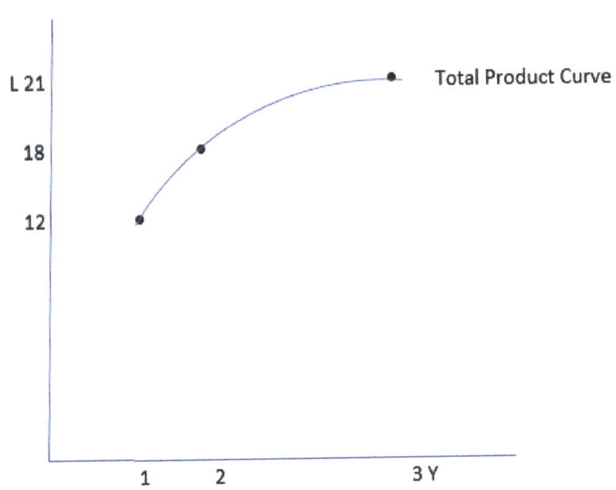

FIGURE 17.3 A Total Product Curve

So why do production increases become smaller with each level of output? This occurs because each resource becomes less efficient and, therefore, less productive. In the example provided, the pizza shop owner only hired workers while leaving all other resources (stove, ingredients, utensils, etc.) at their current level. This has caused each worker to have less space to work and, therefore, each worker became less efficient, as well as less productive. However, each worker would be just as efficient as the others if the pizza shop owner changed all other resources proportionally as he hired additional resources.

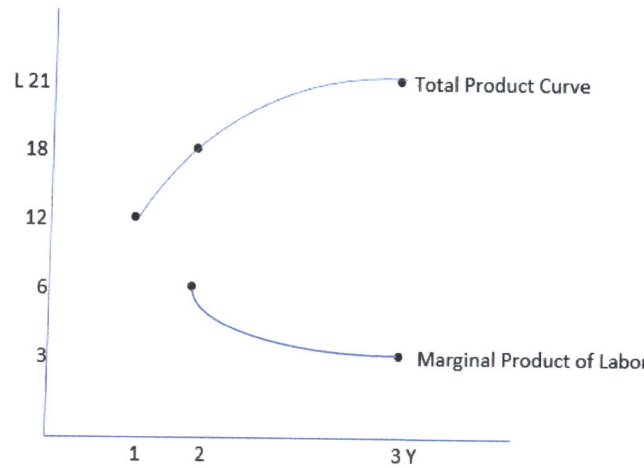

FIGURE 17.4 An Example of the Marginal Product of Labor

Diminishing returns do not occur in the long run. The **long run** is defined as a period of time in which the factors of production can be changed. It is also defined as a period of time in which businesses can build new facilities or modify existing ones. Therefore, during this period, diminishing returns do not occur because businesses are able to change their resources as they hire additional workers. As a result, the additional space created allows each worker to be productive.

During both the short run and the long run, a business will search for labor, equipment, raw materials, and other resources needed to produce. The number of resources purchased will depend on expected sales needed to maximize profits. Therefore, the business's demand for these resources, including labor, are recognized as derived demand. **Derived demand** refers to the demand for productive resources needed to produce that is, in turn, based on the demand for goods and services. Derived demand is based on the belief that an increase in the demand for goods and services will lead to an increase in the demand for productive resources, including labor. This, in turn, motivates businesses to hire more labor. However, using the concept of the marginal principle, the business will use rationality in its hiring decision. This means that in addition to hiring the number of workers at a given price (wage) needed to produce at a level of production where its marginal benefits equal its marginal costs, the business will also only hire more workers if those workers contribute to greater level of production. As a result, rationality ensures the business is hiring additional workers only if those workers lead to greater productivity. This can be measured by marginal physical product. **Marginal physical product** (MPP) shows the change in production for each additional input employed. As such, MPP can be determined using the following formula:

marginal physical product = change in production / change in labor

An example of MPP would be a machine shop owner hiring one worker, who produces 20 machine parts per hour. In this example, the MPP is 20 (20 / 1). If the machine shop owner hired a second worker, who, in turn, increased overall production to 50, the second worker created an MPP of 30. This number is found by taking the difference between total hourly machine parts produced by one worker (20) and the total hourly machine parts produced with two workers (50). Table 17.2 provides a diagram of this example.

TABLE 17.2 An Example of Marginal Physical Product

Labor	Production	Marginal physical product
1	20	20
2	50	30
3	75	25

As production increases due to a rise in labor, the business will seek to understand how the increase affects revenues earned. This can be measured by marginal revenue product. **Marginal revenue product** (MRP) measures the change in revenues for each additional input employed. The formula for determining MRP is as follows:

marginal revenue product = change in revenues / change in labor

Using the previous example of the machine shop, if one worker generates $48 per hour in producing 20 machine parts, the worker's MRP would be $48. If the second worker in combination with the first worker generates $88 per hour in producing a combine 50 machine parts, the MRP would be $40, which is the difference between the first work's change in total revenue and the combined revenues. Table 17.3 shows a table of this example.

TABLE 17.3 An Example of Marginal Revenue Product

Labor	Production	Marginal physical product	Total revenue	Marginal Revenue Product
1	20	20	48	48
2	50	30	88	40
3	75	25	120	32

wage: the amount of money paid and received for work

marginal principle: the belief that one should increase an activity if one's marginal benefits are greater than marginal costs, decrease an activity if the marginal costs are greater than the marginal benefits, and choose the level of activity at which the marginal benefits equal the marginal costs

short run: a period of time in which one or more factors or production remains fixed; a period of time in which a business can't build new facilities or modify existing ones.

principle of diminishing returns: the belief that output will increase at a decreasing rate when one input increases while all other inputs remain at a constant rate

total product curve: a curve that shows the relationship between labor (l) and output (Y)

marginal product of labor: a curve that shows the change in output for each additional worker employed

17.3 The Supply of Labor

The amount of labor workers are willing to supply is dependent on a number of factors including price (wage). All these factors represent the everything that labor is willing to give up in exchange for earning money. Because of this, it can be said that the supply of labor is based on the principle of opportunity cost. The **principle of opportunity cost** is the belief that for one to obtain something, something else must be given up in return. As such, this principle explains that everything has a cost, and therefore, one must make a sacrifice to acquire something else. This principle communicates the trade-offs associated with earning money. Those trade-offs include leisure. In other words, the greater the number of hours worked to earn money, the less leisure one has, which, in turn, makes leisure more valuable. However, as wages increase, labor will be willing to sacrifice greater leisure time (law of supply). This, in turn, creates the substitution effect of higher wages. The **substitution effect of higher wages** is the belief that labor will substitute leisure for work as wages increase. As a result, this creates upward movement along the supply of labor (SOL) curve. Figure 17.5 depicts this effect.

long run: a period of time in which the factors of production can be changed; a period of time in which businesses can build new facilities or modify existing ones.

derived demand: demand for productive resources needed to produce that is, in turn, based on the demand for goods and services

marginal physical product: shows the change in production for each additional input employed

marginal revenue product: measures the change in revenue for each additional input employed

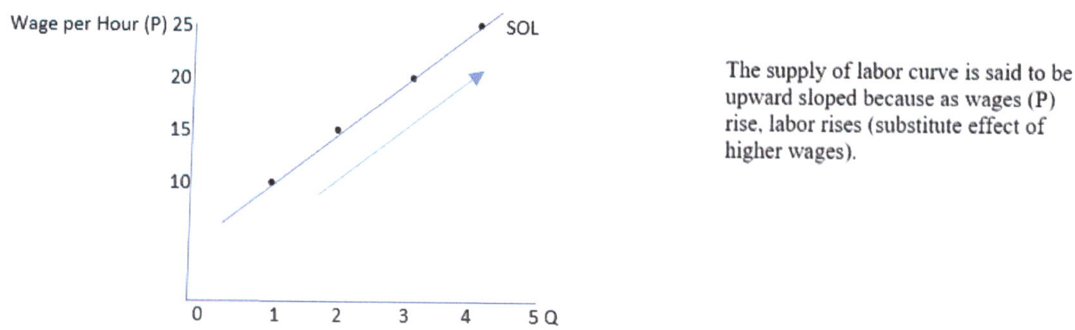

FIGURE 17.5 An Example of Upward Movement Along the Supply of Labor (SOL) Curve

However, as wages rise, labor will feel a greater desire for leisure. This creates the income effect of high wages. The **income effect of higher wages** is the belief that workers will seek greater leisure time without losing money as their income increases. In other words, a worker will seek to take more time away from work as their income increases because they can afford it. Along with this, other factors that affect the supply of labor includes tastes (enjoying work), expectations, prices of consumer goods, and taxes. Such factors will cause the supply of labor (SOL) curve to *shift right (increase)* or *left (decrease)*. Figure 17.6 shows the relationship between the factors other than wage (V) and the supply of labor (SOL).

principle of opportunity cost: the belief that for one to obtain something, something else must be given up in return

substitution effect of higher wages: the belief that labor will substitute leisure for work as wages increase

income effect of higher wages: the belief that workers will seek greater leisure time without losing money as their income increases

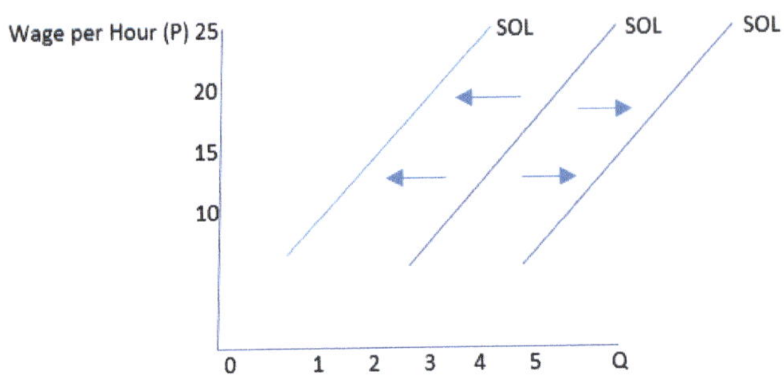

A right or left shift of the supply of labor (SOL) curve is caused by a change in factors other than wage (V).

FIGURE 17.6 An Example of the Relationship Between Factors Other Than Wage and the Supply of Labor Curve

17.4 Labor Market Equilibrium

The demand for labor and the supply of labor meet at the equilibrium wage; therefore, **equilibrium wage** refers to the wage point at which the quantity demanded for labor (QDFL) equals the quantity supplied of labor (QSOL). At this point, the labor market is said to be efficient. In other words, equilibrium wage creates the point at which the greatest number of businesses will be willing hire as well as the greatest number of workers will be willing to supply their labor. Figure 17.7 provides a picture of equilibrium wage.

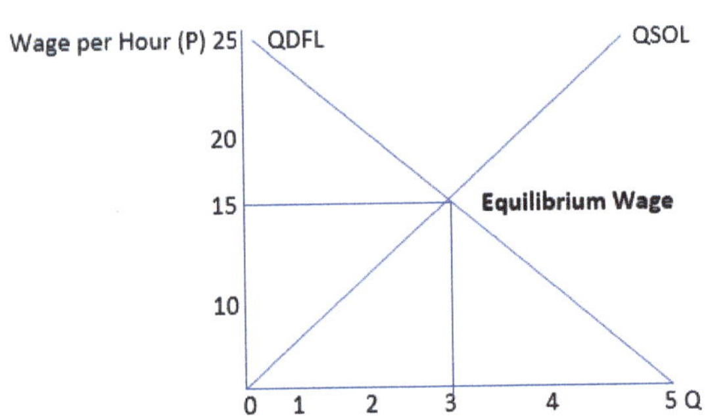

Equilibrium wage refers to the point where the quantity demanded for labor (QDFL) equals the quantity supplied of labor (QSOL).

FIGURE 17.7 Equilibrium Wage

How is it known that the greatest demand for labor and the greatest supply of labor will occur at the equilibrium wage? If wages rise above equilibrium wage, this will create excess supply. **Excess supply** is defined as a situation in which there will be greater supply than what consumers are willing to buy. Pertaining to the labor market, excess supply creates a labor surplus. This means there will be more workers supplying labor than businesses demanding labor. This, in turn, will cause upward movement along the demand curve. As a result, labor will not be earning the greatest profits. Figure 17.8 shows excess labor supply.

equilibrium wage: the wage point at which the quantity demanded for labor equals the quantity supplied of labor

excess supply: a situation in which there will be greater quantity supplied than what consumers are willing to buy

excess demand: a situation in which there will be a greater number of consumers willing to buy than the number of products that is available for sale

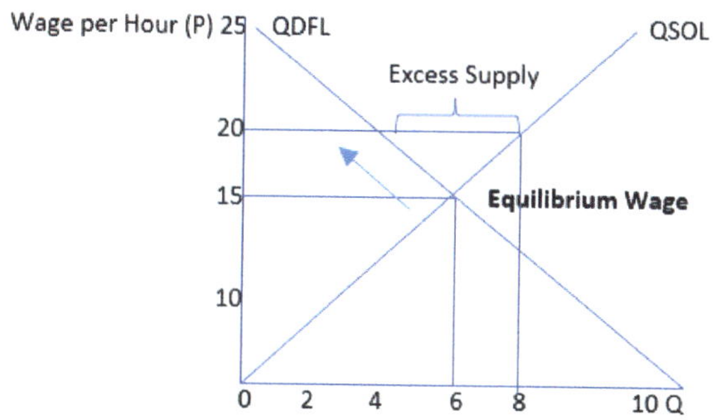

Excess labor supply occurs when wages rise above equilibrium wage.

FIGURE 17.8 Excess Labor Supply

If wages fall below equilibrium wage, this will create excess demand. **Excess demand** is defined as a situation in which there will be a greater number of consumers willing to buy than the number of products that is available for sale. Pertaining to the labor market, excess demand creates a labor shortage. This means not enough workers will be willing supply their labor. This, in turn, will cause downward movement along the supply curve. Figure 17.9 shows excess labor demand.

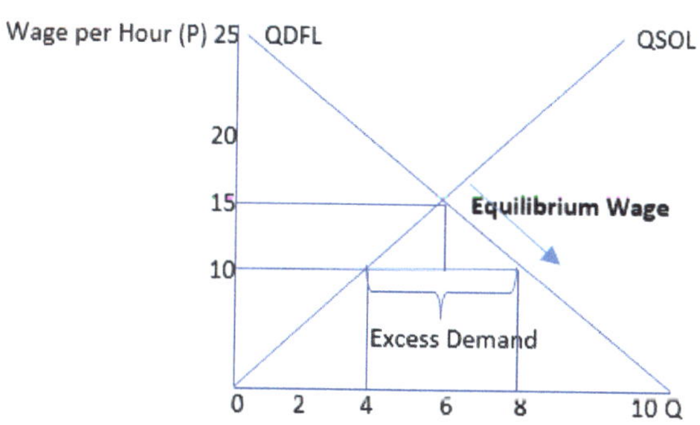

Excess labor demand occurs when wages fall below equilibrium wage.

FIGURE 17.9 Excess Labor Demand

SUMMARY

- The "labor market" is a market that consists of the demand for labor and the supply of labor. (LO 17.1)
- The relationship between price and the number of workers that businesses hire can be seen on a demand for labor curve. (LO 17.1)
- The relationship between price and the number of workers who are willing to sell their labor can be seen on a supply for labor curve. (LO 17.1)
- A "wage" is defined as the amount of money paid and received for work. (LO 17.2)

- A business's decision on the number of workers to hire at a given price is based on the marginal principle. (LO 17.2)
- During the short run, a business's decision on the number of workers to hire is based on the principle of diminishing returns. (LO 17.2)
- A "total product curve" is a curve that shows the relationship between labor (L) and output (Y). (LO 17.2)
- The "marginal product of labor" is a curve that shows the change in output for each additional worker employed. (LO 17.2)
- Diminishing returns do not occur in the long run because businesses are able to change their resources as they hire additional workers. (LO 17.2)
- "Derived demand" refers to the demand for productive resources needed to produce that is, in turn, based on the demand for goods and services. (LO 17.2)
- "Marginal physical product" shows the change in production for each additional input employed. (LO 17.2)
- "Marginal revenue product" (MRP) measures the change in revenues for each additional input employed. (LO 17.2)
- The supply of labor is based on the principle of opportunity cost. (LO 17.3)
- The "substitution effect of higher wages" is the belief that labor will substitute leisure for work as wages increase. (LO 17.3)
- The "income effect of higher wages" is the belief that workers will seek greater leisure time without losing money as their income increases. (LO 17.3)
- "Equilibrium wage" refers to the wage point at which the demand for labor equals the supply of labor. (LO 17.4)
- If wages rise above equilibrium wage, this will create excess supply. (LO 17.4)
- If wages fall below equilibrium wage, this will create excess demand. (LO 17.4)

END-OF-CHAPTER APPLICATION

Comprehension Questions

Directions: Refer to the chapter to correctly respond to the following questions and prompts.

1. Define the labor market. Explain the difference between the demand for labor and the supply of labor. Explain and illustrate how an increase in price (wage) affects the demand for labor and the supply of labor. (LO 17.1)

2. Use the marginal principle to explain how profit maximization affects a business's hiring decision. (LO 17.2)

3. Use the principle of diminishing returns to explain a business's hiring decision in the short run. Explain the effect of diminishing returns on a business' hiring decision in the long run. (LO 17.2)

4. Use Table 17.4 to determine marginal physical product for each worker. (LO 17.2)

TABLE 17.4

Labor	Production	Marginal physical product	Total revenues	Marginal revenue product
1	50		100	
2	85		150	
3	100		175	
4	110		185	

5. Use Table 17.4 to determine the marginal revenue product for each worker. (LO 17.2)

6. Explain the relationship between price (wage) and the principle of opportunity cost for labor. How does the substitution effect of higher wages affect workers' labor decision? How does the income effect of higher wages effect affect worker's labor decision? Explain. (LO 17.3)

7. Define "equilibrium wage." Explain why the labor market is said to be efficient at the equilibrium wage. Explain what would occur to the labor market if price (wage) rises above equilibrium wage. Explain what would occur to the labor market if price (wage) falls below equilibrium wage. (LO 17.4)

Case Scenario: An Analysis of U.S. Hiring Challenges in the Aftermath of COVID-19

Directions: Use what you learned in the chapter to respond to the following scenario.

According to PeopleReady (2022), U.S. businesses are faced with hiring challenges as the economy recovers from COVID-19. This source reports that the number of job openings in the country have increased to the highest level on record. This source also reports that these openings have been caused by factors such as retirements, lack of affordable childcare, greater unemployment benefits, and continuing fear of COVID-19. Among these factors, this source reports that businesses will be challenged with increased minimum wage in 24 states. Answer the following questions:

1. Explain how businesses could respond to their hiring challenges in this case.

2. Explain and illustrate the demand for labor curve and the supply of labor curve in this case.

3. Explain and illustrate how retirements, lack of affordable childcare, and greater unemployment benefits affect the demand for labor curve.

4. In theory, explain how an increase in minimum wage affects the demand for labor and the supply of labor in this case. Explain how the hiring challenges affect the demand for labor and the supply of labor as it relates to the increase in minimum wage.

BIBLIOGRAPHY

Dicitionary.com. (2022). Wages. In *Dictionary online.* https://www.dictionary.com/browse/wage

Marginal physical product. (2022). In *Amos Web Encylonomic Webpedia.* https://www.amosweb.com/cgi-bin/awb_nav.pl?s=wpd&c=dsp&k=marginal+physical+product

PeopleReady. (2022). *Minimum wage set to increase in many U.S. states for 2022.* https://www.peopleready.com/minimum-wage-set-to-increase-in-many-us-states-for-2022/

O'Sullivan, A., Shreffin, S., & Perez, S. (2017). *Microeconomics: Principles, applications, and tools* (9th ed.). Pearson Publishing.

Schiller, B. R. (2016). *The micro economy today* (14th ed.). McGraw-Hill Education.

CREDITS

International Trade

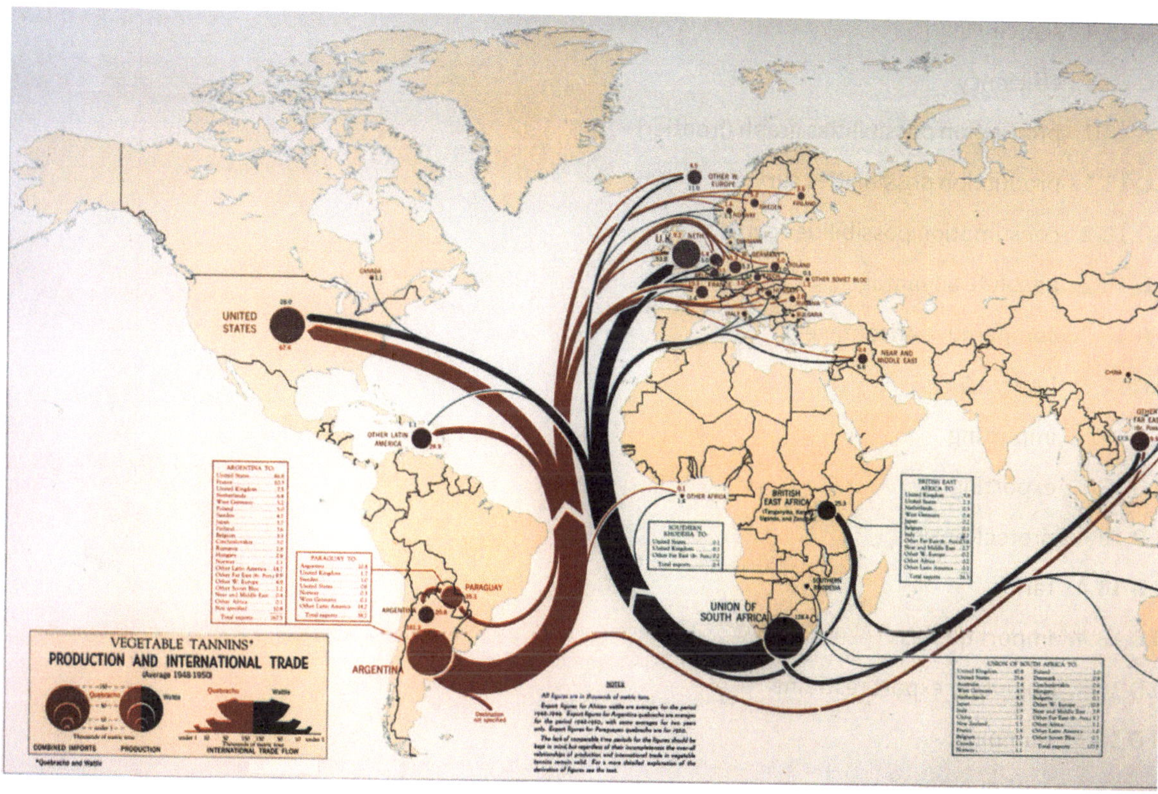

Concept Highlight

Chapter 18 examines the concept of international trade.

Real Life Example: What Does This Mean to You?

International trade is a requirement for nations seeking the resources that they need to have a productive society. An example of international trade is the United States trading with Canada and Mexico. Within such agreements, economists seek to understand the type of trade agreements created by the governments of each country as well as understanding how trade may make all involved nations better off. Furthermore, economists seek to understand how governments protect their countries from trade.

Introduction

Most nations believe in free trade. "Free trade" is an important concept to understand because it provides insight into goal of trading among nations. However, free trade affects employment within a country, which, in turn, affects income and national wealth.

OBJECTIVES

While reading this chapter, readers learn about

LO 18.1. scarcity

LO 18.1. efficiency

LO 18.1. production possibilities graph (frontier)

LO 18.1. production possibilities curve

LO 18.2. consumption possibilities curve

LO 18.2. absolute advantage

LO 18.2. comparative advantage

LO 18.3. free trade

LO 18.3. importing

LO 18.3. exporting

LO 18.4. protectionism

LO 18.4. tariffs

LO 18.4. import quotas

LO 18.4. voluntary export restraint

LO 18.4. dumping

LO 18.4. anti-dumping

OUTCOMES

After completing this chapter, readers will be able to do the following:

- Explain and illustrate a production possibilities graph (frontier).
- Explain and illustrate what the production possibilities curve indicates.
- Explain and illustrate how foreign competition affects domestic demand.
- Explain and illustrate how foreign competition affects the domestic demand for labor.
- Define free trade.

- Define and explain the goal of protectionism.
- Explain how tariffs affect foreign product prices and demand for domestic goods.
- Explain how import quotas affect foreign product prices and demand for domestic goods.
- Explain how voluntary export restraint affects foreign product prices and demand for domestic goods.
- Explain how anti-dumping laws affect foreign product prices and demand for domestic goods.

Key Terms in This Chapter

The following key terms are discussed in this chapter:

- scarcity
- efficiency
- production possibilities graph (frontier)
- production possibilities curve
- consumption possibilities curve
- absolute advantage
- comparative advantage
- free trade
- importing
- exporting
- protectionism
- tariffs
- import quotas
- voluntary export restraint
- dumping
- anti-dumping

18.1 A Review of Efficiency and the Production Possibilities Graph (Frontier)

A nation's economy consists of limited resources (**scarcity**) that are used to produce a variety of products and services to satisfy demand. In producing these products and services, the nation seeks to be efficient in the production process. **Efficiency** refers to having the ability to maximize resources in production. In other words, producing multiple products and services allows a nation to get the most out of its resources. As such, one tool that can help determine possible combinations of goods and service to produce is the production possibilities graph (frontier). As discussed in previous chapters, the **production possibilities graph (frontier**; PPG**)** is a graph that shows the possible combinations of goods and services produced based on the available resources. The production possibilities provide a picture of the different production combinations of goods and services which, in turn, allows people to make decisions on production levels. A review of an example used in chapter 1 allows for greater understanding of this concept. In this example, a nation is deciding on the level of production of agricultural and manufacturing goods to employ with its resources. From this analysis, Table 18.1 shows the nation's production decision for agricultural and manufacturing goods (in tons) based on the resources it possesses:

TABLE 18.1 Production Choices Based on Scarcity

Agricultural goods	Manufacturing goods
100	700
200	600
300	500
400	400
500	300
600	200
700	100

Figure 18.1 provides a listing of the nation's production capabilities in agricultural and manufacturing goods based on the resources it possesses. This shows the production of one good coming at the expense of producing the other good due to limited resources. In doing so, Figure 18.1 demonstrates the production possibilities graph (frontier), which provides a picture of the sacrifices incurred in production associated with limited resources.

Each point on this graph represents a production combination level. When the points are connected, it creates a production possibilities curve. A **production possibilities curve (PPC)** is a curve that shows the possible combinations of goods and services produced based on the available resources. This curve represents what is attainable and what is not attainable. Everything inside of the curve is attainable because the nation has the resources, while nothing outside of the curve is attainable because there are not enough resources. Therefore, the production possibilities curve establishes the boundary between what can be produced and what can't be produced.

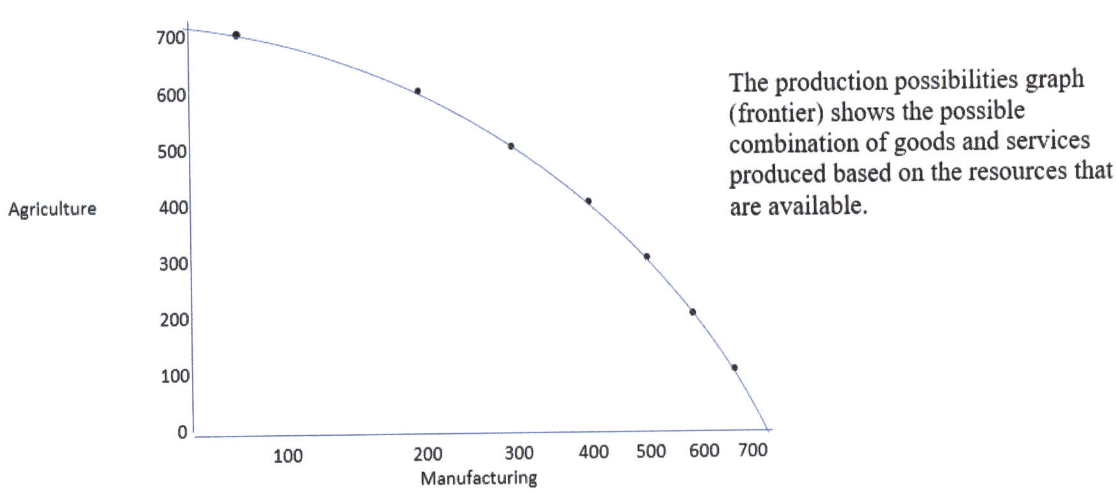

FIGURE 18.1 A Production Possibilities Graph (Frontier)

In Chapter 1, we discussed that the production possibilities curve isn't stationary. In fact, this curve can shift to the right or to the left. The curve will shift to the left if resources are not replaced as they are used. This shift represents a *decline in production*. However, the curve will shift to the right if resources are replaced as they are used. This shift represents an *increase in production*. Figures 18.2 and 18.3 provide an example of the shifts.

scarcity: a situation in which there are limited resources

efficiency: having the ability to maximize resources in production

production possibilities graph (frontier): a graph that shows the possible combinations of goods and services produced based on the available resources

production possibilities curve: a curve that shows the possible combinations of goods and services produced based on the resources available

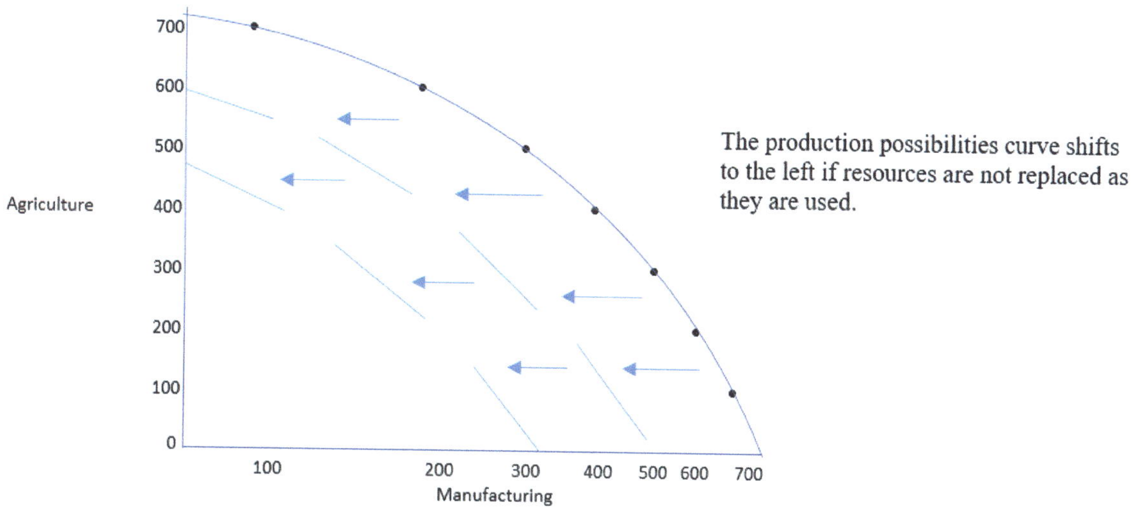

FIGURE 18.2 A Left Shift of the Production Possibilities Curve

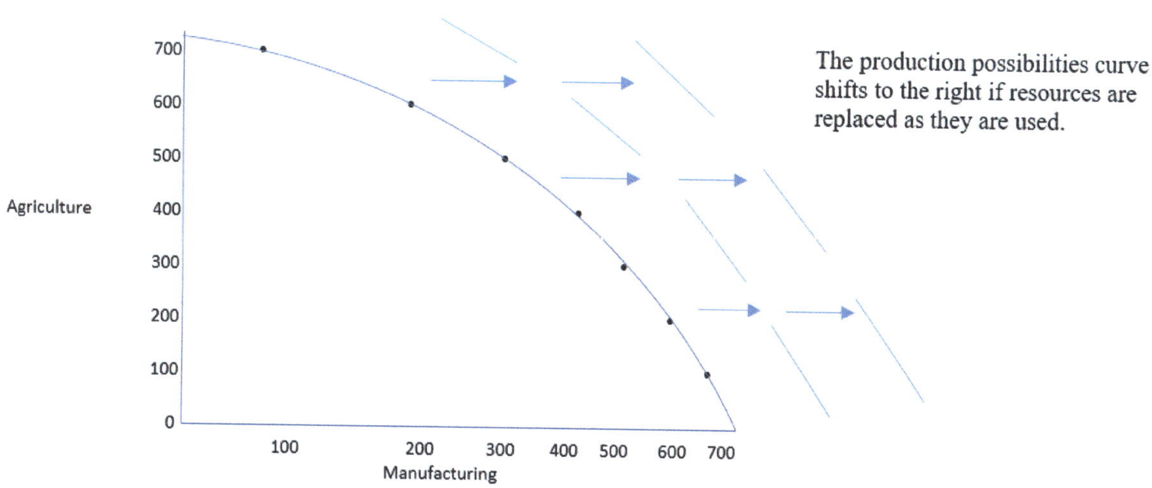

FIGURE 18.3 A Right Shift of the Production Possibilities Curve

18.2 Specialization and Trade: A Review of Absolute and Comparative Advantages

Within the production process, some producers choose to specialize and trade with others. This decision is based on the principle of opportunity cost. As discussed in previous chapters, the principle of opportunity cost explains that specialization makes people better off because it allows them to be efficient in the production process by focusing its resources on producing one or a few goods while trading with others who are also focusing their resources on producing other types of goods. In doing so, this principle demonstrates there will always be trade-offs.

Understanding the concept of specialization and trade, a review of an example from Chapter 3 is reintroduced. This example involves two producers, Samantha and Bobby, who possess the same resources. With her resources, Samantha can produce 6 watermelons and 2 tomatoes. By comparison, Bobby can produce 1 watermelon or 1 tomato with his resources. In this example, Samantha's opportunity cost is 3 watermelons for 1 tomato, while Bobby's opportunity cost is 1 watermelon for 1 tomato. In analysis, the principle of opportunity cost demonstrates that Samantha should specialize in watermelons and Bobby should specialize in tomatoes. In doing so, Samantha can specialize in producing watermelons and trade with Bobby who, in turn, can specialize in producing tomatoes. This allows both to be better off. Table 18.2 shows the production capabilities of Samantha and Bobby.

TABLE 18.2 Production Capabilities of Samantha and Bobby

Producer	Watermelon	Tomato
Samantha	6	2
Bobby	1	1

consumption possibilities curve: a curve that shows the possibilities combination of consumptions resulting from specialization and trade

absolute advantage: an advantage that occurs because one is more productive than another

comparative advantage: an advantage that occurs because one can produce at a lower cost than another

From this example, we can use the consumption possibilities curve to see the consumption possibilities created from specialization and trade. A **consumption possibilities curve** is a curve that shows the possibilities combination of consumptions that result from specialization and trade. Figure 18.4 shows a consumption possibilities curve for Samantha and Bobby. In this illustration, Samantha's consumption options move from 6 watermelons for 1 tomato to 1 watermelon from 6 tomatoes. In doing so, this curve shows the benefits resulting from specialization and trade.

Additionally, in this example, Samantha has an absolute advantage. An **absolute advantage** is an advantage that occurs due to one being more productive than another. However, both Samantha and Bobby can achieve a comparative advantage through specialization and trade. A **comparative advantage** is an advantage that occurs due to one being able to produce at a lower cost than another.

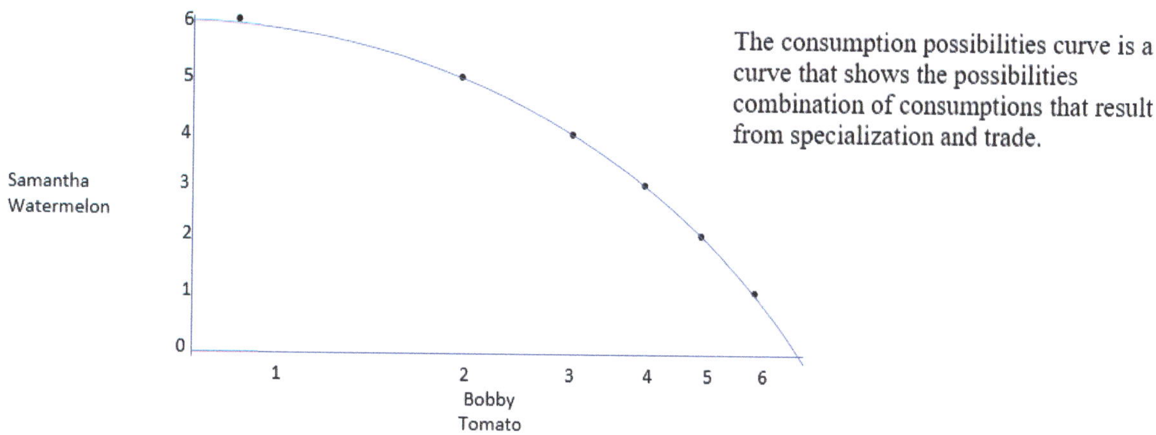

FIGURE 18.4 A Consumption Possibilities Curve

18.3 What Is Free Trade, and How Does it Affect Employment?

Every nation has limited productive resources. Therefore, it becomes advantageous for governments to trade with other governments to ensure their nations acquire the resources needed. In doing so, most nations believe in the idea of free trade. **Free trade** is a situation in which governments agree to trade with each other without trade barriers. Therefore, under this agreement, businesses freely move products, services, and productive resources from one nation to the other through purchases and sales. This movement includes both importing and exporting. **Importing** refers to shipping foreign goods into a country. **Exporting** refers to shipping domestic goods out of a country.

free trade: a situation in which governments agree to trade with each other without trade barriers

importing: shipping foreign goods into a country

exporting: shipping domestic goods out of a country

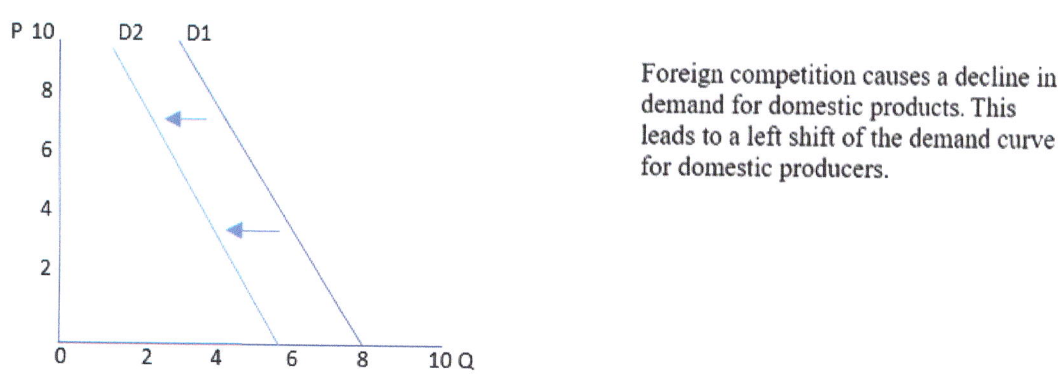

FIGURE 18.5 The effect of Foreign Competition on Domestic Demand

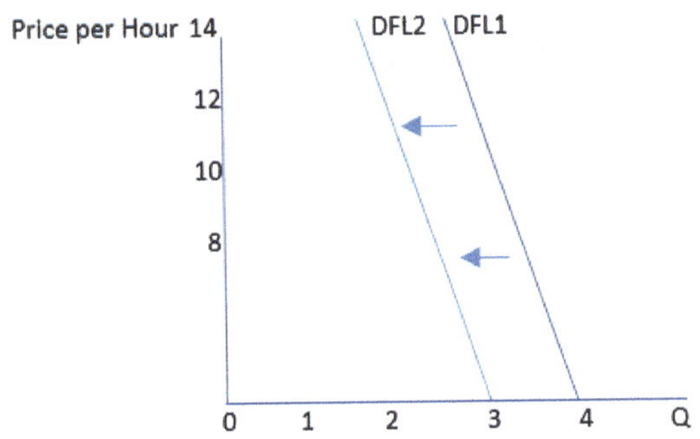

Foreign competition causes a left shirt of the demand for labor curve (DFL) as domestic producers have less demand for workers.

FIGURE 18.6 The effect of Foreign Competition on Domestic Demand for Labor

When foreign businesses export goods into a country, they will compete with domestic producers. As a result of this competition, domestic producers will lose customers, which will lead to a decline in demand. This decline in demand will cause the demand curve to shift to the left. Figure 18.5 depicts this effect.

A decline in demand for domestic producers because of foreign competition will lead to a decline in domestic production. A decline in domestic production will cause a decline in the demand for labor. As the demand for labor declines, unemployment rises. This, in turn, causes the demand for labor curve to shift to the left. Figure 18.6 demonstrates this shift.

18.4 Protectionism

Free trade allows a nation to acquire the resources needed for its society to be productive without the expense associated with trading. However, in exchange, the nation will lose jobs and income as foreign competition enters into the domestic market. This, in turn, leads to the nation becoming poorer. Because of this, although most nations practice free trade, governments use protectionism to protect jobs, income, and national wealth. **Protectionism** is defined as a use of governmental policies to protect domestic producers from foreign competition. Therefore, governments use protectionism to protect domestic jobs and income.

Several protectionist policies used by governments include tariffs, import quotas, voluntary export restraint and anti-dumping. **Tariffs** are taxes placed on imports. An example of a tariff is the Trump Administration imposing a 25% tariff on imported steel in 2018. In imposing this tariff, the goal of the U.S. government was to increase the price of imported steel, so there would be greater demand for U.S. steel.

An **import quota** refers to the process whereby a government limits the amount of goods that can be shipped into the country. An example of an import quota is China limiting the amount of corn into its country to 7.2 million tons in 2020. By limiting this amount, the Chinese government seeks to increase the price of imported corn, thereby increasing demand for domestic corn.

Voluntary export restraint refers to a policy whereby the government limits the number of exports to a country. An example of a voluntary export restraint policy is the Japanese government imposing a limit on the number auto exports to the United States in the 1980s. Although this increases production costs and prices for Japanese automobiles, it also allows it to reduce the level of tariffs imposed, thereby protecting jobs and incomes for the exporting country.

FIGURE 18.7 A Cartoon Depicting Protectionism

Dumping refers to a foreign business strategy of selling goods below production costs or market value. In doing so, the strategy gives foreign businesses an unfair advantage against domestic producers by allowing foreign businesses to sell their goods at a lower price. In response, many governments have enacted anti-dumping laws. **Anti-dumping laws** prohibit foreign businesses from selling goods below production costs and market value. An example of this includes the U.S. Commerce Department finding China guilty of selling solar panels below production costs in 2011. The result of this finding led to the U.S. government imposing tariffs up to 250%, which caused a sharp decline in Chinese solar panel exports to thc United States.

SUMMARY

- A nation's economy consists of limited resources (scarcity) that are used to produce a variety of products and services to satisfy demand. (LO 18.1)
- "Efficiency" refers to having the ability to maximize resources in production. (LO 18.1)
- The production possibilities provide a picture of the difference production combinations of goods and services, which, in turn, allows people to make decisions on production levels. (LO 18.1)
- A "production possibilities curve" is a curve that shows the possible combinations of goods and services produced based on the resources available. (LO 18.1)
- A "consumption possibilities curve" is a curve that shows the possibilities combination of consumptions that result from specialization and trade. (LO 18.2)

- An "absolute advantage" is an advantage that occurs because one is more productive than another. (LO 18.2)
- A "comparative advantage" is an advantage that occurs due to one being able to produce at a lower cost than another. (LO 18.2)
- "Free trade" is a situation in which governments agree to trade with each other without trade barriers. (LO 18.3)
- "Importing" refers to shipping foreign goods into a country. (LO 18.3)
- "Exporting" refers to shipping domestic goods out of a country. (LO 18.3)
- "Protectionism" is defined as the use of governmental policies to protect domestic producers from foreign competition. (LO 18.4)
- "Tariffs" are taxes placed on imports. (LO 18.4)
- An "import quota" refers to the process whereby a government limits the number of goods that can be shipped into the country. (LO 18.4)
- "Voluntary export restraint" refers to a policy whereby the government limits the number of exports to a country. (LO 18.4)
- "Dumping" refers to a foreign business strategy of selling goods below production costs or market value. (LO 18.4)
- Anti-dumping laws prohibit foreign businesses from selling goods below production costs and market value. (LO 18.4)

END-OF-CHAPTER APPLICATION

Comprehension Questions

Directions: Refer to the chapter to correctly respond to the following questions and prompts.

1. A country produces the following goods (in tons) with its resources. Draw a production possibilities graph (frontier). Explain what the production possibilities curve indicates. (LO 18.1)

Clothes	Jewelry
20	100
30	80
40	60
50	40
60	20

2. Bobby can produce 4 melons and 2 stalks of corn with his resources. Ken has the same resources and can produce 3 melons or 1 stalk of corn. What are Bobby and Ken's opportunity cost? Who should specialize in which product? Determine production possibilities through specialization, and draw a consumption possibilities curve from the resulting data. (LO 18.2)
3. Define "free trade." Explain how free trade affects employment and the demand for labor. Draw the curves to illustrate this effect. (LO 18.3)
4. Define "protection." List the protectionist policies identified in the chapter. Explain how these policies affect imports and domestic demand. (LO 18.4)

Case Scenario: Analyzing a U.S. Tariff on Canadian Aluminum Imports

Directions: Use what you learned in the chapter to respond to the following scenario.

In 2020, the Trump Administration announced it was imposing tariffs on aluminum imports from Canada. As a result, this tariff was placed on $2.5 billion worth of Canadian aluminum, which resulted in $250 million tax increase incurred by Canada. Answer the following questions:

1. What would be a possible goal of the U.S. government in imposing the tariff?
2. How does the tariff align with the traditional free trade relationship the United States has maintained with Canada?
3. How would the tariff affect Canadian aluminum imports?
4. What would the effect of the tariffs on demand for U.S. domestic aluminum be? Draw a demand curve to illustrate this effect.

BIBLIOGRPAHY

Garver, R. (2022, April 4). US to investigate use of Chinese materials in imported solar panels. *VOA*. https://www.voanews.com/a/us-to-investigate-use-of-chinese-materials-in-imported-solar-panels-/6515081.html

Gu, H. & Patton, D. (2020, May 13). China hands out more grain import quotas to increase purchases – sources. *Reuters*. https://www.reuters.com/article/china-grains-imports-quota/china-hands-out-more-grain-import-quotas-to-increase-purchases-sources-idUSL4N2CV0CC

Hargrave, M. (2021, February 17). *Voluntary export restraint (VER): Definition, uses, example*. Investopedia. https://www.investopedia.com/terms/v/voluntary_export_restraint.asp

O'Sullivan, A., Shreffin, S., & Perez, S. (2017). *Microeconomics: Principles, applications, and tools* (9th ed.). Pearson Publishing.

Schiller, B. R. (2016). *The micro economy today* (14th ed.). McGraw-Hill Education.

York, E. (2022, April 1). *Tracking the economic impact of U.S. tariffs and retaliatory actions*. Tax Foundation. https://taxfoundation.org/tariffs-trump-trade-war/

CREDITS

IMG 18.1: Central Intelligence Agency, https://commons.wikimedia.org/wiki/File:1950_International_Trade_(30583518780).jpg, 2016.

Fig. 18.7: Nathaniel Lloyd and Company, https://commons.wikimedia.org/wiki/File:Free_Trade_and_Protection.jpg, 1910.

Printed and bound by CPI Group (UK) Ltd, Croydon, CR0 4YY
13/09/2026
14961053-0001